Satire *and the* Threat of Speech

Publication of this volume has been made possible through
the generous support and enduring vision of Warren G. Moon, with
additional support from the Institute for Scholarship in the Liberal Arts,
College of Arts and Letters, University of Notre Dame.

⇛ *Satire and the*
Threat of Speech ⇚

Horace's *Satires*, Book 1

CATHERINE SCHLEGEL

THE UNIVERSITY OF WISCONSIN PRESS

The University of Wisconsin Press
1930 Monroe Street
Madison, Wisconsin 53711

www.wisc.edu/wisconsinpress/

3 Henrietta Street
London WC2E 8LU, England

5 4 3 2 1

Library of Congress Cataloging-in-Publication Data
Schlegel, Catherine.
Satire and the threat of speech : Horace's satires, book 1 /
Catherine Schlegel.
p. cm.—(Wisconsin studies in classics)
Includes bibliographical references and index.
ISBN 0–299–20950–4 (alk. paper)
1. Horace. Satirae. Liber 1. 2. Verse satire, Latin—History and criticism.
3. Rome—In literature. 4. Speech in literature. I. Title. II. Series.
PA6393.S8S35   2005
871′.01—dc22   2004028325

Contents

Acknowledgments

Roman satire, once relatively neglected, enjoys more attention from Classicists these days than it has perhaps since the eighteenth century. Our appreciation has surely changed in temper since that era which prized urbanity, but the protean nature of Roman *satura* serves our own preoccupations just as well. I hope that I have contributed to the contemporary look at this genre of the Romans' own making and have perhaps introduced another register into our current discourse on satire. For any virtue in that contribution I have many to thank.

I am grateful to Adam Mehring and Barbara Wojhoski of the University of Wisconsin Press for their great care and infinite patience in the preparation of this book. My sincerest thanks too to Blythe Woolston, indexer supreme.

The University of Notre Dame has given me a generous home in the Classics department, all of whose members offered me support in their special ways. Dan Sheerin and Martin Bloomer gave me meticulous and thoughtful suggestions on early renditions of the project, and the Institute for Scholarship in the Liberal Arts provided me with an extra portion of Notre Dame's resources for help in the book's completion. Versions of chapters four and two appeared in *Arethusa* and the *American Journal of Philology*, and I am grateful to their readers and reviewers for shrewd readings and critiques. Eleanor Leach and my dear graduate school comrade Mary Depew each kindly invited me to present portions of this work at crucial stages.

I would like to thank teachers and mentors, some from long ago. Ralph Johnson introduced me to the concept of choral poetry, and maybe even of poetry. J. P. Sullivan introduced me to the many voices of Roman satire and himself enacted its best precepts as he lived and died. Phil Levine taught me about the moral dimensions of education and academia, not to mention a passion for Latin literature. To Kenneth Reckford and Daniel Hooley I owe great thanks for spontaneous and generous support.

Good fortune has dogged me in my friends. Liz and Tadeusz Mazurek have been marvelous colleagues and interlocutors. Doris Bergen and Laura Crago cast their keen historians' eyes over the introduction, to its great benefit. In different ways but to similar ends Naomi Cassirer and Daniel Mattern each supplied their formidable editorial skills to this author's need. Under Paulene Popek's careful guidance I learned to think about violence in news ways; among numberless other intellectual and emotional gifts Rebecca Resinski taught me to do the same. Lannie Abrams and my brother Tom Schlegel gave me general life-support to keep thinking. Tom Habinek, besides giving me employment at a critical time, has been a friend in more ways than I think I actually know. Keith Bradley has been a friend and a *patronus* in all the best senses of that complicated word. Henry Weinfield, an extraordinary colleague, read every word of this manuscript, and had a comment on quite a few of those words. Carole Newlands, *anima candida,* lent her numinous support to all elements of this project; she has my everlasting gratitude and respect.

Satire *and the* Threat of Speech

Introduction

Satire and the Threat of Speech

The violence of Roman public life has a canonical beginning in 133 BCE, when Tiberius Gracchus, the tribune of the Plebs, was murdered by his political opponents. The person of the tribune was designated as sacrosanct by Roman tradition, and there is a special alarm in this murder that inaugurated a course of increasingly bloody political solutions in Rome. These solutions culminated in the long years of the civil wars. Julius Caesar crossed the Rubicon in January of 49 BCE to fight the armies of his old friend and former son-in-law, Pompey the Great, and there was little peace until after Octavian, soon to be Augustus, settled matters with Antony and Cleopatra in 31 BCE.

This public violence was the social practice and the reality of the society in which Horace wrote his *Satires*. For a long time—in fact since Horace's texts have had readers—critics have speculated and made assertions about who the poet Horace was, his temperament, economic circumstances, family background, and so on; but they have had little to say about things concerning Horace that are more knowable, such as what the world that Horace inhabited was like. Our sources for the *realia* of Horace's Rome may be exiguous, but they are more verifiable than the character of the "real" Horace. Yet it is that "real" man whom readers confidently sought and reconstructed from the canny beauty of Horace's poetic art.

This book is a literary exploration of that art, in the first book of Horace's *Satires*. The purpose of the book is not to present a historical picture nor to offer an analysis of such a picture (others have done this). But if the climate in which Horace wrote offered violence as the prevailing solution to public conflict, then this would be a powerfully influential

paradigm, and any artistic effort would be necessarily informed by it. The
genre of satire flirts with verbal violence and has literary-genetic roots
in speech genres of attack and coercion (iambic verse and magical incantation). Horace is remarkably defensive about writing satire in his first
book; he defines the genre by putting forward the expectations his audience has and then insisting he has no capacity to fulfill these expectations.
I suggest that the extreme violence of political life in Rome while Horace
was living there and writing the *Satires* figures profoundly in his use of
satire. Once Horace has opened up his thesis in *Satires* 1.4 that satire is a
genre that does harm and makes people afraid, he has introduced a model
that is surely informed by the harmful and frightening acts perpetrated
against people that were everywhere visible in Rome.

Satire has never been congenial to category. While epic, tragedy, and
comedy rest securely in our minds as literary entities and as recognizable media of the impulse to praise, to ponder, or to laugh, satire shifts
and turns. Quintilian's famously confident statement, "satura quidem tota
nostra est" (satire is all our own), claims a Roman birth for the genre of
satire, but does not address satire's unsteady generic state. It is perhaps
only in that characteristically equivocal Latin particle *quidem* that Quintilian lets in a whiff of satire's uncertainty.[1] The confused etymology of
the name *satura* bespeaks the genre's uncertainty: is "satire" born of the
root *sat-*, meaning "full, full of mixture," as a sacrificial plate filled with
a mixture of herbs, or as a sausage filled with various food stuffs, or even
as a law packed with codicils to please a variety of interests? Or does satire
derive from satyr plays, the frisky conclusions to an Athenian day of tragedy viewing?[2] Modern scholars favor the first etymology, but both attempts
at fixing the history of the genre's name reflect satire's cloudy nature, mark
its difference from a clear literary tradition. Indeed, the first etymology
notes satire's nonliterary nature, drawn from a homely realm of food and
made metaphorical in law. Variety is the essence of this derivation, a neutral comment that satire is unfixed and contains many elements. To connect satire with "satyr" notes another element, which is the unconstraint
of the satyr figure and the plays associated with it in the Greek dramatic
tradition, not strictly comedy but performing some of comedy's service
to liberate the audience by permitting the speech and action that social-
ized life suppresses. The undogmatic nature of satire's definition allows
satirists to move about freely in their genre, and I will argue in this work
that Horace is especially manipulative of satire's generic boundaries and

expectations and that, indeed, he is offering a definition of satire in each poem of the first book of his *Satires*.

It is deemed necessary in any modern work of scholarship on Roman satire to speak first of the indefinability of this genre, as I have just done, but it is also evident that readers and critics have no trouble recognizing satire when they see it. The genre of satire has proved to be one of remarkable durability; its flexibility has allowed satire to continue to serve literary needs from the Romans to the present day. Perhaps satire has endured as a genre partly because of its flexibility; fullness and satyrs are never out of fashion, that is, variety and unconstraint always need expression. But an element not contained in the ancient etymologizing of satire's name, though belonging to unconstraint, persists in satire to this day. Satire expresses a certain hostility toward its subject, a critical edge, an opinion expressed by the satirist at variance in some part from the community he observes. We can think of the satirist as a kind of reversed version of the choral poet: like the choral poet the satirist speaks publicly to a group about that group, but in the place of praise the satirist speaks blame, and the harmonious relation between the praise poet and his audience is for the satirist an antagonistic one.[3] The choral poet expresses to a community its highest values and through praise teaches the community about itself, telling its value to the audience. Praise speech links the object of praise with the speaker: the community and its poet together share positive values, and the choral poet is thus not differentiated from the community he sings about; rather he participates in the community by being the medium through which its values are articulated and made eternal in words. The audience is gratified by the speech of the poet.

The satirist, like the choral poet, speaks about and to his community, but where the choral poet praises, the satirist blames. While the choral poet, at least temporarily, joins the audience-community whose virtues he shapes in words, the satirist is inevitably differentiated from his community by virtue of having verbally assailed his audience. While the choral poet is identified with the community by his praise of it, the satirist pushes himself apart from that community with his criticism. His reproachful speech separates the satirist from his audience. The result of this separation is that the satiric speaker himself is a much more clearly differentiated and articulated figure than the praise speaker; the praise speaker's attractive speech, rather than prompting scrutiny, allows the audience to contemplate themselves and to leave unexamined the congenial voice of praise.

If all speech functions in some sense as a means by which a speaker identifies himself, blame speech does so with special clarity: it is implicit in a statement of blame that the speaker does not share in that blame. Statements of attack identify the object of attack, but they equally clearly identify the speaker of the attack. If the speaker has authority with his audience, that authority derives from an assumption that the speaker is free of the faults he notes. Blame speech overtly identifies the other, the one who is the blameworthy object, but blame speech equally identifies the speaker, as one who does *not* deserve blame. The listeners, under attack, naturally question the speaker's assumption of blamelessness.[4] In this respect too the satirist reverses the situation of the choral poet, who praises his community. The audience evaluates the giver of praise for the skill of his speech, not for his personal authority for delivering praise, because the poet gives voice to what the listeners already wish to believe; the dissenting voice of the satirist, by contrast, attracts attention to the satirist himself as he speaks against some element of the community. What authority inheres in the satirist that justifies his hearers' attention? Why does the satirist have an audience at all? What is there in the satirist's speech to persuade his audience to listen? The listener looks to the source of the speech, the speaker of blame, to justify his attention to such speech; and the result is that the satirist himself is as much the object of attention as his speech.

I argue that Horace creates a persona for himself, as the satiric speaker in book 1 of the *Satires,* which can be understood as a response to the tensions inherent in the operation of hostile speech. Readers of Horace's *Satires* have often seen his poems as anomalous to the genre of satire. Horace's satire is mild, not harsh, and presents none of the risky sting that we expect from satiric speech; Juvenal, far better than Horace, conveys the tone we associate with satire. Yet the poems of *Satires* I delve more deeply into the crucial issues inherent in the genre than do those of any other Roman satirist. Horace's poems in book 1 make a commentary on the satiric genre in which Horace overtly attempts to resist the practice of biting speech: he presents the bite but does not do the biting. Horace's anxiety at, and interest in, being a speaker of blame in the genre of satire directs his attention in the *Satires* toward an articulation of his own persona. The poet of the *Satires* is uniquely aware of the dangers of satiric speech and the consequent potential alienation of the listener; Horace is constantly hedging against the alienation of satire and against the biting of the satiric poet by manipulating his satire through his moderating persona.

Horace has chosen, however, to write in a genre that has an inheritance of blame speaking, and if his persona mitigates the negative effects on the audience of such speech, Horace's satire does not ignore or deny the issues of invective and conflict that belong to satire. Nor, I argue, does Horace entirely wish to relinquish the powerful voice of the satirist, despite the work of his persona in the poems. Critics distinguish Horace from other Roman satirists for his milder tone, by the fact that he does not use the critical voice of the satirist as Lucilius or Juvenal does and instead exploits the "fullness" of satire and its mixed nature.[5] While this is true, it is also misleading, for it fails to account for much of the activity of the *Satires*. Horace writes his satire against the expectation of the genre, and the poems of *Satires* I very often acknowledge the conflict-based nature of satire, even if the poet is not participating in the conflict. We will see in the course of looking at the poems of book 1 how Horace double-deals with his satiric genre, how he puts *satura* into *sermo*, and how he writes against satire as he is writing in satire.

What the poems of book 1 do, rather than enacting conflict—that is, speaking invective against an audience—is to present the issues of powerful speech and domination that inhere in satire. The allure of self-articulation that comes with attacking another person is a pleasure of domination and of self-expansion. In modern terms, uncontained power over another, whether verbal or material, is a loss of boundaries; in Horace's Epicurean terms it is a failure to live within nature's limits (*Sat.* 1.1–3). Invective strives to exert this kind of power over another and is, for its speaker, a self-aggrandizing pleasure that to Horace is inconsonant with human happiness. Horace seems to suggest that the necessary passivity of listening (what he calls the burden to the ears) is always an opportunity for a speaker to dominate, always a threat to the hearer and a temptation to the speaker; he seems to suggest, that is, that all speech, hence all poetry, entertains the menace of unequal power between speaker and hearer. This problem then in satire will be acute, since the genre's invective and coercive properties rely on the power of speech to menace, control, and overpower the hearer. The speaker of satire will always be one who cannot observe limits.

Horace's treatment of satire puts its focus on the speaker of satire rather than on its object, the passive listener. Although the danger may *seem* to be to the victim of satiric speech, in Horace's manipulation of the genre, it is the speaker who is most endangered. The reckless speaker of satire is mad, has lost the idea of boundaries, of nature's limits, and has hence lost his relationships with others; friendless and incontinent, the satirist lives outside human society, gratifying his appetite for self-identification, for self-expansion. The desire to be invulnerable that hostile speech enacts by attempting to obliterate the other is a blurring of the distinction between self and other—a loss of those Epicurean limits.

To relieve the audience of satire's potential burden on it, one of Horace's strategies is to illustrate the competitive nature of powerful speech by locating it within the mouths of different speakers (not his own): he does this in *Satires* 1.7, for example, when he pits two invective speakers against each other, and intermittently throughout *Satires* I he focuses on competition between poets. The purpose of competition is to decide who wins, who dominates; the prize for winning this competition is the audience, and in the final poem of book 1 the prize Horace wins is the most powerful audience, the denizens of Maecenas's household. But the first poetic competition that Horace offers us to regard, in *Satires* 1.4, is his own competition with his satiric predecessor Lucilius. Horace wins, and perhaps unfairly. Lucilius provides the model for the satiric speaker against whom Horace can shape his own restrained, benign, and stylish speaker of satire, and Horace's carefully drawn persona works to attract our attention first to the issue of satire's force and then to Horace's refusal to deploy that force. The controlled and limited persona that Horace constructs as his speaker in *Satires* I embodies the theory of satire that we see operating in these poems. Paradoxically, however, Horace shapes the persona of that speaker within a competitive context of the very sort that his principles of satire would eschew. Horace dominates Lucilius in this genre, which deploys powerful, dominating speech, despite going to significant lengths in book 1 to offer us a different kind of satire. Horace's competition with Lucilius belongs to Lucilian, not to Horatian satire, and contradicts the design of his noncombative poetic persona in the *Satires*.

That satiric persona is informed by a principle of balance in Horace's satire, and this principle is his fundamental means of controlling satiric excesses. The name of the genre, *satura*, provides Horace with a pun that plays on the word *sat* (full, enough), and the idea of the limitation that must be embraced if one is to be content with merely *enough* establishes a principle for Horatian *satura*. Horace uses this punning idea of sufficiency to check all of satire's impulses toward power as domination. Though uncontrolled passion and the use of words as instruments of power may be the wellsprings for satire's original force, Horace will offer a concept of *satis*-faction and sufficiency to make his satire controlled and rational.

As the poems of *Satires* I progressively reveal and develop Horace's idea for this genre, however, the confidence with which this controlled satiric stance is maintained begins to waver. I will argue that Horace's project for satire in the first book is only equivocally a success, and that the anxieties of the relation between speaker and hearer, poet and audience, grow too great for his structure to contain. Even the benign, controlled figure of Horace's persona in *Satires* I does not quite keep his balance, and the clarity and confidence of the opening to the book has little counterpart in its final poem.

The opening three satires are genial and definite and also include very little of the figure of "Horace" that will become so important a factor in shaping the satire of book 1. The speaker of the first three poems is a confident, impersonal narrator who is sure of the wisdom he speaks and is contained by a deferential relation to Maecenas, to whom the opening poem is addressed. Each of these poems articulates Horace's principle of satire as a genre of what is *sat,* and each suggests restraints on human appetites to permit contentment and pleasure. The first poem sets the theoretical stage, and the next two demonstrate the precept: 1.2 in terms of sexual desire, and 1.3 in terms of friendship. One must limit one's desires for oneself (1.1), limit one's desires for an erotic object (1.2), and limit one's desire to expand the self by diminishing another (1.3). In each poem the satiric voice counsels that to recognize reality means to limit the longings of the imagination; human happiness belongs to the realm of material sufficiency. In the third poem, Horace illustrates the way friendship requires us to limit our desire to criticize others, and his exemplar of this friendly behavior is Maecenas (63–65), who tolerates Horace's foolish interruptions without rebuking him. The latter instance is the only moment we see our narrator in the first three poems, a narrator firmly knowing his place with Maecenas.[6]

In the fourth satire the little-visible narrator of the first three poems enters with a personality, opinions, anxieties, a biography, and a father. This poem continues the theme of limitations by looking at the limits of the invective impulse in satire itself, but "Horace," the maker of the poems and a character in this poem, enters the *Satires* when the subject is satire. He enters as a figure who, because of who he is (or "what he is," as he says of himself in *Satires* 1.6), crucially limits and defines his genre. The "ego" of Horace's satires stays in the rest of book 1, sometimes in disguise. The persona of the poet is part of the control structure for the genre, and every attribute granted to this figure, from his tiny verbal output to his low social status, acts as a counterweight to the expectation of a satiric speaker who exercises clout, *auctoritas* of an overweening kind, over his listener. The figure of himself that Horace here puts forward is one who lacks both the capacity and the inclination for the controlling and uncontrolled speech of satire.

In the first chapter of this work I offer a reading of the first three poems of book 1 that demonstrates the theoretical program Horace articulates for his satiric practice. In the subsequent chapters, I then look closely at *Satires* 1.4 through 1.10; I consider how the second triad of poems, *Satires* 1.4, 5, and 6, progressively elucidates the poet's satiric persona, and how the definition of the poet's persona in these three poems allows for an investigation in the following triad, *Satires* 1.7, 8, and 9, of the satiric elements that Horace excludes from his own satiric speech. Each of the poems in the latter triad depicts speech deployed to gain control over another person and explores the power in satiric speech to dominate its hearer. The reader will notice that certain lines of *Satires* 1.4 recur in the discussion of these poems, because those moments in which Horace describes himself and his satiric predecessor Lucilius continue to function in the latter poems of book 1 in the voices he gives to himself and to other figures in these satires. Contrary to Eduard Fraenkel's suggestion that these poems are casual additions by Horace drawn from his portfolio to fill out the book (1957, 119), I will demonstrate that *Satires* 1.7, 8, and 9 are fundamental to the meditation on satiric speech that emerges in *Satires* I. The last poem, *Satires* 1.10, articulates the unease concerning the speaker's relation to his audience that is increasingly apparent in *Satires* 1.7, 8, and 9. In the course of book 1, Horace's persona grows increasingly vivid *and* uncertain, as the appeal of satiric unrestraint becomes more evident. The satiric principle of limitation and restraint is supposed to grant to the satirist and to his audience the pleasure of satire without its pain and is supposed to restrain the grandiose impulses of coercive speech and invective; but limitation begins to strain the poetic enterprise in 1.10, and the pinch of Horace's perfectionism threatens the poetic imagination. Horace's invective against other poets in *Satires* 1.10 is another skilled manipulation of his poetic self in *Satires* I. Horace allows himself to indulge in invective and presents the appeal of satiric speech. He also thereby undoes his own principle of satiric restraint and enacts the longing to take out the threatening other—the other who in 1.10 is embodied by bad poets.

Thus Horace's own figure in the poems enacts the issues of competition and control in terms of his fellow poets. He endows his satiric persona with intense emotions and invites his reader to respond in kind. This strategy has given rise among critics to an insistently biographical reading of the *Satires*. There is a certain irony in the fact that Horace's poetically, generically motivated focus on his own persona in the *Satires* has prompted an irresistible desire in readers to take the *Satires* as the poet's autobiography. It is a measure of the success of Horace's satiric strategy that the *Satires* have been relentlessly mined for details of the historical Horace's life, and that the poems themselves have been interpreted so that their meaning would be congruent with the autobiographical account Horace supposedly intends to give. From the earliest commentaries of Horace onward, suggestions are made about the reality of the *Satires*, that conflicts in the *Satires* correspond to actual conflicts in Horace's life.[7] Horace's account of his freedman father and his consequent insecure social status has held a fascination for readers who see a reflection in those details of their own culture's class distinctions.

The literary concept of a persona, to render the distinction between the actual poet and the voice he adopts in his poetry, is hardly new, but its application by critics came tardily to the figure of Horace in the *Satires*. The work of W. S. Anderson and J. E. G. Zetzel and critics following them, in recognizing that Horace deploys his persona in the *Satires* as an ironic speaker and in seeing the activity of the artist behind the persona of the satirist, invaluably illuminated the poetic operations of these poems. What is remarkable is that these observations came so late to Horace's *Satires;* although literary studies of ancient poetry had grown skeptical of reading the life of the poet out of and into his poetry, the criticism of the *Satires* long persisted in this habit.[8] Fine treatments of Horace's *Satires* by Eduard Fraenkel and Niall Rudd nevertheless unselfconsciously interpret these poems according to the statements the poet makes about himself in the *Satires*. Anderson himself occasionally falls prey to the temptations of a biographical reading of the *Satires* (1974, 33–56). The persistence of such a reading speaks to the effectiveness of Horace's poetic construction of himself in these poems. But Horace's construction of that satiric persona belongs to his close observation of the activity of satire, and if we fail to see the art of that construction, we will also fail to understand the nature of satire as Horace sees it.

Yet before we condescend to the autobiographical reading of Horace's *Satires* as hopelessly naive, we might take account of two factors that make such a reading compelling, if ultimately misleading. The first, which is true of all ancient literature, is that in interpreting Horace's poetry we are trying to reconstruct a world that, for all our efforts, is elusive and largely unknowable. Ancient literature poses a constant temptation to be used as documentary evidence of a place to which we will ever remain strangers. In the *Satires*, Horace offers us in abundance what seem to be the concrete details of his life (and material details are characteristic of the genre of satire), and it requires restraint on the part of the modern reader— given the dearth of information about Horace's actual world—not to gratefully accept the whole poetic portrayal as "truth" or "reality." The second reason for the critical reluctance to abandon the autobiographical reading of Horace's *Satires* in particular pertains to Horace's special genius in treating his genre. The personal statements the poet makes about himself in the *Satires* are deeply woven into his satiric program and are cast within an invitation to know the satirist, to trust him, and not to fear him. Horace invites the reader to believe his autobiographical account for the express purpose of making his persona safe and unthreatening to the reader, and he gestures intimately toward the reader so as to engage the reader's sympathy. His satiric speech is thus produced in a context that elicits the audience's sympathy and works against the impulse of satire to alienate its audience; Horace is so successful in this that he intriguingly disables principles of critical reading.

Thus, to find in the *Satires* a Horace who is just like us, a fleshed-out human being we believe we know, is to respond to the invitation of the poems.[9] The problem with the biographical reading is that our desire for "real" information and our sense that the poems give us that information prevent our recognition of what Horace is doing artistically in the *Satires*. But it is interesting to see that fissures in the autobiographical narrative— Horace's father, for instance, was not the lowly *libertinus* that the *Satires* portray—and a sometimes palpable disingenuity have not prompted readers to change their interpretive habits. Rather it is Horace who is found wanting, as Amy Richlin summarizes:

Meanwhile the "real Horace" awaits readers as he always has, tangled in the contradictions of his contorted self-exegesis. If he confided his "whole life" to these books, he did not do so lucidly, and this cannot be accidental; like a raconteur whose only real subject is his mysterious self, he forces the reader to wonder about the poet—not really about life, or other people. This is the same man who wrote *"exegi monumentum aere perennius."* He had, of course, some justification for his self-absorption; but, as many have remarked, the format of the *Epistles* was much better suited to his temperament. There he could devote the entire poem to himself.[10]

It is not Horace's temperament that motivates his self-portrait in the *Satires* but instead the project of solving the problem of the effect that critical speech has on an audience. A critical distance in reading the *Satires* is crucial; as Phebe Bowditch notes, the "Horatian speaker continues to project a seductive believability."[11]

Horace designed the persona of the poet in the *Satires* to serve his poetic program, not to reveal the "real" Horace; to treat the *Satires* either as a biographical or a sociohistorical resource misses the generic context of Horace's presentation of his persona. Horace's persona in the *Satires* is constructed to reassure the reader by undermining the threat of satiric speech and by revising the genre he has inherited from Lucilius. The persona mitigates a menace to the audience that satire, as a version of blame speech, inevitably poses. Horace identifies his persona in *Satires* I not only as the maker of the poetry but also as equivalent to the satire itself. Questions of both style and content in the *Satires* are therefore answered by referring the reader to the poet's life and character. It is thus necessary for Horace to articulate and rearticulate "himself" in the progressive operation of defining his satire. As I noted, critical speech makes the satirist's voice particularly audible, because it attracts the audience's suspicious attention to the speaker. In Horatian satire, the satirist needs to delineate his persona in order to deliver his speech credibly and justifiably, in order to define his relationship to his audience, in order to have an audience, and in order to define his genre. It is not "Horace" we see in the *Satires* but a satirist.

The approach of recent scholarship on the *Satires* in general expresses more faith in Horace as a poet in the *Satires* than previous scholars were prone to do; among the latter one frequently finds the lurking assumption, as Kirk Freudenburg says, "that Horace only turned into a poet in the *Odes*" (1993, 126). Just as the earlier fond interpretation of Horace as the ideal of European gentlemanly urbanity has its roots in the sociology of earlier centuries, likewise recent interpretations of Horace's *Satires* owe their disposition to prevailing cultural conditions of the late twentieth century and the accompanying critical appreciation for absurd, comic, unsettling, and complex literary efforts.[12]

In seeing the poet's persona as an artifice of the poetry, critics have displayed a concomitant tendency, however, to regard the whole enterprise of the *Satires* as fraudulent and to fail to see the service that Horace's artful use of his mask performs. It is as if these readers declare, upon discovering the device of the poetic persona, that they will not be fooled again, and are inclined to read the poems as arch renderings in which meaning is undermined by artifice. This too, like the reading that looks to the *Satires* for a coherent biography of the poet, deprives the poems of their pleasure and heft. Zetzel and Freudenburg, for example, discount the ethical statements in the *Satires* as pure posturing because they view these statements as subverted by the parodic impulse evident in Horace's presentation. The portrait of Horace's father in 1.4, seen as an artistic creation with echoes of the father Demea of Terence's play, becomes an ironic joke about both the satirist and filial piety. I think this impulse is mistaken, and that the *Satires* present a more complicated field of meanings than either faithful self-portraiture or relentless self-caricature reveals. An interpretive balance is necessary between the extremes of credulity and artifice. Within the play of Horace's persona, one finds an ethical orientation and meaningful meditations on threatening speech, the problematic nature of communication, and the unease of human relations expressed in speech.

One has to note that it is Horace's immense craft that makes the interpretive balance difficult to maintain. The point of Horace's enormously sympathetic satiric persona is to collapse the critical distance between poet and reader and to quell any suspicion in his audience that the satirist will bite. The conventional wisdom about the autobiographical elements included in Horace's satiric persona, particularly concerning his social status as the son of a freedman (*Sat.* 1.6), held that Horace, unlike his aristocratic predecessor Lucilius, does not have the social confidence to make open attacks on members of Roman society and to adopt the free-ranging (and raging) voice of a satirist.[13] That is, Horace the parvenu was in no position to attack a society he was grateful to have the opportunity to join, and his strategy as a satirist is not a poetic choice but one forced on him by the circumstances of his status in Roman society. It is true that Horace may have been making a virtue of necessity; but this view of Horace's poetic activity as a satirist distracts our attention from the virtue and focuses it on the necessity, and inhibits recognition of what that persona, the marginally accepted arriviste, enables Horace to do as a satirist, and how that persona manipulates the impact of his speech. The observation that Horace was constrained by social necessity ignores the fact that it is Horace who has given us this biographical information, and that this is a poetic decision; the issue is not the fact of Horace's birth but why he tells it to us.

Horace portrays himself explicitly as socially inferior by birth, and this is first of all consistent with a biographical tradition that puts blame speakers on the periphery of their communities; the poet's biography reflects the alienation and alienating powers of their speech and informally explains the psychology at work in alienation. That Archilochus was supposedly illegitimate is somehow consistent with the distancing ferocity of his iambs; in some part the poet does not belong to the social structure of the world he regards.[14] This kind of biographical tradition has a double meaning: while it explains the alienation of the poet, it also discounts the force of his speech, locating the cause of that speech in circumstances peculiar to the poet and not in the justice of his view. In this way the blame is placed back on the poet, and his listeners are safe. Horace's construction of his own autobiography in *Satires* 1.6 suggests an awareness of this blame phenomenon, and Horace can place himself within the tradition of blame speakers who are in some way at a remove from their community. He can use this claimed status of outsider as proof of his satiric *bona fides*. But in addition, since he makes his own poetic persona the source of this biographical information, he gives further evidence that he is not a menacing speaker—and perhaps he is acknowledging that the listener needs protection from blame speech. Horace tells his listeners that he has a social disability and thereby deprives himself as a poet of the dominating potential of social authority.

The single most striking feature of Horace's strategies in *Satires* I is a continuous double-dealing, a trick that applies to nearly every move he makes that involves his reader or his genre. In the same satire in which Horace speaks of his social disadvantages, Horace is also describing his acceptance into the circle of Maecenas, the ultimate social insider (as

Horace points out, 1.6.1–2: "Non quia, Maecenas, Lydorum quidquid Etrus-
cos / incoluit finis, nemo generosior est te" [though of all the Lydians that
are settled in Tuscan lands none is of nobler birth than you]).[15] Horace
thus puts himself back inside the social circle and by doing so takes back
power for his persona. The move is characteristic of Horace's manipulation of his persona in the first book of the *Satires* and adequately represents the bivalent version of satire he produces. Readers of Horace's *Satires*
rightly note that Horace is unlike Lucilius or Juvenal, that his use of invective is limited and his satirist's voice is mild, not harsh. His emphasis
on friendship, along with his socially enfeebled, sometimes laughable persona, produces a kind of satire and a satirist that do not menace. He is
a more effective moralizer if he is more an insider. But just as in his
relationship with Maecenas, he wants it both ways, to be inside the inner
circle while noting that as the son of a freedman he also stands outside
that circle. Horace retains the rights of the satirist should he choose to use
them, and he recognizes the inalienable power of the satirist's voice.

Horace is conscious throughout of both the genre and of the "self," the
speaker, of the genre. The making of his own persona in the *Satires* allows
Horace to expose the workings of satire, and in so doing he allows the
reader room to avoid being put in the situation of the coerced, passive
listener. Critical speech is uncomfortable to hear. Horace recognizes but
does not discuss the coercive capacity of speech, however much he does
discuss the question of fault-noting and its effects in *Satires* 1.4. Speaking
is voluntary; hearing is not. Speech has a powerful life in the exercise of
magic, since magic attributes to words a material force. The potency of
incantation relies on a profound human belief in the power of words as
actual instruments that can achieve certain ends, ends determined by the
speaker, against which the listener is helpless.[16] In *The Power of Satire*,
Robert Elliott advances the thesis that satire in all its literary forms grows
from verbal magic, which expressed the primitive belief that thought, and
then words, have the power to prompt action and particularly have the
power to do injury or to kill.[17] As magic becomes art, Elliott argues, in its
more sophisticated environment satire has the power to do worse than kill:
it can make the life of its object unlivable by producing pain and humil-
iation. This conception assumes that speech is active and listening is passive, and that to hear is to be powerless. One need not subscribe to Elliott's
theory of literary evolution to acknowledge that the power of speech to
evoke emotional responses in the listener may readily seem magical.[18]

Horace gives much evidence in the *Satires* that he recognizes not only that this power of speech exists but that the satirist has a share in it. The figure of aging female menace, Canidia, plays the part of an alternate satirist, along with the ithyphallic god Priapus, in *Satires* 1.8; and *Satires* 2.1 makes its appeal to her as a model for the satirist in the use of defensive weapons; most significantly, Canidia's breath closes the *Satires* in the last line of *Satires* 2.8. I will look at Canidia's role in *Satires* I in more detail later, but I allude to her here simply to note that the *Satires* show an awareness of a nonliterary, popular element that Horace seems to acknowledge belongs to his genre.[19] The coercive power of speech is not confined to the magical, incantatory realm; the least of Horace's heroes in the *Satires*, the Troublesome Talker of *Satires* 1.9, is humorously granted the power to end the poet's life by talking. Careless, endless speech, oblivious to the desire of the unwilling hearer, is a force that gives no quarter to the hearer's desire and for the hearer becomes the equivalent of death.

What, then, is the situation of the speaker and the hearer of *sermo* in the first book of Horace's *Satires*, where the poet is reproducing conversational speech without an interlocutor and doing it in the genre of satire? The reader/listener plays the part of the interlocutor, but he cannot speak. There is an internal contradiction in a conversational genre of writing in that there can only be one speaker, the poet. While imitating the sound of conversational speech, the poet cannot include its crucial element, the exchange of speech. The exchange in conversation allows the power of speech to flow between both parties and so makes it a reciprocal event in which each participant plays the active role of speaking and the passive role of hearing. Writing does not permit exchange. The dialogues of the second book of the *Satires* suggest to me an attempt by Horace to redress the problem of a silent hearer by providing the persona of the poet with an interlocutor within the poem itself; but this too is a compromise that does not entirely relieve the satirist of the burden of overpowering speech, since the voice of both speakers is still the satirist's in disguise. This is a problem for Horace in the *Satires* because the genre's inherited nature, blame speech and the binding power of folk satire linked to magical incantation, exert a power over the hearer, and Horace is always wary of that power. Horace's wariness, I suggest, is also an aspect of his persona, a mistrustful construction that serves both to alert the reader to the dangers of satire—in fact, to teach his listeners about his genre—and to protect himself, as the satirizing poet, from the return of blame that coercive speakers attract.

It is part of the larger program of the *Satires* that the reader be with Horace, not alienated from him, and part of his satiric program to reduce the alienation of the reader that comes with invective. In *Satires* 1.7–9 none of the solutions to coercive speech are in fact accomplished through rational speech: a pun, a fart, and a rescue by Apollo in those poems save the listener. If these are the only kinds of solutions to conflict-based speech, the speaker and the listener are left in a situation where speech is merely the exercise of power, and such speech cannot achieve any of the kinder aims of communication and friendship that Horace proposes in *Satires* I.

I suggest that ultimately Horace is uneasy with the role of the satirist, and that his manipulation of his persona and consequently of his genre is insufficient protection against the menace to the hearer of satiric speech. All speech embodies a degree of coercion of its hearer, and speech in satire is loaded with the weight of its generic inheritance. In the experiments with dialogue in the second book of the *Satires*, Horace may address the problem of the powerless listener, but this still does not finally solve the problem of the satirist's inherited menace to a silent listener. Later in his life Horace returns to hexameter poetry in the *Epistles*, which are often said to be not very different from the *Satires*.[20] But there is a very great difference of genre between the two. The satirist is gone, replaced by a writer with a single addressee. The reader stands outside the correspondence, looking in, unable to be harmed by the coercive power of the speaker's address. Having tried out all the approximations to conversation in the *Satires*, Horace's solution to the contradiction in the genre may perhaps be the *Epistles*, where the genre explicitly admits the unavailability of an interlocutor.

The Limits of Satire,
Iam satis est

Satires 1.1–3

If you fail to refer each of your actions on every occasion to nature's end [τὸ τέλος τῆς φυσέως], and stop short at something else in choosing or avoiding [φυγὴν ... δίωξιν], your actions will not be consequential on your theories.

—EPICURUS, *Key Doctrines* 25

Whenever intense passion is present in natural desires which do not lead to pain if they are unfulfilled, they have their origin in empty opinion [κενὴ δόξα]; and the reason for their persistence is not their own nature but the empty opinion [τὴν κενοδοξίαν] of the person.

—*Key Doctrines* 30

He who knows the limits of life [τὰ πέρατα τοῦ] βίου knows how easy it is to obtain that which removes pain caused by want and that which makes the whole of life complete. He therefore has no need for competitive involvements [πραγμάτων ἀγῶνας κεκτημένων].

—*Key Doctrines* 21

Satires 1.1, 2, and 3 are called the "diatribe satires," because they conform to the cajoling moral philosophy that is the pattern of diatribe, or as Albin Lesky defines it, "the propaganda speech declaimed with sharp wit and aggressive satire and enlivened with polemic in fictional dialogues" (1966, 670). They are probably milder than the lost works of Bion of Borysthenes, the Cynic associated prominently with diatribe; but long after Horace wrote the *Satires,* he called them his *Bionei sermones* (*Epistles* 2.2.60). The evident fact that these first three poems of the *Satires* are recognizable genre pieces of popular philosophizing, however, does not help to illuminate their function in Horace's first book.[1] I shall argue in this chapter that in the first three satires of book 1, Horace is concerned with the idea of limitation in an ethical or experiential sense. Beginning in *Satires* 1.4, however, Horace will turn this ethical concern with limits self-reflexively upon the genre of satire itself, a genre that he will thereby transform.

Horace is writing satire against an expectation that he is largely responsible for creating. The satiric genre of biting and abrading, of noting faults and scaring the audience, is at issue in Horace's satire because it is what Horace says he doesn't want to write; his treatment of satires is a sort of extended *praeteritio*. Readers of Roman literature are likely to assess Lucilius's writings on the basis of what Horace says about Lucilius, rather than on the basis of the twelve hundred lines of fragments left to us from Lucilius. Similarly, we form the idea of satire as a genre of menace and harsh speaking from the warnings Horace issues in *Satires* 1.4 about the fear and hatred the genre inspires, rather than from a comprehensive assessment of the republican history of Roman satire. But before Horace issues those warnings, he provides a conceptual frame in the first three satires of book 1 to demonstrate the need to abide by human limitations and to show the dangers of going beyond the limits that our material circumstances impose on us. The first three *Satires* articulate a view of human happiness that is familiar to any student of ancient moral philosophy: if we live within realistic limits we can live a contented life; we already possess what is sufficient unto the day. Each of the first three *Satires* takes a slightly different turn on the concept of sufficiency, of what is *satis*. The outlook of these three poems expands from the point of view of one's relation to oneself, outward to one's relation to others. Horace's pun on *satura*, through his use of the word *satis* and its affines, points to the theoretical path he will follow in his satire. If fullness is possible, then there necessarily are borders or limits (*fines*) that delineate this condition of satiety. The first three satires consider these limits and the consequences of living within and without them: they present what, according to Horatian satire, is *satis*.

Each of the first three satires explores the context of a certain limit on human desire, and the discussion moves outward from the narcissistic situation of one's relation to desires for objects that gratify the self, to one's relation to the desires of other human beings. In Horace's satiric conception, the desires most in need of limitation are those that belong to satire's genetic forebears, invective speech and the speech of magical incantation. These are both verbal ways to control a listener, ways to exploit the passivity of listening in order to gain control over another, and to expand the (speaking) self past its viable boundaries. Even speech without anger or hostile intent can easily be a weapon against the hearer. Horace takes pains to show the reader that he recognizes the danger of excessive talk, talk that invades the listener, that breaks him with exhausting words. Horace repeatedly reassures the reader that he will remain within the boundaries of speaking and thus will not ruin the listener's pleasure; he will observe his own principle of moderation in speech. The conceptual outline of limitation (what is *satis* within those limits) that emerges in the first three poems will then operate for book 1 as a whole.

Satires 1.1: Limiting Desire

Horace begins the *Satires* by examining the problem of desire, as it pertains to the self in general, and the ways in which the self can satisfy its desires; he focuses, in *Satires* 1.1, on the desire for wealth and domination, which, though we believe they will make us happy, invariably wreck our happiness. Why, Horace asks Maecenas in the opening poem, and following the convention of μεμψιμοιρία (blaming fate), is no one able to live content with his lot?

> Qui fit, Maecenas, ut nemo, quam sibi sortem
> seu ratio dederit seu fors obiecerit, illa
> *contentus* vivat, laudet diversa sequentis?
>   *Sat.* 1.1.1–3

> How does it happen, Maecenas, that no one lives content with the lot that either planning has given him or chance has thrown in his way, but instead he praises those who follow other paths?

The answer, Horace asserts at the end of the poem, is that people live life as if it were a chariot race, aware only of who is ahead and discounting those they have overtaken:

> illuc unde abii redeo, qui nemo, ut avarus,
> se probet, ac *potius* laudet diversa sequentis,

quodque aliena capella gerat *distentius* uber,
tabescat, neque se *maiori pauperiorum*
turbae comparet, hunc atque hunc superare laboret.
sic festinanti semper *locupletior* obstat,
ut, cum carceribus missos rapit ungula currus,
instat equis auriga suos vincentibus, illum
praeteritum temnens extremos inter euntem.
    Sat. 1.1.108–16

So I come back to where I began, how it is that no one can like himself, being greedy, but, *rather*, praises those with different lives; because his neighbor's goat has an udder that stretches *bigger*, he's eaten up with envy; and he wouldn't compare himself to the *bigger* crowd of those *worse off*, but works only to get ahead of one after another. There's always a *richer* man to stand in the way as he hurries—it's the same as when the horses' hooves sweep the chariots free of the gates, and the charioteer presses against the horses defeating his own, and takes no note of whom he passed and left among the stragglers.

The first satire bristles with comparative adjectives that characterize the envy of competitive desire: "It is *better* to be in the army"; "nothing stands in your way so long as some other is *richer* than you are"; "his neighbor's goat has an udder stretched *bigger*." What another has is the measure of what you lack. Because of this envy you cannot love what you have and can never feel complete: "at bona pars hominum decepta *cupidine falso* / '*nil satis est*' inquit, 'quia tanti quantum habeas sis'" (1.1.61–62, but the better part of mankind, taken in by *false desire*, says "*it's not enough, because you are only as much as you have*"). False desire—that is, desire for what one does not need, or what Epicurus calls empty or false belief (κενὴ or ψευδὴ δόξα [*KD* 30])—makes people think in this way. Fear grips the one who lives like this, fear of losing what he has, and fear that always recalls the ultimate loss, the loss of life itself. This fear makes for distortions and confusions: a rich man, hated, goes home and gives himself a round of applause, alone with his piles of money; another sleeps with his cash and suffers a confusion about the sacred—he worships his heaps of money as if they were votive tablets (1.1.64–72).

The only cure is living inside nature's boundaries; it is profitless to attempt a life beyond those limits:

milia frumenti tua triverit area centum,
non tuus hoc capiet *venter* plus ac meus: ut si
reticulum panis venalis inter onusto
forte vehas umero, nihilo plus accipias quam
qui nil portarit. vel dic quid referat *intra*
naturae finis viventi, iugera centum an
mille aret? "at suave est ex magno tollere acervo."

    Sat. 1.1.45–51

Even though your threshing floor pounds out a hundred thousand bushels
of grain, your *stomach* will still hold no more than mine. It's this way: if you
were the slave who happened to carry the weight of the bread bag on your
shoulder, you'd get no more bread than the one who carried nothing. Or,
explain what difference it makes to him who lives *within nature's boundaries,*
whether he ploughs a hundred acres or a thousand?

The interlocutor has responded with the unreason of appetite: "but it feels
good." Nevertheless the stomach supplies the limit to appetite, and thus
supplies this moral philosophizing concerned with limits with a metaphor
ready to hand: all desire has natural limits in the same way that the desire
for food has the material limit of the stomach.

est *modus* in rebus, sunt *certi* denique *fines,*
quos ultra citraque nequit consistere rectum.

    Sat. 1.106–7

There is a *mean* in things, there are, in fine, *sure boundaries:* past these or
short of them the right path cannot go.

If the borders of the stomach are the model for nature's limits, then
food—its kind and use—is the model for the objects of desire. The ant
(the only *sapiens* in the poem, 38) lays up the food it needs as the year
turns and knows when it has what it needs for the winter. In contrast there
is no season that stops the ant's greedy and desperate human counterpart
from his quest for gain ("lucro," 39), as long as someone else is wealthier
(as long as there is a horse ahead in the chariot race). Plain food (74) is
all that human nature wants, and little cakes can make a child learn its
lessons:

praeterea ne sic ut qui iocularia ridens
percurram: quamquam ridentem dicere verum
quid vetat? ut pueris olim dant crustula blandi
doctores, elementa velint ut discere prima.
    Sat. 1.23–26

[A]nd besides—not to scamper on, laughing like a joker—but, what's to stop
one from telling the truth while laughing? It's just the way kindly school-
teachers sometimes give little cakes to children so they'll want to learn their
lessons.

Horace here recalls Lucretius's famous trick of lining the cup with the
honey of poetry in order to make his Epicurean philosophical medicine
more palatable.[2] By comparing the laughter of his satire with the little
cakes that teachers give children, Horace links himself to Lucretius and to
the latter's poetic program; Horace says, in effect, that his laughter will do
good, not harm, because it belongs to a world of limits and satisfaction.
Like Lucretius, he alludes to the very medium in which he is speaking, in
order to draw attention to his method. Moreover, this Lucretian figure
lays the ground for the paraphrase of Lucretius that the reader encounters at the end of the poem. In *De Rerum Natura*, Lucretius writes:

Cur non ut *plenus* vitae *conviva* recedis,
Aequo animoque capis securam, stulte, quietem?
    De Rerum Natura 3.938–39

Why don't you withdraw from life, like a full dinner guest, and take your
rest, you fool, carefree with a tranquil mind?

Horace's paraphrase both reinforces the gastric metaphor of his poem and
enlists Lucretius's philosophical program in the workings of Horatian satire:

inde fit ut raro qui se vixisse beatum
dicat, et exacto *contentus* tempore vita
cedat uti *conviva satur*, reperire queamus.
iam *satis* est. ne me Crispini scrinia lippi
compilasse putes, verbum non amplius addam.
    Sat. 1.1.117–21

And so it is that rarely do we find one to say that he has lived well, and, *content* with his span of time, takes leave of life like a *filled-up* dinner guest.

Now this is *enough* [full]. So that you won't think I've rifled the desk of half-blind Crispinus, I'll add not one word more.

Horace's *fines* have reprised Epicurean borders and boundaries, but he also then applies them to his own writing. Just as Lucretius's dinner guest in *DRN* leaves the table of life *plenus*, Horace's doppelganger for this ideal in *Satires* 1.1 leaves *satur*. The figure who said "nil satis est" now says "iam satis est" and says no more. Horace, true to his much-repeated precept, will stay inside the boundaries of the poem and will not burden the reader with words to bore, exhaust, or harm him.

Although one great impulse that breaks boundaries in satire is anger, the only anger in *Satires* 1.1 belongs to Jupiter, and even the god seems merely exasperated. When Jupiter offers humans the chance to switch lives, those humans are immobile (1.1.15–22). The sky god appears as an indulgent parent, blowing annoyed wind from heaven, but no worse. There is obviously no danger to the audience from *this* satire of the menacing, outsized voice of invective. But we will see how Horace plants the idea of invective potential, and of the unbounded self that speaks invective, into the satiric program that he builds out of his pointed omissions.

Satires 1.2: Limiting Desire for Erotic Objects

nonne cupidinibus statuat *natura modum* quem,
quid latura sibi quid sit dolitura negatum,
quaerere plus prodest et inane abscindere soldo?
num tibi cum fauces urit sitis, aurea quaeris
pocula? num esuriens fastidis omnia praeter
pavonem rhombumque? tument tibi cum inguina, num si
ancilla aut verna est praesto puer, impetus in quem
continuo fiat, malis tentigine rumpi?
non ego: namque *parabilem* amo *venerem facilemque*.
    Sat. 1.2.111–19

Doesn't it surely do more good to find the limit that nature puts on desires, what she will tolerate and what she will miss, if it's denied; and isn't it better to clearly distinguish void and substance?

You're really going to claim that when your throat burns with thirst, you need a golden goblet? That when you're starving you spurn all but peacock and turbot? That when you've got a gigantic hard-on, though there's a housemaid or a slave boy right there to go at it at once with, you'd prefer, engorged, to burst? Well, not me—I like sex right at hand and easy.

The second satire continues to consider the trouble that comes when desire leaps over the borders of reality and drives men to extremes.[3] Continuing his focus on the *satis* principle of correction, Horace examines sexual desire in the context of the generic human problem—that the imaginings or false beliefs of desire substitute for reality and the limits of nature. The poem begins as if it will continue to dilate on the theme of 1.1, the pursuit of excess—how men go to wild extremes of prodigality or self-imposed penury: "dum vitant stulti vitia, in contraria currunt" (1.2.24, While fools avoid one fault, they run to its opposite).[4] But two examples of sartorial excess (25–27) lead us abruptly to the problem of sexual excess, which is the poem's subject:

> nil medium est. sunt qui nolint tetigisse nisi illas
> quarum subsuta talos tegat instita veste;
> contra alius nullam nisi olenti in fornice stantem.
>   *Sat.* 1.2.28–30

There's no middle ground. Some men don't want to touch a woman unless her ankles are hidden under a flounced robe; then there's the other kind who won't touch any woman unless she's standing in a stinking brothel.

In the first satire an excess of *having* breeds the fear of *losing*: because the threat of loss is so great, the money that one has becomes desperately precious—to the extent that the fear prompts a confusion about what is sacred (1.1.70–72). A similar confusion of boundaries—or in other words, confusion between appearance and reality—is the focus of 1.2, but here the problem is that men choose their sexual objects badly. False belief commandeers desire, and men confuse social status, spurious beauty, or a general self-deceit with the reality of their need. As the stomach, hunger, and food supplied metaphors for desire, need, and satisfaction in the first satire, so here too the penis supplies the limit to need. In a reversal of the modern view, according to which a man's reason is blotted out by his member,[5] Horace's sexual blunderer gets a stern word from his penis:

huic si *mutonis* verbis mala tanta videnti
diceret haec animus: "quid vis tibi? numquid ego a te
magno prognatum deposco consule cunnum
velatumque stola, mea cum conferbuit ira?"
quid responderet? "magno patre nata puella est."[6]
   Sat. 1.2.68–72

If his brain—of this guy who's seen all this trouble—spoke to him with
the words of his prick, this way: "What do you want? When my blood is up,
do *I* ever crave pussy that's offspring of a brilliant consul, who's wrapped up
in a stola?" What would he reply? "But this girl's the daughter of a big shot."

The voice of reason comes from his body; the body's material reality is
sanity and is the measure of *satis:*

at quanto meliora monet pugnantiaque istis
dives opis *natura* suae, tu si modo recte
dispensare velis ac non fugienda petendis
immiscere.
   Sat. 1.2.73–76

But how much better, and how much at odds with this, are the things that
nature recommends—she rich in her own stores—if you would only make
good use of her and not confuse what to avoid with what to want!

In reality, barriers abound in the pursuit of the wrong objects of desire—
angry husbands, severe jurors, shame, and plain physical impediments:

si interdicta petes, vallo circumdata—nam te
hoc facit insanum,—multae tibi tum officient res,
custodes, lectica, ciniflones, parasitae,
ad talos stola demissa et circumdata palla,
plurima, quae invideant pure apparere tibi *rem.*
   Sat. 1.2.96–100

If you're after the forbidden, what's surrounded by a rampart (and this
makes you crazy), then so much gets in your way: guards, the litter bed, hair-
dressers, parasites, the clothes covering her from head to foot; a thousand
things work against your seeing *reality* clearly.

None of this stops the man who is the victim of this particular madness; he is insane precisely because he will not see reality, cannot abide its limits and barriers and so proceeds in his self-destructive boundary breaking. The girl wearing transparent Coan silk who is visible and for sale (101–3) hides nothing and also prompts no madness; there is in that unmysterious interaction no loss, no fear of loss, and no confusion of appearance and reality; she is the remedy to the madness that this satire examines, the available, known object. No appetite is so linked to unreason as the erotic one, and yet it can be tamed by the principle of *satis*.

Here it is useful to consider the second satire of book 1 in a historical and also an ideological context. Because of the way it deals with sexual matters, in the European tradition this poem has often been expurgated or simply omitted from Horace's oeuvre. Even Fraenkel, though he pronounces Horace's treatment of the subject masterful, remarks that the subject itself is not only unpleasant but a hackneyed aspect of the diatribe repertoire (1957, 76, 79). *Satires* 1.2 does much more than merely reproduce the "folly of adultery" theme of diatribe, however. Horace is not attacking loose morals in this satire in a conventional way; true, he exploits the conventions of diatribe to attack adultery, for example, but this is subordinate to a larger perspective, one that has not always been understood. In 1746, Philip Francis wrote in his commentary on the *Satires* that the poem could be used to dissuade boys from misbehaving in the current age of vice (1746, ad loc.). But Horace's concern in the poem is not with the moral implications of adultery or sexual excess per se but with the way in which sexual excess exemplifies a refusal to live within nature's boundaries and hence a refusal to abide by the reality principle.

Our own views concerning the self, love, and sexual experience are as much at variance with Horace's view in this satire as Philip Francis's were. In Horace's formulation, sexual appetite matches the appetite for food, and the fact that a sentient human being gratifies his sexual needs, and in whatever way that is expedient for him, is not at issue here. While sexual desire involves another self, in the formulation of this satire that other self has no role except as an object. The choice of a slave boy or girl as the object of your desire is different from the choice of another man's wife or the daughter of a senator or an expensive freedwoman, but only because of how that choice defines *your* experience. The social configuration/status of the object of your desire changes *your* circumstances, but the object has yet to come to life. Horace's treatment is notably free of any consciousness of the "power politics" that is so central to the contemporary discussion of sexual interaction—and of course this is true for other ancient writers as well. Horace is keenly aware of the operations of domination and power—indeed, more so than most writers ancient or modern—but in *Satires* 1.2, sexuality is not a sphere in which that awareness is manifest. This is only to note that the Romans articulated their ideology about sexuality, if we may even say such a thing exists for the Romans as a discrete entity of the personality, differently from the way we do.[7] We make different claims for sexuality when we moralize on the subject, whether or not that moralizing is tongue-in-cheek.

I would argue that this satire, seemingly in the form of a diatribe, has no overt moral content, or, at most, is unstable and thrown off course by Horace's examples. Horace makes no real objection to adultery; his argument is against stupidity, lack of realism and self-knowledge—the failings that give rise to a distorted idea of need and its satisfaction. The poem toys with the conventions of diatribe rather than really reproducing the vehement tone of the Cynic philosopher. The ethical point of view that the poem does convey is embodied in Horace's concept of satire as a genre that inhabits the sufficient space between boundary lines and that argues how and why human happiness is found within those boundaries.

At the end of *Satires* 1.2, Horace provides a final example of sufficiency when—in contrast to the adulterer caught midstroke as the husband returns, with the consequent bedlam and injury—Horace, or his narrator, speaks of lying with a girl who, without disguises, is the genuine article, a choice well inside nature's boundaries:

> candida rectaque sit; munda hactenus, ut neque longa
> nec magis alba velit quam dat *natura* videri.
> haec ubi supposuit dextro corpus mihi laevum,
> Ilia et Egeria est; do nomen quodlibet illi.
>   *Sat.* 1.2.123–26

I want her fair and shapely, and made-up—but not so much that she appears taller and blonder than nature made her. When this girl lays her body down next to mine, flank to flank, she is my Ilia and my Egeria—give whatever name you like to her.

"I don't like girls who want to seem taller and blonder than they really are": Horace is giving voice to the old anxiety, articulated in its genuine color by Hesiod in the *Works and Days* (for example), that men are the dupes of their own desire, and women—who are the objects of desire but are substituted for the desire itself—can make monkeys out of men by appearing different than they are. Where Hesiod's account of the creation of Pandora is forthrightly drenched in the male fear of female deceit and consequent loss of control, Horace presents a suave confidence that, Epicurean as he is, he knows the difference between fraud and honest dealing, and the girl he chooses will be his for the renaming. If the object of desire has no "self," it also poses no threat.

By having his narrator call this girl who fulfills his reasonable need Ilia or Egeria, Horace is making his point that the *fulfillment* of desire makes an ordinary girl into Romulus's mother or King Numa's divine paramour—in other words, that happiness is always easily within our reach, in the consoling realm of reality, if we would only see it. But this also brings him to the following satire's particular point about the boundaries that reality offers.

Satires 1.3: The Other as Limit

Satires 1.3 is the first poem of this book to consider limits to behavior in terms of the desires of others and in terms of social interaction. The self here inhabits a world of other selves. *Satires* 1.3 makes a small move away from the self that limits its desires only for the sake of its own health and toward a self that limits its appetites for the sake of someone else. The poem articulates the other *as* a self, shows that what the self needs is also what the other needs. "Call your friend by names that make his faults benign" in the same way a father speaks of his son or a lover of the beloved. In the previous poem Horace calls the girl who fulfills his modest desires Ilia or Egeria in order to make his point that natural desires can easily be gratified.[8] The object of his desire who has satisfied him has a perfect pedigree *because* she has satisfied him; *his* fulfillment defines the girl. In 1.3, Horace again speaks of giving generous names to another, but this time in relation to another who also needs to feel satisfied.

Satires 1.3, like the two previous poems, lays the ground for the work of satire in the other seven poems of book 1, and, in doing so, it looks beyond the self with its appetites, its excesses, and modes of correction. *Satires* 1 and 2 consider the limits on the extent to which the self may legitimately grasp for objects of gratification; overreaching gorges the self, makes it burst its borders, results in unhappiness, madness, envy, and the whole array of miseries characteristic of the human condition. But in these two poems the concern is with the self and the self alone; in 1.3 the self lives among others, and others also constitute boundaries that are dangerous to cross.

The poem is concerned with how to handle the failings, the *vitia,* of our fellows. We have an impulse to reject friends, or scorn them, for trivial failings—which is to say that we have a satiric impulse. In the next poem, *Satires* 1.4, *vitia* are connected to satire, *vitia* that have moral and ethical implications and have to do with the human being and his character, his ethical outlook, and, finally, with how the ethical outlook of the poet controls his poetry. Horace's character, as constructed by the poem, will be the delimiter of his poetry. The desire to mark faults in others, Horace will assert, is the deep genetic impulse that makes his satiric predecessor Lucilius the offspring of Athenian Old Comedy. But the desire to mark faults is also apparently a universal impulse. It is one that we need to curb if we want to have relations of any warmth and pleasure with others. It is important to note that as soon as Horace begins to speak of our desires and our relations with others, he speaks of the desire to diminish the other, to exploit the *vitia,* the failings, of the other in order to congratulate ourselves. Maenius's uncritical self-love, which feels no inhibition about picking at others, deserves to be censured. This love is *stultus* and *improbus:*

Maenius absentem Novium cum carperet, "heus tu"
quidam ait, "ignoras te, an ut ignotum dare nobis
verba putas?" "egomet mi ignosco" Maenius inquit.
stultus et inprobus hic amor est dignusque *notari.*
cum tua pervideas *oculis* mala *lippus inunctis,*
cur in amicorum vitiis tam cernis acutum
quam aut aquila aut serpens Epidaurius? at tibi contra
evenit, inquirant vitia ut tua rursus et illi.
   Sat. 1.3.21–28

When Maenius was picking at Novius behind his back, someone said, "Look, what about you, don't you know yourself, or do you think you can flim-flam us as if we didn't know you?" "Oh, me, I forgive myself (I don't know myself)," Maenius says.

This self-love is stupid and shameless, and ought to be censured. Given that you view your own misdeeds as if you had pink-eye, your sight obscured by ointment, why then do you discern the shortcomings of your friends with sight as sharp as an eagle or an Epidaurian snake? But it'll come back at you, and they'll be looking into your shortcomings in return.

The folly of Maenius's self-forgiveness is couched in practical terms: you will get the same treatment you deal out. There is, in a sense, a remarkable justice in human dealings: contempt, mockery, and criticism of another get you the same in return, and so do affection and tolerance. If you are so foolish as to indulge faults in yourself that you can't indulge in another, you deserve to be censured—*notari* (24). What you deserve, in fact, is the action of satire.

Satires 1.3 proposes that the model for right behavior, of the self in relation to the other, is, first, the lover to the beloved and, second, the father to the son. The bad eyesight of the beholder works to a positive end:

illuc praevertamur, *amatorem* quod amicae
turpia decipiunt caecum vitia, aut etiam ipsa haec
delectant, veluti Balbinum polypus Hagnae.
vellem in amicitia sic erraremus, et isti
errori nomen virtus posuisset honestum.
at *pater* ut gnati sic nos debemus amici
si quod sit vitium non fastidire.
    Sat. 1.3.38–44

Let's consider this instead, that the blind lover is deceived about his girlfriend's nasty flaws—or he even takes pleasure in these very flaws—the way Balbinus feels about the wart on Hagna's nose. I wish we went astray like that in friendship, and that goodness gave a fine name to such mistakes. Just as a father is with his son, so should we, as friend to a friend, not be squeamish about some failing of his, whatever it is.

The relationships of father to child and lover to beloved are paradigmatic for friendship. In those relationships the feeling you have for the object of your love transforms his or her faults into endearing traits; the cross-eyed child is called Winky, the wart-ridden Hagna turns into "my little chickadee." It's all in a name, or rather all in the way you construct the features of the other. What counts is that you see the other as a self. We are, after all, endlessly generous with our own failings. The other has the same needs for love that you have: give to another the love you give to yourself. The father indulges his children's failings and gives them gentle names to make them endearing. Define the other as a self, the way fathers do their children and lovers do the beloved. This is how the friend ought to regard the failings of a friend, and yet in this very way we fail by doing the opposite in friendship:

> opinor,
> haec res et iungit iunctos et servat amicos.
> at nos virtutes ipsas invertimus atque
> sincerum cupimus vas incrustare. probus quis
> nobiscum vivit, multum demissus homo: illi
> tardo cognomen, pingui, damus.
>   *Sat.* 1.3.53–58

This is the way, I think, both to make friends and keep friends. But we turn this very goodness upside down and can't wait to dirty a clean dish. Someone who lives among us is a fine human being, and terribly shy; we nickname him loser, fatty.

We make a friendship into what Epicurus in *Key Doctrines* 21 calls a competitive involvement and suffer the consequent loneliness and incompletion: "He who knows the limits of life [τὰ πέρατα τοῦ βίου] knows how easy it is to obtain that which removes pain caused by want and that which makes the whole of life complete. He therefore has no need for competitive involvements [πραγμάτων ἀγῶνας κεκτημένων]." It appears that our own self-love should be our real guide. The only way for us to measure ethical treatment is to consult our own experience. What is pleasure to us is pleasure to another. This also requires us to grant that the other is another self and simultaneously to see that this sameness is what constitutes difference: other human beings are selves in their own right and different from us precisely insofar as they possess a selfhood made up of desires and plans devised in relation to that self, in the same way we do. The other has a commitment to the self just as we have a commitment to our selves. Out of this awareness one develops an ethical view of reality in which one places limits on one's own desires according to how those desires impinge on others. In this way, self-love is the guide to understanding the other: our own self-love teaches us about the self-love of others; our own self-love then has to accommodate the self-love of another. Consequently, Maenius deserves to be marked, noted, and censured because his self-love, foolish and wrong, fails at the boundary and crosses over so that he sees no wrong in indulging himself and carping at others—sees no wrong in granting himself a different standard than the one he applies to others. Maenius fails to see the nature of the difference between selves, fails to see that the difference lies in the distinctions or boundaries between entities who are constituted in the same way.

In the first poem of his second book of *Satires*, Horace opens by alluding to a "law" of satire that he claims (though disingenuously, we might note) his critics say he has transgressed (2.1.1–2). But there is already a law in *Satires* 1.3 that will serve as a conceptual foundation for Horace's satirical practice. That law here consists of an agreement between two parties—between two friends, self and other—which is an agreement that one will recognize the other as a "self" and will agree to the same conditions of communication and judgment for the comfort of the other, in order to gain that comfort for the self (when he weighs my faults, let his be placed, according to this law, in the same balance: "hac lege in trutina ponentur eadem," 72).

> eheu,
> quam temere in nosmet legem sancimus iniquam!
> nam vitiis nemo sine nascitur: optimus ille est
> qui minimis urgetur. amicus dulcis et aequum est
> cum mea compenset *vitiis* bona, pluribus hisce—
> si modo plura mihi bona sunt—inclinet, amari
> si volet: *hac lege in trutina ponetur eadem.*
> qui ne tuberibus propriis offendat amicum
> postulat, ignoscet verrucis illius; aequum est
> peccatis veniam poscentem reddere rursus.
>   *Sat.* 1.3.66–75

Good lord, how recklessly we levy the same unfair law against ourselves. For no one is born without faults; he is best who is burdened with the fewest. A kind friend will weigh my virtues against my faults, it's fair, and he'll favor the first since they are more numerous—if indeed my virtues *are* more numerous—if he wants my love: *according to this rule he will be weighed in the same scales*. If he wants his friend to tolerate his blemishes, he had better forgive his friend's warts: if you demand indulgence for your failings it is fair to grant it in return.

While the other is in fact a version of the self, that other also provides a boundary to the self. The boundary is a boundary to anger, a limit placed on the impulse to mock and scorn, a fence placed about the desire to dominate another. *Satires* 1.3 first looks at this human figure that Horace constructs out of impulses and desires that need restraining and sees him as one who lives among other humans; in order to have a happy life, he must regulate his own desires according to what others desire: the desire of another is as firm a boundary as the limit of the stomach. The reward is that you will not be the reciprocal target of the anger that you feel toward others, if you restrain that anger, that is, if you follow this condition: "hac lege" (72). The long passage on human evolution, vv. 99–124, is Horace's satiric founding myth that tells how justice arises from the fear of injustice, which is another way to say the same thing: fair action arises from the wish to be dealt with fairly. It is also another advance notice of the satirical program that Horace will explicitly reveal in the following poem, *Satires* 1.4, where the poet will assure his audience that the exchange of satiric speech will do no harm.

Satires 1.3 is concerned with a justice that is enacted in the appropriate assessment of failings, and from this point of view the discussion veers into the lunacy of the Stoic position that puts all failings on the same level. The attack on the Stoic *sapiens* is a means of shoring up the satire's view that to criticize others unduly, to refuse to be generous to the other who is, after all, a version of the self, is to refuse to recognize reality. Horace's constructed Stoic *sapiens* of 1.3 fails to see distinctions between *vitia*.

> denique, quatenus excidi penitus vitium irae,
> cetera item nequeunt stultis haerentia, cur non
> ponderibus modulisque suis ratio utitur, ac res
> ut quaeque est ita suppliciis delicta coercet?
>   *Sat.* 1.3.76–79

In short, insomuch as the fault of anger, like the rest of the faults that cling so deep in witless humans, cannot be completely cut out, why can't reason use her own weights and measures and, for each given situation, restrain the crimes with the punishments that fit?

The failure to see the difference between self and other, and the failure to see the likeness of self to other, is the same as the failure to distinguish between faults. Both failures are an inability to see how life works its distinctions, and are failures to see how the world is arranged. To judge right and wrong takes common sense, as does recognizing that others need the same forgiveness you do; how to judge what's right takes some work, some *sensus* and *mores* and *utilitas* (the mother of fairness, 1.3 96–98).

Finally the poem's stoic *sapiens*, the king and *dives*, is alone, and this appears to define the failure of his philosophy. The first-person speaker of the poem, the Horace of 1.3, contrasts himself to the *sapiens*: with friendships that rely on forgiveness, he is embedded in a world of comfort; the stoic *sapiens* barks and growls (36) and is alone except for the unattractive Crispinus, who accompanies him to his bath. Horace, again, is also already telling us about the satirist he will turn out to be in *Satires* 1.4, when he is more likely to be the victim of satiric bark and bite.

This poem that introduces the needs of the other, and presents those needs as another limiter on the expansive desires of the self, at the end expresses the poet's pleasure in his community of friends and mocks the rigid philosopher, who pays the price for his rigidity by living alone. The next poem, *Satires* 1.4, will apply the problem of the needs of the other to the needs of a satirist's audience and will consider what kind of poet can avoid doing harm to his audience when he writes satire. In 1.4 the poet is the "self" that must restrain its desire for coercive or threatening speech in order to have a relationship with the "other," his audience. *Satires* 1.4 will be about desire in speech and the desire to violate the boundaries of the listener. As *Satires* 1.3 makes *vitia* and how to judge them its subject, the next satire will make *vitia* into faults of both behavior and poetry, and will assert an identity between the poet and his poem in order to argue that the audience of his satire is safe. The persona of the speaker is unnecessary until he begins to address the issues of satire itself; then that persona is required to protect the audience. This persona will also support the useful conceit that satire is a potentially dangerous genre, even in Horace's wily hands.

And once again a father, this time Horace's own father, will enact the model of satirical behavior with his son. Horace's enticing allusion to "himself" in 1.3.64, where he slips a gentle address to Maecenas into the poem, and offers a glimpse of that famous relationship, is a tiny harbinger of the full-blown artfulness of his autobiography in *Satires* 1.4. He will offer that self-portrait as a way to demonstrate and prove the limits he wishes to place on the outsized desires of satiric speech.

❯❯ 2 ❮❮

Horace and His Fathers

Satires 1.4 and 1.6

Fere nulli alii sunt homines qui talem in filios suos habent potestatem qualem nos habemus.

There are virtually no other human beings who possess such power over their sons as we do.

—GAIUS, *Institutiones Iuris Civilis*, 1.55

No ancient poet offers the sense of affectionate intimacy that Horace grants to his readers with his account of his father and his upbringing in the *Satires*. It is consequently with some initial regret that readers recognize that Horace tells us very little about his life, and that furthermore the "information" he supplies is motivated by its poetic context, rather than by the impulse that Horace beguilingly alludes to, of confessing his life to his books.[1] *Satires* 1.4 and 1.6 are the well-known loci of Horace's upbringing by his father, told in the context of Horace's relation to Lucilius, his satiric forbear, and to Maecenas, the man conventionally known as Horace's patron. All four figures—father, son, satiric predecessor, and patron—are artifacts of the poet's generic construction, dramatis personae structured to provide a definition to Horace's satiric art. The freedman father who so famously raised his son, by hand as it were, serves to organize the relation between Horace and the two figures Horace makes to loom in his poetic life, Lucilius and Maecenas. Paired in their respective poems with Horace's father, Lucilius and Maecenas are given a fatherly relationship to Horace only to be displaced by the biological parent. More remarkably, Horace's biological father emerges from the poems as Horace's poetic father too, and this leaves Lucilius and Maecenas deprived of the poetically crucial role that they seemed bound to assume in the satire and life of the poet. These paternal maneuvers in *Satires* 1.4 and 1.6 make the persona of

Horace the poetic cause of his art, make the constructed "self" of Horace the unshakable source of his poetry, and secure a particular disposition for his satire. Although Horace appears to subordinate art to life, extracting the causes of his persona and his poetry from his father's training and social status, the eventual outcome works in reverse, and it is the poet's life that is subordinated to his art.

Satires 1.4: Who Is the Father of This Genre?

It is especially important to recognize the artful selectivity of Horace's self-portrait in the *Satires*, because the satirist's persona emerges as a crucially defining element of the genre of satire for Horace. In *Satires* 1.4, Horace uses his own persona to explain, justify, and limit the satiric poetry he writes. Although Horace begins the poem by distinguishing himself from Lucilius stylistically, what evolves in the course of the poem is a contemplation of human character in which poetic style is only one outcome of that character. Horace's defense of his satire in 1.4 rests on a self-description couched in ethical, not poetic, terms. The merging of poetic style and personal character produces a picture of the satiric genre that is identified with the poet himself; the poetry is the inevitable outcome of the man. When Horace asks whether his poetry is justifiably *suspectum* (1.4.65), he answers by telling us who he is; the poet *is* the answer to the question about the genre. Style and ethos are thus made indistinguishable.

That art can be wholly identified with its human source is in some sense a radical view, but this view is congenial to Horace's satire, which he fixes in the ordinariness of life and whose muse is, as Horace says later, *pedestris*.[2] As satire constantly finds its wisdom, parody, or bite in ordinary material reality, so Horace's strategy of equating the poem with its material cause, i.e. the poet, is perfectly consistent with the genre's orientation. It is a genre, after all, whose name can be derived from a food, the stuff of life.[3]

If the portrait of Horace's father is determined by its poetic context in 1.4, as I suggest is the case with all the dramatis personae of these poems, the portrait of Lucilius is in turn determined not only by the poetic context but also by the portrait of Horace's father. Lucilius enters *Satires* 1.4, and the *Satires* as a whole, on the heels of the Old Comic poets Eupolis, Cratinus, and Aristophanes; Horace begins his discussion of his genre in the opening six lines of *Satires* 1.4 with a discussion of Lucilius's lineage. The Greek comic poets, Horace says, "noted with great freedom" ("multa cum libertate notabant," 1.4.5) the faults of any who deserved it ("quis erat dignus," 3). From these poets Lucilius is entirely descended; he follows them in all but metrical form (6–7). *Satires* 1.4 will demonstrate that ultimately Horace and Lucilius have separate genealogies. While Lucilius enjoys descent from the Old Comic poets, who freely noted human failings, Horace learned the same practice of noting faults from his father but learned it for very different ends (and with little freedom). Though Horace writes in Lucilius's genre, they have no common ancestors.[4] Horace disowns his satire's literary pedigree in order to make his genre widely distinct from that of Lucilius, his literary parent.

The path that *Satires* 1.4 takes to relocate Horatian satire, however, is a winding one. Although the problematic nature of Lucilian satire and its practice of noting faults is the issue the poem resolves, Horace is quick to establish that the first failing to address is in Lucilius's style. Having granted that Lucilius was elegant, had a keen nose, and was a tough writer of verse ("durus componere versus," 8), traits themselves decreasingly positive in Horace's poetic lexicon, Horace also states that Lucilius was *vitiosus:* he wrote too much too fast, and, too lazy to write correctly ("garrulus atque piger scribendi ferre laborem, / scribendi recte," 12–13) produced a muddy river.[5] Lucilius's distinguished status as a direct descendant of the Greek Old Comic poets takes a swift fall with Horace's catalog of his predecessor's stylistic failings, which ends with a terse reference to the quantity of Lucilius's verse ("nam ut multum, nil moror," 13).

By way of an invidious comparison between himself and the blowhard Crispinus (13–16), Horace tells us that the gods made him by nature incapable of Lucilius's "vitia: di bene fecerunt, inopis me quodque pusilli finxerunt animi, raro et perpauca loquentis" (17–18). The words *raro* and *perpauca,* key words of neoteric aesthetics, suggest that Horace's nature is "poetically correct," and that he is unable, by nature, to produce large, lumbering verses. It emerges, however, that no one reads Horace's writings, not because they are tightly crafted and the product of a taste uncongenial to the crowd, but because the content of satire ("genus hoc," 24) displeases people: like the audience of Old Comedy, they deserve blame ("culpari dignos," 25) and do not like to have this pointed out. Horace confesses, or appears to confess, that no one reads his writings and that he is in fact afraid to recite to the public ("vulgo," 23). The poem opens with a question of style that becomes a question of the relationship between the satirist and his audience, and the ethical issues involved therein. Horace identifies the freedom in noting faults that Lucilius inherited from Old Comedy as a danger that will redound upon the satirist.[6] The audience fears the genre of satire, as Horace inherits it from Lucilius, because that audience is likely to exhibit the faults that the satirist, like the Old Comic writers, found blameworthy. If we believe what Horace says, this dubious crowd has never even heard Horace's version of satire. Horace grants that most people have faults that deserve blame, but not that he in fact writes the same kind of satire Lucilius does; on suspicion of association with this genre, he is an unheard poet.

Horace's discussion of Lucilius's stylistic failings and of his own freedom from such failings had created the expectation that he was about to mark out his poetic territory as a poet of the elite, one whose style is fitted to a more refined taste. What Horace says instead, however, suggests that he is *unfairly* treated by the crowd, which, given to greed, ambition, and intemperate passion (traditional moral failings reprised in vv. 25–32), fears poetry and hates poets:

> omnes hi metuunt versus, odere poetas.
> "faenum habet in cornu; longe fuge: dummodo risum
> excutiat, sibi non, non cuiquam parcet amico;
> et quodcumque semel chartis illeverit, omnis
> gestiet a furno redeuntis scire lacuque,
> et pueros et anus." agedum, pauca accipe contra.
>   *Sat.* 1.4.33–38

All of these fear poetry, hate poets. "He's got straw on his horn [he acts like a crazed bull]; steer clear: if he can squeeze out a laugh he'll spare no one, not a friend, not himself; and as soon as he's scratched it onto his page, he's dying for everybody, every slave and old woman coming back from the bakery and the watering-hole, to know it." Well now, come hear a few words from the other side.

The section of *Satires* 1.4, in which Horace presents the putative accusation against himself and his rebuttal to that accusation, is a piece of the *Satires* whose humor has been too little grasped by critics.[7] The leap from Horace's restrained style to the moral failings of his potential audience (23) has come as a surprise, and the further suggestion that the vice-prone *turba* (25) fears poetry and hates poets (33) is an unlikely one, given the popularity in antiquity of both Greek Old Comedy and Lucilius. The characterization of the poet, in vv. 34–38 (where he supposedly quotes the audience he has already said he doesn't have), if Horace means himself, is utterly implausible for this poet who scorns the challenges of Crispinus to a writing contest (14–16) and sneers at Lucilius for writing while he "stands on one foot" (9–10). Horace's conclusion that his possible audience fears poetry and hates poets casts an improbably wide net for poetry; it is surely not poetry but this genre of poetry that makes the audience nervous. Horace gives a long and illogical rebuttal (39–62) to this, however, saying that he, Lucilius, and writers of comedy should perhaps not be considered poets at all. His defense "answers" the initially untenable statement that the audience of dubious morals hates poets, with the result, if one chooses to follow the "logic" of Horace's argument, that it is right to fear Ennius but not Horace, or conceivably that this untutored and fearful crowd is unable to make generic distinctions thanks to the baneful effects of fault-noting comics and satirists. Either way, the suggestion that Horace does not write poetry when he writes satire seems to be no solution to the problem Horace claims to have with his audience, nor does that audience seem a likely one for Horace to court, since he has disdained poets, like Fannius (21), who are eager for any audience at all.

Horace's rebuttal is hardly brief ("pauca," 38). In the argument of vv. 39–62, Horace proposes to remove himself from the ranks of poets, taking Lucilius with him ("nos," 41). There are those who question whether comedy is poetry, for it lacks a fierce spirit and force in both diction and substance, and differs from plain talk only in meter (39–48). To demonstrate the point that comedy differs not at all from real life—and that, like satire, it possibly should not be accorded the status of poetry—Horace gives a rendition of a conventional scene out of comedy, in which a father helplessly rages at his son's disgraceful behavior (48–56).

The scene Horace paraphrases is knowingly chosen. The rescue of Horace's satire will be accomplished in this poem by his own, real-life father; this comic father and son belong to a genre that, for the moment, links the narrative of living to the nonpoetic. The comic father burns with rage; the son is crazy ("insanus," 49) with passion for a prostitute. It isn't enough, says Horace, to write plain words in verse, with the result that, if you broke apart the meter, any angry father would rage the very same way that the father in the play does. And the same goes, Horace continues, for what Lucilius and he write. The comic scenario contributes to the

argument that the genre of Lucilius and the genre of comedy are dis-
qualified as true poetry because their speech is too much like the speech
of life itself, where fathers rage at their wastrel sons. This is only life, not
the stuff of great poetry such as Ennius writes. With a grotesque image of
the dismembered Ennius, or the dismembered satirist, Horace abandons
this line of defense, such as it is, by saying he will figure out the true
status of this poetry another time ("hactenus haec: alias iustum sit necne
poema, / . . . quaeram," 63–64).

What has this cheerfully illogical argument concerning the status of his
own genre achieved? Why devote twenty-three lines to a self-contradictory
question that is then irresolutely abandoned? For the moment Horace has
placed himself generically with Lucilius; the element, shared with comedy,
that defines the genre stylistically is its use of plain (but not inelegant)
speech: "sermoni propiora" (42), "sermo merus" (48), "puris versum . . .
verbis" (54).[8] The final reference to Ennius conveys a sense much closer
to Lucilius's parodies of the tragic poets Accius and Pacuvius than to a
sincere tribute to the great writer of the *Annales*.[9] The reference in v. 43
to the poet and his large-sounding voice, "os / magna sonaturum," recalls
Callimachean mockery of epic and the subsequent Roman enlargement of
the hundred-, then thousand-tongued epic writer.

But Horace maintains that the genre he has inherited from Lucilius is
suspect and to be feared; leaving for another time the question of whether
this genre is poetry, he now says he will content himself with an inquiry
into whether satire ("genus hoc," 65) *deserves* the suspicion cast upon it
("meritone tibi sit / suspectum genus hoc scribendi," 63–65). Horace
undertakes this inquiry, however, by considering not the poetry he is
writing but his own character. "Why fear me?" he asks. "My books aren't
out on stalls for the masses to thumb through; I read only to friends, and
only when coerced and in private, not in public or at the baths" (71–78).
In arguing that he does not deserve to be feared, Horace shows disdain
for the poets of the *vulgus* (72) and what is more, insists that he recites
his poetry only to his friends.

In his attempt to remove the suspicion and fear that have attached
themselves to the Lucilian brand of satire, Horace himself poses as the
moral counterweight to Lucilius. To the accusation that he delights in
doing harm ("laedere gaudes," 78), Horace provides examples of people
who truly do harm, those who betray friends for a laugh or for popularity. Beware of such a man as this, O Roman, says Horace in an over-heated

moment ("hic niger est, hunc tu, Romane, caveto," 85).[10] In this part of
the response to the question whether *hoc genus* is fairly *suspectum*, Horace,
offering his own character in rebuttal, develops a picture of the moral life
of friendship; and in reply to the suggestion that he delights to do harm,
he asks whether anybody with whom he has *lived* makes this assertion
("est auctor quis denique eorum vixi cum quibus?" 80–81). It is from the
community that knows Horace himself that Horace asks for a witness—
the living is the proof—and his examples support his contention: a friend
who cannot defend an absent friend (81–82 and 93–100); the dinner guest
who abuses his fellow diners and the host; people who faithlessly betray
friends in quest of laughter (83) and popularity (90 and 93–100). These
betrayals of the people with whom one lives constitute the *vitium* that
Horace forswears in poem and heart ("chartis atque animo," 101–2), the
"black ink of the cuttlefish, pure bile" (100–101). Horace makes explicit
the link between poetry and poet by describing how he is not *vitiosus*
(100–103).

When he equates his *animus* and *chartae,* Horace introduces his father
to the poem. The characteristics of the *vitium* Horace swears to avoid,
the license and laughter of the bad friend ("risus," 83; "Liber" [wine], 89;
and "liber," 90) who is three times called "black" ("niger," 85; "nigris," 91;
"nigrae," 100), have a counterpart in his own speech:

> liberius si
> dixero quid, si forte iocosius, hoc mihi iuris
> cum venia dabis: insuevit pater optimus hoc me,
> ut fugerem exemplis vitiorum quaeque *notando.*
>   *Sat.* 1.4.103–6

> If I speak a little too freely (*liberius*), or maybe joke a bit too much (*iocosius*),
> it is fair that you indulge me for this: for the best father instilled this in me
> so that, *by noting* examples of faults (*vitiorum*), I might flee from them.

The verb *notare* describes the activity of both progenitors of satire in this
poem; Lucilius is the offspring, as it were, of the writers of Old Comedy
who noted with great liberty the failings of others ("multa cum libertate
notabant," 5), and Horace is the offspring of a father who likewise noted
faults.[11] The poem gives the two satirists, Lucilius and Horace, different
family trees.

The Lucilian activity of noting faults with freedom, inherited from Old Comedy, was the pedagogic cornerstone of Horace's own upbringing ("insuevit pater optimus hoc me, / ut fugerem exempl vitiorum quaeque notando," 105–6), that Horace Sr. practiced with the explicit aim of teaching his son how to avoid the moral failings the poet has enumerated in the poem (25–102, passim). The practice was a success, and Horace, having internalized his father, now goes about the world replicating the practice, instructing himself in correct living (133–38); thanks to this method, his poetry and his heart are free from *serious* flaws. The poet adds that his father's intentions in teaching his son to note moral flaws differed from the intentions of the writers of Old Comedy and hence from those of Lucilius. By pointing out to his son living examples of human failings, Horace's father aimed to illustrate the type of behavior the young Horace should avoid. His method was both personal and pragmatic. Moreover, Horace Sr., a practical man, relegated a theoretical concern with virtue and vice to the philosopher; he felt it sufficient to pass on to his son the custom (*morem*) of the ancients (ancestors—*ab antiquis*) and to keep his son's life and reputation safe, so long as his son needed a guardian. Horace movingly quotes his father's words in vv. 115–21.

This psychologically exemplary father understands not only what the function of a Roman father must be but also that he will not forever be his son's guardian; he is a protector until such time as the child is sturdy enough, in limb and spirit, to swim without a cork. The child, father to the man, is raised according to the Roman ideal that the past is the model for *mos*.[12] Yet the father denies himself the blunt temptations of *patria potestas,* the power to own a son for life, and knows that his words will send his son off secure on the waves, to be his own guardian. He knows that it is not the force of law but the power of words that will hold a son.

"This way he formed me with his words," says Horace, who goes about reproducing in himself his father's precepts and practice, forming himself with words, noting what to avoid and what to imitate in what he sees of life (133–38). Horace's father has given him, through words, his ethical shape as a man, and Horace in turn now shapes words—poems—according to this ethos. With lips pressed together (*compressis labris,* 138), Horace rehearses his father's lessons.[13] In leisure time, he tells us next, he toys with his pages, one of those trivial faults that you would forgive in him. And so he ends the poem:

ubi quid datur oti
illudo chartis. hoc est mediocribus illis
ex vitiis unum; cui si concedere nolis,
multa poetarum veniat manus auxilio quae
sit mihi (nam multo plures sumus), ac veluti te
Iudaei cogemus in hanc concedere turbam.
    Sat. 1.4.138–43

. . . when there is time I mess with my pages. This is one of those ordinary
failings of mine, and if you didn't allow it a great gang of poets would come
give me help (for we are the greater number by far), and just like the Jews
we'd force you over to our throng.

A conversion of language has occurred during the course of this poem.
At the beginning of the poem, Lucilius, Horace's model in satire, is characterized by his stylistic *vitia*—namely, that he was careless in his writing,
too lazy to write correctly: "garrulus atque piger scribendi ferre laborem,
/ scribendi recte" (12–13). Rightness at the end of the poem is for Horace
rightness in living; it is applied to actions that will make life better, and
the poet says to himself: "rectius hoc est: / hoc faciens vivam melius"
(134–35, this way is better: I shall live better doing this). Just as Horace is
free of Lucilian garrulity (14–21), so, far from being *piger*, his diligence
proves him free of the grosser *vitia* of human character: "ex hoc ego sanus
ab illis, / perniciem quaecumque ferunt, mediocribus et quis / ignoscas
vitiis teneor" (129–31, because of this [upbringing] I am free from those failings and have only the ordinary ones that you would forgive). Lucilius,
lazy with words, is ultimately no model for the father-made, word-made
Horace ("sic me / formabat puerum dictis," 120–21); the son continues to
practice his father's precepts on himself in order to be likable to his
friends, to his poetic audience, and to the people among whom he lives.
Horace, like his father, notes *vitia* with a purpose unrevealed in the activity of Old Comedy and in the satire of Lucilius ("multa cum libertate
notabant. / hinc omnis pendet Lucilius, hosce secutus" 5–6). And the *vitia*
themselves, initially presented as characterizing the stylistically *vitiosus*
Lucilius, are transferred from the poetic to the moral realm.

Vitium, in v. 101, is applied to the activity of a man who cannot be a
friend, where it is entirely ethical in connotation and corresponds to what
Horace pledges will be absent from his pages and his heart: "quod vitium

procul afore chartis / atque animo, prius ut, si quid promittere de me / possum aliud vere, promitto" (101–3, If I can promise anything honestly about myself, I promise this, that this vice will be far away from my pages, and before that from my heart). *Vitium* also comprehends the behavior that Horace's father taught him to shun by noting its examples, as did the writers of Old Comedy: "insuevit pater optimus hoc me, / ut fugerem exemplis vitiorum quaeque notando" (105–6); and, "sic teneros animos aliena opprobria saepe / absterrent vitiis" (128–29, this way the disgraces of others often can deter the unformed soul from faults). Faults of the same type, ethical rather than stylistic, but of a more trivial nature, still bedevil Horace ("mediocribus et quis / ignoscas vitiis," 130–31), but the poet hopes that age, the honest friend, and his own counsel—the latter gained by practicing his father's art (133–38)—will remove them. Of the ordinary *vitia* remaining in the poet's character, Horace mentions only one specifically, and that is, remarkably, composing poetry: "illudo chartis. hoc est mediocribus illis / ex vitiis unum" (139–40).

The discussion has come full circle in one way, in another not at all. The poem began by characterizing the stylistic failings of Lucilius as *vitia,* proceeded to doubt whether the genres of satire and comedy even qualified as poetry, and then moved into the realm of *vitia* as moral failure. The genre of satire, nearly denied the status of poetry (39–62) and initially characterized in the poem in terms of its *vitia,* is now restyled as itself an ethical failing, but of so minor a sort that the poet may be forgiven for it. The satirist who claimed such timidity in v. 23 that he would not read out loud to the crowd now cheerfully threatens anyone intolerant of this minor failing with a gang of proselytizing poets ("multa poetarum veniat manus," 141).

The *turba* (25), too full of ethical failings to endure satire, is reconstituted as the *turba* of poets (143) to which Horace himself belongs, and it is this *turba* that is the last word of the poem. The fearful nonlisteners, full of their moral troubles, have become a throng of speakers, poets, not fearful but sure, coercive, ready to force the nonbeliever to join. The throng, earlier characterized by its vices, is now characterized by its poetry. The license of harmful speech, first in the *libertas* of Old Comic writers, Lucilius's ancestors, then in the speech of the abusive dinner guest (his true nature revealed by wine ["Liber," 89], seemingly "comis et urbanus liberque" [90], but in fact black to the core), becomes the benign *liberius* of Horace's speech (103) and finally the valuable quality of a friend, honesty,

that will help take away the faults that yet remain in the poet's nature
(132). The *membra* of verse (62), Ennius's or the satirist's, scattered about
when the words of verse are tossed out of their meter and order, become
the limbs, the *membra*, of the boy Horace (120), made strong in spirit over
time by his father's speech, speech that has enabled him to swim by himself in an ethical fashion. The adjectives to describe satire's language,
"sermo merus" (48) and "puris verbis" (54), have their metaphorical counterparts in moral terms: one can spurn accusers if one lives with clean
hands ("at bene si quis / et vivat puris manibus contemnat utrumque,"
67–68); the backbiting friend, who can do no better in defending his friend
(according to his custom, "ut tuus est mos," 95) than to impugn his character, is "aerugo mera" (101), unadulterated vitriol. Literary and moral
terms are forced into identity with each other by the poem, and an equation is made between literary and moral traits by the use of words.

In this conversion of language, the most striking aspect is the poet's
reconstitution of what it means to be a poet. Though the poem has dwelt
on the possibility that satire, *genus hoc*, is not poetry, Horace says without hesitation at the poem's end that he belongs to a *turba poetarum*. The
turba (143) is reconstituted. The meanings of words initially associated
in the poem with the literary realm shift to the moral realm, and satire is
thereby reinstated in the ranks of poetry; but this shift has essentially been
effected by the account given of Horace's father, which also forms the basis
for Horace's presentation of his persona. Horace's playful suggestion that,
in writing satire, he is not writing poetry prepares the reader for a re-
definition of satire that he accomplishes in the second half of the poem
when he makes his father's ethical training the basis, the equivalent, of his
own satirical poetic activity.

Horace's demonstration that his genre is not *suspectum* is argued
straight out of real life, and the most artfully "real" part of the second half
of the satire is in the autobiography of the poet, through the picture he
gives of his "real-life" father. The father of the poet, in contrast to the *pater
ardens* in the comic scenario Horace earlier describes (48–56), has a son
who is *sanus* (129). As a father, Horace Sr. adheres to the custom of Roman
fathers ("traditum ab antiquis morem," 117); he cautions his son away from
profligacy, from passion for a prostitute, from adultery, from gaining an
evil reputation (109–15); and he does so by means of the satirist's art, noting faults in others to instruct his son. The father and son of the poem's
comedy piece present the inversion of this relationship: the son ignores

the financial arrangements of the father; he is crazy (*insanus*), is in love with a prostitute, and courts disgrace ("quod dedecus . . . ," 51–52). The comic son defies the father and leaves him powerless and raging, while the filial Horace represented in the poem maintains his allegiance to his father and reproduces the father's ethos in both his character and his poetry. Horace as a son reproduces his father's perfect authority twice, first in his character and second in his poetry—"chartis / atque animo" (101–2). Horace fulfills the demands of comedy by presenting himself as the restored norm and supplies relief from the anxiety of chaos; the comic father and son are replaced with the father and son of Horatian satire, and this is now "real life." Such a reality, which includes living among friends, a reality shaped by the father whose authority is unquestioned and embraced by his son, is this satirist's material, and it deserves to be called poetry, with a Roman imprimatur worthy of Ennius.

In a poem preoccupied with Lucilius's satiric model, the impulse behind Lucilian satire is repressed, and Lucilius himself is excluded as a formative influence. Horace's satire is akin to that of Lucilius, but the account given of his father defines Horace's satiric practice not as the result of imitating Lucilius (or Old Comedy) but as the result of the poet's character, a character that permits friendship to flourish and is incapable of serious vices. The pure noting of faults is endowed by Horace's father with an ethical goal: satire is no longer the mere exposition of vice but the creation of virtue in its hearer. The father as source of this genre is by definition an ethical, not a literary, source, so that the resulting poetry will have a deep structure, a DNA if you will, of ethical orientation. Horace could not have built a more protective architecture for his satire. The responsible agent for this is Horace's father; the literary father, Lucilius, is duly overthrown, but by the biological father.[14]

Horace's strategy of posing father against father achieves several ends. By making his own father the debunking agent, Horace can indulge the impulse for a son to debunk a father without incurring a reproach of impiety; he achieves his distance from the literary father Lucilius in an action of such clarified Roman piety that it cannot be protested. The distance Horace takes from Lucilius lies in the conception he develops of his own satire as ethically motivated, a conception that establishes the pedigree for the motivation and gives an account of the source of his satiric ethos as one that cannot be separated from the person(a) of the poet himself. As Horace tells the tale, he cannot produce harmful speech; his account binds speech to character and makes them inseparable, so that speech is merely a symptom of character.

The restoration of the cultural norm that Horace offers, by showing us a father revered by his son and respected for his authority, performs the reassuring function of demonstrating that Roman values really do work; the stratagem, with all its overt cultural rectitude, disguises the fact that Horace has made Lucilius irrelevant to his poetic enterprise by reducing him to a weak impulse, a model largely to be avoided. Whereas, when joined with Lucilius (56–57), Horace suggests that he is not writing poetry, once he has demonstrated that his father is the satirist who has made him the poet he is, he is restored to poetry by this paternal ethical influence. Horace is a poet and will call up his trusty band of marauding poets and force any objector to become one of them (140–43). Lucilius, father of the genre of satire though he may be, is ejected by a better father who is apparently a more profound satirist, one who, with perfect Roman credentials, earns his son's reverence and is hence a support for patriarchy, the fundamental model for social order. Horace could not have devised a more thorough, persuasive, and conservative method for rejecting the influence of Lucilius on his satire.

In *Satires* 1.4, Horace creates a distance between himself and Lucilius, his literary father, by making his biological father critical to his development as a satirist, endowing the fault-noting habit of satire with a Horatian bent to engender virtue. The actual father is a wedge between Horace and his figurative, literary father Lucilius, and the Roman patriarchal context of this strategy gives Horace's satire a pedigree that enhances his redefined genre. Although the impulse to reject a parent to make space for oneself is consistent with the manner in which Horace treats Lucilius in *Satires* 1.4, it is vital to recognize the quality of this rejection, that it is done in the context of writing in Lucilius's genre, done in a poem that marks Horace's poetic activity as inside the tradition of the older poet. The rejection of his model coincides with Horace's embrace of his model, and the embrace as well as the criticism is reinforced in the following poem, *Satires* 1.5, a Lucilian *imitatio*.

What does it mean to write inside the genre of other writers? You inhabit their skin, you feel them all over; you admire and revere what they have done and who they are, but when you come to doing it yourself, you resent their mastery, their wholeness next to your incompleteness, their confidence next to your hesitation. You look for ways to mitigate your own fear by diminishing them; you find ways to be disappointed in them so that you have a chance, a space to enter. It is no wonder that Horace is kinder to Lucilius at the end of his first book of satires, in 1.10,[15] and can be wholly generous to him at the beginning of the second book, when he has accomplished something, a whole book of satires finished, and can begin to trust his own powers. He has room to praise Lucilius and grant him his due as the *inventor* of satire when the virtue of his predecessor no longer threatens to overwhelm his own efforts. It is very like a parent's power over a child; the parent is loved and longed for but occupies the place of power the child wishes to enter. Growing up means finding one's own place and at the same time assigning a new place to one's parent.[16] To write in the inherited genre is to use the predecessor's substance; the son is the material of the father in a new version.

Satires 1.6: Who Is the Father of This Satirist?

The second appearance of Horace's father in the *Satires*, in *Satires* 1.6, belongs to Horace's account of and meditation on his relationship with Maecenas. Horace tells a story of his father different from but consistent with the portrait in *Satires* 1.4, how his father, from unprepossessing circumstances, brought his son to Rome and supervised the education of the child's mind and character among the sons of senatorial and equestrian fathers. As in *Satires* 1.4, the portrait of the father appears in the second half of the poem as an explanation of the issues raised in the first half, and, as in 1.4, the account of Horace's father both articulates and challenges the fatherlike status of the poem's major figure. In 1.6, Horace again takes his distance from a figure of authority, who is paired with his father; it is important to see here not only the delicacy of the rejection but the simultaneous embrace of Maecenas, the father counterpart, as he is set alongside Horace Sr.

Satires 1.6 begins, as did *Satires* 1.4, by providing a lineage for the father counterpart. Lucilius's lineage was literary, Maecenas's sociohistorical. Horace introduces Maecenas through an address to him that points out the difference in their social status and that connects that difference to the respective conditions of their fathers. Maecenas does not, as many do, "turn up his nose" at nobodies like Horace, born to a freedman father (1.6.1–6).[17] The opening articulates what emerges as the poem's task: to consider the meaning of the difference, established by the conditions of their fathers, between Horace and his friend and patron Maecenas. The phrase "me

libertino patre natum" is the refrain of the poem's first half.[18] Maecenas
believes "that it makes no difference what a man's parent is, so long as he
is free-born," but the problem is with the crowd, with the *populus,* which
is dazzled by fame and does honor to the undeserving. What, asks Horace,
has this to do with us, far, far removed as we are from the common crowd
("quid oportet / nos facere a vulgo longe longeque remotos?" 17–18).

In his work on Roman poets and their literary patrons, Peter White
(1978 and 1993) notes that while the relationship of *amicitia* was invariably between persons of greater and lesser status, these social distinctions
are not acknowledged by the language of the relation (which uses the
terms *amicus, sodalis,* and the like equally to describe both partners in the
relationship), and this convention is part of the etiquette of that relation.
White usefully points out that the terms "patron" and "client" (*patronus*
and *cliens*), while used in Latin to describe political relationships, are rarely
employed to describe the social relationships of *amicitia.* It is thus interesting to note that Horace introduces Maecenas in *Satires* 1.6 with a very
clear statement about the difference in social status between them. Horace
breaks the etiquette of the language of *amicitia* by speaking immediately
of their fathers and by observing that while Maecenas has a line of ancestors reaching backward to the Lydian settlement of Etruria, Horace, as
son of a freedman, has in effect no ancestors. The direct treatment of this
question lends intimacy to the address to Maecenas; Horace breaks with
linguistic etiquette to treat a subject that the public descriptive terms of
their relationship suppress, thereby demonstrating the private context of
this discussion with Maecenas. This is the matter of the poem, the issue
of what a private life is and what one loses in a public life, and Horace
comes down squarely in favor of the private life for himself. In the private
realm Horace's father is not a liability but a pure advantage to his son;
in the public realm Horace's father is simply a *libertinus,* with the result
that the son's success can only make Horace the subject of *invidia,* envy.[19]
Horace carefully distinguishes between *justifiable* envy of him for his public good fortune as commander of a Roman legion ("ut forsit honorem /
iure mihi invideat quivis," 49–50), and unjustifiable envy over his friendship with Maecenas, which has not come about by luck or accident ("felicem dicere non hoc / me possim, casu quod te sortitus amicum," 52–53).
In the private arena, which pertains to Horace's friendship with Maecenas,
Horace's father is the stated cause ("causa fuit pater his," 70) because he
is the maker of his son's character and person. In the public arena the

crowd sees only the birth and status of a man, whereas in the private arena Maecenas sees Horace's life and the heart (64), his father's product. As Horace makes his case, he would, as he says, be crazy, *demens*, to choose a public life, to choose a father whose birth would set him in the center of a troublesome, expensive public life.

The distance that Horace measures between himself and Maecenas is his distance from public life, for Maecenas is engaged in public life. In the process of establishing this distance, however, Horace confides the causes of his private disposition to his friend, demonstrating that the relationship with Maecenas belongs to the intimacy of private life. Within the context of this private relation of *amicitia* with Maecenas, Horace reverses the procedure he has taken in 1.4 with Lucilius, where Lucilius was displaced by Horace's father as the author of his character and hence of his satire. Maecenas is paired with Horace's father to mark the similarities between the two men and their roles in Horace's life. The disparity between them in birth and social status and the importance of this disparity in the public realm are presented by the poem. For the private realm, however— that is, within the context of their friendship—Maecenas's relationship to the poet has a fatherly aspect. Horace's entrance into friendship with Maecenas is told as a birth (56–64): Horace is *infans* with *pudor* when he first meets Maecenas, speechless as an infant. *Infans* describes both speechlessness and the state of infancy, the situation of the newborn as marked by its relation to language. Horace takes leave of Maecenas while the potential friendship gestates for nine months in Maecenas's mind, after which he is recalled by Maecenas and taken into the latter's friendship (61–62). The result of entering into this friendship is the security of an assured place for the poet and for his speech.[20] In Horace's account, both his father and Maecenas have focused on his virtue; neither is said to have an opinion about his poetry. Modesty ("pudor," 57) blocks Horace's speech in his successful interview with Maecenas, and modesty, the first attribute of virtue, is what Horace's father strives to preserve in his son ("pudicum, / qui primus virtutis honos, servavit ab omni / non solum facto, verum obprobrio quoque turpi," 82–84).[21] Maecenas can see this in the son and thus makes Horace a friend ("magnum hoc ego duco / quod placui tibi, qui turpi secernis honestum, / non patre praeclaro sed vita et pectore puro," 62–64).

Of course, if it had not been for his poetry, Horace, however blameless his nature, would never have been introduced to Maecenas. If he had not been a poet, Maecenas is not likely to have cared about his character. As

W. R. Johnson wryly remarks about Maecenas: "Horace became Maecenas' friend because of that enormous poetic talent for which he seems to have had a jeweler's eye (his eye for what most people, then and now, would call rectitude seems to have been, as it were, not wholly trained)" (1993, 28). In *Satires* 1.6, however, the poetic construction of this relationship is entirely subordinated to Horace's character. Again, Horace substitutes ethos for literary concerns in his poetic/generic autobiography.

Horace's contrived omission of his poetic talent, when he tells in 1.6 of Maecenas's adoption of him, is frequently explained as consistent with the portrait he gives of himself and of his father, a portrait designed to deflect the envy of those who resent Horace's social ascent. From this point of view, envious detractors, whether real or imagined by Horace (that is, imagined by the poet as a convenient rhetorical maneuver for his poetic purposes, or, imagined by the historical paranoid Horace, etc.), are seen as motivating Horace's unprepossessing self-portrait.[22] But Horace's autobiography also belongs to the requirements of his satiric genre as he has cast it, and it is helpful to the practitioner of that satire to appear to be unpowerful in order to be unthreatening. If Horace has a father with no ancestors, if he cannot be envied, he has no social authority with which to wield satiric control over others. Furthermore, when Horace withholds his poetry as a cause of his friendship with Maecenas, he withholds from his own persona the very means by which a satirist may wield power, i.e. his poetry, despite now occupying a position of potentially greater social control. It seems unlikely the envy of the crowd would truly deter Horace from saying anything he chose to say; the subordination of his poetry to his character here is a poetic choice designed to construct his satiric persona.

It is important too to consider how Horace negotiates and makes use of the formal aspects of his relation to Maecenas, constructed as it is in terms of fatherhood. A relationship of literary patronage in Rome in Horace's day, even if practiced by its participants in a language neutral with respect to status issues, nevertheless is based on a social structure that existed to support the interdependent needs of the weaker and stronger members of the society.[23] In the more explicit context and terminology of political patronage, the model for the *amicitia* relationship is derived from the relationship that results from the manumission of a slave.

The designation *patronus* (etymologically derived from *pater, patris*) itself indicates the link to the model of a father who supports his children, and who, just as in the relationship that imitates it, gains prestige from the existence of his children.[24] The exchange of protection and obligations suggests certain legal and social similarities between the patron-client relation and the father-son relation. An important respect, however, in which the two relationships differ centers on the relative social ranks of the two parties in each: whereas a father bequeaths his social position to his son (as Horace insists in *Sat.* 1.6), the status of a patron depends on the inferior situation of his clients and is in fact defined by the existence of lower-placed clients who depend on the greater social authority of the *patronus.* The situation between Horace and Maecenas is different, of course, but the relations of *amicitia* imitate the structure the Romans devised for ex-slaves and their former masters and in a characteristically conservative way keep those relations stable. In 1.6, Horace exploits that conservative impulse, by maintaining that he will never be the social equal of Maecenas.[25] Though Maecenas is gratefully embraced as a second father into whose household Horace is accepted as one of the number of his *amicorum,* and though Maecenas's function in the poem is structured like that of Horace's own father (for both recognize Horace's essential nature, and neither is said to care about poetry), the poet also insists on his allegiance not just to his actual father but also to his father's social rank.

Horace's insistence on the social gap between himself and Maecenas serves his satiric program. While it may be that Horace is in fact saying to Maecenas that he prefers to be who he is, we should recognize again that his claim of preferring his status as son of a freedman over Maecenas's status functions above all poetically to solidify the satiric persona he is constructing. The cause of Horace's refusal to identify himself completely with Maecenas and his elite coterie is his father, Horace tells us, and the (poetic) virtues that the private life permits him. Horace's refusal can be explained from his poetic stance; he could not be a satirist if he held Maecenas's position and status. According to Horace's construction of his poetic persona, the material simplicity of his life and his humble status are necessary conditions of satire, a "low" genre. If he were to strive for a higher social place than he was born to, he could not plausibly claim the virtues of contentment he praises in *Satires* 1.1, and he could not claim the private and separate status of a satirist, which he so eloquently delineates at the end of 1.6.

Thus, in *Satires* 1.6, as in 1.4, Horace approves and embraces Roman social reality in expressing his loyalty to his father and his contentment with his place in his society (he thinks Appius would be right to exclude him from the rolls, "censorque moveret / Appius, ingenuo si non essem

patre natus: / vel merito, quoniam in propria non pelle quiessem," 20–22).
One should recall that the satirist is, in the traditional realm, a figure at
some distance from his community, that his critical role (however miti-
gated by the desire to engender virtue, as Horace's claims to be) places
him apart from the run of men and makes him solitary. Horace does
something noteworthy in this regard. He has presented his relation to
his audience (or at least his potential audience) in 1.4 as uneasy; he is a
poet of the elite writing in a popular (low) genre who worries about the
reaction of the mob to his satires. He resolves the problem in part by not
answering it, but in part by establishing the persona he constructs on the
basis of Roman rectitude, so that his satire has an explicit stamp of common Roman values. He thereby sets the satirist's voice in the protective
setting of cultural values that are acceptable to all Roman orders.[26] Horace
can make himself "belong" to all levels, to the low as a writer of satire (a
low genre) and as the son of a freedman, to the high as a Callimachean
poet (18, far, far from the mob) and friend to Maecenas. The Callimachean
poet makes his peace with his bifurcated status by claiming his low status
as poetic territory and by praising the privilege of the private, solitary life
as the bulwark of the satirist's art.[27]

Just as Horace's father is made the cause of the satirizing impulse in
Horace in 1.4, with all its beneficial effects and ironically presented shortcomings (i.e., that Horace's speech is occasionally "iocosius" and "liberius," 1.4.103–4), this father is also the cause of Horace's friendship with
Maecenas. Just as the character that the father formed in Horace makes
the son's satire harmless (not deservingly *suspectum*) and adequate to the
condition and status of poetry, so Horace's character allows for the relationship with Maecenas. The persona Horace presents, humble, upright,
and honest, reinforces the ethical nature of his satire. This is a strikingly
apt conflation for a satirist to make. The genre of satire is earthbound, its
style *humilis,* its observations embedded in the stuff of life; to make the
poet's character materially equivalent to his writing fits the genre's relation to dailiness and its quotidian sense that life makes art.[28]

Horace's account of his father, vv. 71–88, is moving. The warmth of the
passage derives in part from the revelation of the father's social vulnerability in his yearning for his son's promotion beyond his own social status.
And while he reveals that paternal vulnerability, Horace simultaneously
protects it by casting his father's ambition for his son as a desire for his
son's ethical character.[29] Much as this father in 1.4 protected his son in life

and reputation ("dum custodis eges, vitam famamque tueri / incolumem possum," 1.4.118–19), so here he protects the boy's modesty from stain in deed and thought ("pudicum, / qui primus virtutis honos, servavit ab omni / non solum facto, verum opprobrio quoque turpi," 82–84). Horace sets the achievement of his own life into the passage with sweet subtlety— "at hoc nunc" (87, but for this now)—*hoc* being the life he does have, its scope enclosed in a quick demonstrative pronoun, subordinated to the idea of the praise and the thanks due his father. As long as he is in his senses ("sanum," 89), Horace then continues, he could never regret such a father; nor does he need the consolation that some do for parents of low status, that he did not choose his parents, reasoning that is abhorrent to him. And if nature were to bid him to reenact his life, he would not, out of pride, choose illustrious parents. Horace's father had a value not to be traded for the superficial symbols of power and office ("fascibus et sellis," 97). This may be crazy in the judgment of the mob, yet perhaps sane ("sanus," 98) in the judgment of Maecenas (89–104).

Horace's loyalty and gratitude to his father are cast as proofs of the character the father nourished in him. Horace's tribute to Maecenas here is that Maecenas, in contrast to the *vulgus*, recognizes that it is a choice of moral health for Horace to choose the parents he had and is consistent with the earlier statement that Maecenas saw in the poet not the station of the father but the life and the heart ("magnum hoc ego duco / quod placui tibi, qui turpi secernis honestum, / non patre praeclaro sed vita et pectore puro," 62–64).

In the final passage of the poem (110–31), the poet's account of his life from one afternoon to the next, Horace tells how his life is governed according to his desire ("quacumque libido est, incedo solus," 111–12). The meticulously itemized conditions of Horace's living (the foods he eats, the details of his tableware, the quality of the oil with which he anoints himself, his preference against playing ball in the Campus Martius) constitute once again a statement about the genre in which he writes. The material conditions of life shape consciousness, and this is a precept of satire: the truth lies in the immediate physical world. Horace chooses the details of his autobiography and constructs his persona knowingly, instructing us thereby that a life of public duty, devoted to care of the city, the command of Italy, the temples of the gods (35–36), would deprive the satirist both of the dignity of his father's upbringing and of the life that allows him to take his moralizing satirist's stand.

In *Satires* 1.4, Horace's father is linked to an explicitly poetic issue to determine the sort of satirist Horace is, as compared to Lucilius; in *Satires* 1.6, this father is connected with the social issue of Horace's low status and his relation to the nobly born Maecenas. In both poems the virtue with which Horace's father endowed his son is an explanation of the son's relationship to the key figures of the poems, Lucilius and Maecenas. In both poems Horace's father is a man who raised his son impeccably, but his parental role has a different emphasis to match the context and the competing father figure of each poem. Bearing in mind that there must have been much other personal information that Horace could offer if personal autobiography were his goal (Horace had a mother and might have had siblings), we should not ignore the poet's choices in telling about himself. In *Satires* 1.4 and 1.6, then, Horace's focus on his father serves his poetic program and contributes importantly to the task of identifying his genre with his persona. The appearance first of Lucilius and then of Maecenas alongside Horace's father emphasizes that Lucilius and Maecenas are themselves fathers of a sort to Horace, Lucilius his literary father in Roman hexameter satire, and Maecenas the patron who made Horace's life as a poet possible. The predecessor and the patron are each put into competition with the actual father, always to the advantage of Horace, *père et fils.*

Horace transfers to both Maecenas and Lucilius a certain negative aspect of the fatherly role. The distance a son needs from his father for the formulation of his own identity is accomplished by Horace in a curious way: he takes his distance from the two figurative fathers, Lucilius and Maecenas, by emphasizing that his actual father is the first cause of himself, the precursor without whom he would have no relationship with either Lucilius or Maecenas. Horace constructs Lucilius and Maecenas as father figures to his poetic life and then points out that his biological father is the true poetic cause. This rebellion against the two profound influences of Lucilius and Maecenas leaves the original socially burdened father-son relationship free of its traditional competition and tyranny. Horace portrays a relationship with his father that epitomizes the Roman ideal, one free of the notorious tensions that Roman comedy boisterously exploits.[30] The relation between Horace and his "real-life" father is the only relationship Horace could evoke in order to distance himself without reproach from his two "poetic fathers"; and the quality of that father-son relation invests the satirist's voice with an authority no amount of moralizing could accomplish.

❧ 3 ❧

Practicing Theory, or,
Perils of the Open Road

Satires 1.5

From the theoretically equivocal situation of satire that Horace presents in *Satires* 1.4 follows *Satires* 1.5, a poem quite free of any of the rambling commentary and contradictory diagnoses that abound in the previous poem. Altogether different in kind, it tells the story of a journey Horace made from Rome to Brundisium in 37 BCE during the tense political era of the decade before Actium, accompanying Maecenas and other top lieutenants of the Roman world.[1] The ultimate goal of the journey, not explicitly alluded to in the poem, was to effect a reconciliation between Antony and Octavian. The poet, however, is preoccupied with the material details of the trip, and his narrative never shifts its focus to the political purpose, or indeed to any purpose of the trip. Any journey, literal or metaphorical, has a goal, but in 1.5 the goal is suppressed to keep our attention riveted on the unfolding pleasures and miseries of travel, and revealed only with the simultaneous end of the poem and the journey. Though Horace is not a player in the political context of the trip, he is traveling with men whose sole purpose is political, and his remote, chatty treatment of the trip to Brundisium has left readers tantalized by absent details.[2] The details the poet does give us in this satire are thick with realism, travel notes of the first century BCE on barges, mules, sailors, frogs, rural officials and entertainment, a missing girl, bad water, good bread, burned food. Moreover, Horace's account of the mundane phenomena of travel is further removed from the political circumstances of the journey through his adoption of a mock-epic style that conveys a certain self-parody, as if the poet endures an Odyssean journey, all the way from Rome to Brundisium. But this very self-parody, in which the satirist plays the low epic poet, provides a clue

59

to a reading of the poem that might relieve our frustration that the satire offers no political revelation. The poem's revelation is of the narrator's identity and disposition, which in turn reveals the poet's satiric agenda. The poem is crafted inside a frame, the journey to the summit meeting at Brundisium. But the political goal of this journey is studiously ignored by the narrator in favor of the humdrum details of his own experience. These details form the substance of satire, for the narrator's view is a satirist's, and they fashion a poem that functions as a satiric *recusatio* of epic, a poem that denies epic and its world of public affairs.[3] It is precisely by telling a story that seems inappropriate to its context that Horace can instruct us about his choice of material and narrator.

The narrator defines his satiric identity in this poem with an account of his personal experience, set in a context that begs for comment on its public meaning. By inviting the reader to want what is not there, Horace can draw more than casual attention to the material that replaces the information not given and to the meaning of the poet's willful choice. That choice denies the usefulness of political conflict, of invective, of a narrator with a harsh voice, and puts in their place an attention to life's immediate frustrations and satisfactions, voiced by a narrator whose greatest pleasure lies in the harmony and health found in friendship.

The poem has a Lucilian model, lost as a whole but preserved in fragments by the faithful grammarians of a later age;[4] from what we know, *Satires* 1.5 seems to be a closer *imitatio* of a Lucilian poem than any other of the *Satires*. Porphyrio says, in his commentary on the first line of *Satires* 1.5, "Lucilio hac satyra aemulatur Horatius iter suum a Roma Brundisium usque describens, quod et ille in tertio libro fecit, primo a Roma Capuam usque, et inde fretum Siciliense."[5] The Lucilius we know from Horace's *Satires* 1.4 is the poet who created our expectation that the satirist freely note the faults he sees in others ("multa cum libertate notabant," 1.4.5), and against whom Horace reacts in 1.4 with his debate over whether his poetry is deservedly *suspectum*—suspected of doing harm and causing fear (1.4.64–65). While Horace has distinguished himself in both style and content from his literary mentor in the preceding poem, he is here evidently using Lucilius's poem as his model. The model provides an opportunity to continue Horace's relation to his literary predecessor, and it can be no accident that this poem follows the introduction of Lucilius in *Satires* 1.4. But we are forced to consider too what is the claim of likeness to Lucilius here as well. Can Horace write in the same genre, and write a poem to echo the earlier satirist's, and at the same time deny his affiliation with Lucilius's temper, which he describes in *Satires* 1.10 as having "rubbed Rome down with a lot of salt" ("quod sale multo / urbem defricuit," 3–4)?

Horace says in *Satires* 1.4 that he is accused of having a destructive tongue. After the poet's self-justification that he doesn't abuse the public by hawking his books, as Hermogenes Tigellius does, or by reciting his poems in the Forum or the baths, Horace presents the following accusation and his own defense:

> "laedere gaudes"
> inquit, "et hoc studio pravus facis." unde petitum
> hoc in me iacis? est auctor quis denique eorum
> vixi cum quibus? absentem qui rodit amicum,
> qui non defendit alio culpante, solutos
> qui captat risus hominum famamque dicacis,
> fingere qui non visa potest, commissa tacere
> qui nequit, hic niger est, hunc tu, Romane, caveto.
>   *Sat.* 1.4.78–85

"You love to do harm," they say, "and you're perverse, you do it on purpose." Where did you get this charge to throw at me? Is your informant anyone of the people I've lived among? I'll tell you, the one who backbites his friend when he's not there, who wants to get a lot of laughs and be thought of as a wit, who can make up what he hasn't seen and can't keep a secret when someone has trusted him—now this, Roman, is a black-hearted soul, of this one you must beware.

Satires 1.5 provides a narrative rebuttal of these charges, where the poet sets about establishing a persona for himself, the poem's narrator, which demonstrates how far he is from being *hic niger*, and elevates, above all, the virtue of friendship. We see him among "those with whom he has lived" ("eorum vixi cum quibus"), we see his passion for his friends, and we see to a fault that he neither invents what he never saw nor betrays a single secret of the operations of those mighty friends (Reckford 1997, 584).

At the same time, in keeping with the "low" status of his genre, and as if to offset any lofty expectations from this ethical rectitude, the poet mocks himself; he characterizes his own figure, in the drama of the journey, through the medium of his own body. He is *lippus* (30, 49)—plagued with eye trouble, has stomach problems (7–8) and insomnia (15, 82–85); he is keenly aware of, and makes us aware of, his appetites for food, sex, and rest. He is an ideal travel guide, if battling discomfort is your primary interest when you travel. In his preoccupation with his own body, he is innocent of doing harm to others. In addition, he offers us other figures in the story who are subtly associated with his own comic persona: the *nauta* (16) on the barge, the *praetor* (34) in Fundi, and the *scurra* Sarmentus (51–70), who provides entertainment in Cocceius's villa. These figures, all of a low mimetic level, all figures of fun to the narrator or to the group to which Horace belongs on the journey, contain elements of the figure of the narrator. They serve to recall that the satirist is a humorous character himself and provide a further illustration of Horace's claim in *Satires* 1.4 that this satirist does not create fear; he is not the deliverer of satiric barbs and in this context is likelier to be their object. The low status of these alternate Horace figures is not designed to reflect Horace's real status so much as his harmlessness. Thus, the account itself of the journey establishes its narrator as an unthreatening speaker.

The poet reveals no more about the great men who join the journey—the most powerful men of the era and the most artistically enticing ones—than he reveals about any of the low-life figures who serve to recall the identity of the narrator in the poem. Horace is very much able to keep quiet ("commissa tacere," 1.4.84), almost ostentatiously refusing to assume the authority of an insider's knowledge. The satirist of 1.5 is himself not a figure of either menace or importance, and his subject for satire is the humdrum quirkiness of human existence, even when he has provided himself with a dramatic scenario rife with opportunities for the freewheeling satiric commentary that he suggests in *Satires* 1.4 (and 1.10) belonged to Lucilius.

The maker of this poem does not appear to enjoy traveling. We are alert to the narrator at once in the opening line of *Satires* 1.5 as Horace starts his trip in the first-person singular: "egressum magna me accepit Aricia Roma."[6] Though he says next that his companion was the rhetor Heliodorus, the most learned man of all the Greeks, what pleasure Horace derives from his company we never know, for we never hear of him again.[7] With the important exception of his reunion with Vergil, Varius, and Plotius (39–44), the personal experiences Horace narrates on this trip are unhappy ones. These unhappy experiences are all material, solitary, and connected with the physical body, whereas the happy ones, having to do with friends, a dinner party, and laughter, are social. The poet's physical distresses attract our attention to the experience of the narrator rather than to the objective account of the journey. Likewise, the suppression of the destination, Brundisium, involves the reader in the moments of the trip rather than its goal. The narrator's attention to his bodily troubles, while they may indeed recall Lucilius's rendition of similar experiences in his satire on the journey to Sicily, as some commentators of *Satires* 1.5 have suggested, make Horace, the narrator, the unenviable focus of the poem.[8] This narrator assures us that he is too absorbed in himself to assume the authority of a speaker inclined to expose, humiliate, or attack others.

Like an army, Horace travels on his stomach, and after he has broken the journey to Appii Forum ("hoc iter ignavi divisimus," 5) with the stop in Aricia, the awful water at Appii Forum gives him diarrhea, which makes it impossible for him to eat and forces him to wait impatiently ("cenantis haud animo aequo / exspectans," 8–9) while his companions dine. We are confronted early in the poem by a very real and insistent narrator, who, isolated from human company and nourishment, wants us to pay attention to him with his testy spirit and his rebellious gut. Horace draws our attention to his digestive problems with an epic rendition of mind-body dualism: "ventri / indico bellum" (7–8, I declare war on my belly); he declares war and has no mental peace. Satiric epic phrases move us to the next stage of the journey, by barge, where humans, bugs, and frogs make sleep impossible (14–19).

The trip proceeds with lively tedium; the party (as yet unidentified except for the poet) finds kinder water at Feronia, for dipping their faces and hands in, not for drinking, and they eat ("pransi," 25). At Anxur, where he joins up with some of the most powerful men on earth, we are drawn again to Horace's bodily experience as he notes that he is coating his eyes with a pharmaceutical cream.

> huc venturus erat Maecenas optimus atque
> Cocceius, missi magnis de rebus uterque
> legati, aversos soliti componere amicos.
> hic oculis ego nigra meis collyria lippus
> illinere. interea Maecenas advenit atque
> Cocceius Capitoque simul Fonteius, ad unguem
> factus homo, Antoni non ut magis alter amicus.
>   *Sat.* 1.5.27–33

The distinguished Maecenas was coming here, and Cocceius, who were both ambassadors sent on an important matter, men accustomed to reconciling hostile friends. This is where I smear some black ointment on my eyes for my pink-eye. Meantime Maecenas arrives, as do Cocceius and at the same time Fonteius Capito—a fellow who's groomed to the last detail, no one a better friend to Antony.[9]

We learn that Maecenas and Cocceius will come to Anxur, that they are ambassadors sent on extremely significant business, *legati*—there on some-one else's behalf; they are adept as peacemakers, men accustomed to rec-onciling antagonized friends. Horace interrupts to say that here he smeared his eyes with black ointment, *collyria nigra,* because he is *lippus* (blear eyed), and then says that Maecenas arrives, as do Cocceius and Fonteius Capito.[10] The latter he describes as "ad unguem / factus homo, Antoni non ut magis alter amicus." This is all the poem says explicitly about the expe-dition; Fonteius Capito is explicitly linked to Antony as his most loyal friend, and his one explicitly mentioned trait is that he is carefully turned out, a bit too neatly tailored, one infers. Of the three men mentioned, only Antony's friend Capito is described: "ad unguem factus homo." By draw-ing attention to his meticulous appearance and thereby focusing on his body—Capito is "a dapper fellow" (literally, "trimmed to the fingernail")—Horace performs the same operation on Capito that he has performed on his own figure in the poem: he has reduced Capito's significance by focus-ing on his bodily aspect. Maecenas and Cocceius are allowed to be known only by their skill at reconciliation, "aversos soliti componere amicos." No mention of Octavian occurs nor of the purpose of the trip apart from what is alluded to in Maecenas's and Cocceius's skill with *aversos amicos.* Our satiric narrator hastens to remind us of his ocular ailment; he can see Capito close up, but his half-sight can see no further to tell us more.

At Capua, Maecenas goes to play ball while the two poets, Horace and Vergil, go to sleep, united by their physical disabilities:

lusum it Maecenas, dormitum ego Vergiliusque;
namque pila lippis inimicum et ludere crudis.
   Sat. 1.5.48–49

Maecenas goes to play ball, Vergil and I to nap; for to the purblind and the dyspeptic there's no pleasure in a game.

The physical activity and nonactivity of all three figures here occupy the poet's account, again tempting us with the names of the figures involved but emphasizing the narrative's intent to leave the principals named but unrevealed except in details that distinguish them not at all from common travelers.

The account remains obstinately fixed on its physical details. The near-disastrous kitchen fire at Beneventum prevents the eating of what promised to be an inadequate meal in any case ("macros turdos," 72), and they stay at a villa near Trivicum that is full of the smoke of a green-wood fire ("lacrimoso non sine fumo," 80), a probable further irritation to the *lippus* narrator. Here Horace is stood-up by what seems to be a call girl or the equivalent, maybe just a flirtatious but shrewd local girl.[11] The poet brings us in again to his immediate physical experience, this time one of sexual annoyance and, again, poor sleep. He tells us he waits alone for the girl ("exspecto," 83), just as early in the poem he has told us he waited ("exspectans," 9) alone for his eating companions, and of how his dreams discharged his frustration as he slept, and left him lying on his back in a soiled nightshirt.

> hic ego mendacem stultissimus usque puellam
> ad mediam noctem exspecto: somnus tamen aufert
> intentum Veneri; tum immundo somnia visu
> nocturnam vestem maculant ventremque supinum.
>   *Sat.* 1.5.82–85

Here like a total ass I waited half the night for a girl who lied to me; sleep finally came, and I still wanted sex, so dreaming stained my nightshirt with its salacious imagery as I lay on my back.

The striking physical detail insists that the reader recognize and identify with a personal, intimate experience, again drawing the narration back to the narrator and to a level of his experience that is physical, banal, and unenviable. Horace's stomach, so often abused on this trip, here is soaked by the *immundo visu* (84) of his dreams, the wrong filling for his stomach and his spirit.[12]

The next stop, which follows the villa at Trivicum, is a little town that Horace says cannot be pronounced in hexameter verse (it does not fit the meter) but which he characteristically describes in terms of its food.

mansuri oppidulo quod versu dicere non est,
signis perfacile est: venit vilissima rerum
hic aqua; sed panis longe pulcherrimus, ultra
callidus ut soleat umeris portare viator.
  Sat. 1.5.87–90

We were going to stay the night in a little town whose name can't be said in
verse, but is very easy to identify: they sell water here—the cheapest item—
but the bread is the very best, so good that the canny traveler will carry it
on his back quite a way beyond.

Where the shape of words fails the poet, the nourishment promised supplies the need to poet and traveler alike. The canny traveler, Horace tells
us, will bear the extra load of bread and water and carry it on to Canu-
sium, where the bread is gritty and the water scarce. The materiality of life
has occluded the meaning of the trip to Brundisium consistently, claiming our attention again and again, and here subsumes even the poet's art.
This is not accidental to Horace's program in the satires, where his premise for happiness is contentment with one's lot and where the basis of
one's lot is material: the limits of the stomach should set the limits of one's
desire, as in *Satires* 1.1.45–46: "milia frumenti tua triverit area centum /
non tuus hoc capiet venter plus ac meus." Even poetry, to the satirist of
this journey, can be subordinated to the greater matters of life—hunger,
thirst, and their adequate satisfaction.[13]

The personal details contribute to the formation of a "low" narrator
whose aims and preoccupations are consistent with satire's requirements
as Horace wishes to define them. Indeed, the low mimetic level of the narrator is more important in the dramatic situation of this poem, where the
narrator's preoccupations need to be very far away from the poetically
obscured purpose of this journey, than in the other satires of book 1. To
emphasize the point that the narrator and his experiences are the substance
of the journey, and to reinforce the idea that as a figure dramatically
opposed to epic norms, he poses no threat to either his companions on the
journey or to the reader, we glimpse throughout the poem characters who
possess traits that remind us of this narrator. All these figures are subject
to ridicule, by the poet or by the whole party on the trip, and their presence, with their odd likenesses to the persona of the poet, serves to remind
us that Horace the narrator, not the journey, is the subject of the poem.

Early on, when Horace is describing the nighttime barge trip through the Pomptine marshes (11–23) and all the noises that keep him awake, among these noises is the singing of the drunken boatman, the *nauta*, about his girlfriend who isn't there: "absentem ut cantat amicam" (15). The *nauta* eventually falls asleep and replaces singing with snoring, lying on his back, *stertitque supinus* (19). Later in the poem and the journey, when Horace is thwarted by the *mendacem puellam* (82), in the smoky villa near Trivicum he lies on his back and dreams: "tum immundo somnia visu / nocturnam vestem maculant ventremque supinum" (84–85). Just as the *nauta* had sung about the absent girl and fallen ignobly asleep, so later Horace sings to us of a missing girl and falls ignobly into sleep. Horace the wayfarer is on his little odyssey singing his own love lament, an odyssey and lament carefully scaled to the level of satire and replete with physical details. He is at once Odysseus and the pastoral Cyclops, the spurned and unfit suitor singing his epic-parodic song of wandering.[14]

Likewise at Fundi (34) the figure of the local official, Aufidius Luscus (*luscus*, blind in one eye), seems to recall the satirist-narrator; by giving us his name and calling him a *scriba* Horace reminds us of our sight-impaired, quondam *scriba* narrator. Luscus's name means "vision-impaired," which is what the *lippus* Horace is on this trip, and he is a *scriba*, the would-be profession of our satirist Horace, were he not a poet and were Maecenas not his patron.[15] The foolish municipal pretensions of this official amuse Maecenas's party: "Fundos Aufidio Lusco praetore libenter / linquimus, insani ridentes praemia scribae, / praetextam et latum clavum prunaeque vatillum" (35–37). This lowly country treasury-clerk wears the *praetexta*, worn in Rome by high magistrates, and the broad purple stripe of a senator, and he carries, presumably, a pan of hot coals (*prunaeque vatillum*) that suggests his intention to perform a sacrificial ceremony to honor his noted visitors.[16] To the distinguished urbanites from Rome, Aufidius's pretensions to higher status are risible; but Horace is keenly aware in other satires that the danger of such pretensions can be applied to himself. Indeed, as a member of a pretentious company who laughs at this official, he flirts with this very danger here; yet by identifying him as *insanus*, Horace separates himself from the traits that make Aufidius laughable. But the elements of his persona that Horace shares with Aufidius Luscus again limit the narrator's satiric threat. To the extent that Horace fashions a narrative self in the poem who is laughable and excluded from the society of Maecenas, he makes a satirist who is the safe object of ridicule, not the unsafe source of critical, satiric speech. The figure Horace crafts for himself is an ingenious poetic creation, one impossible in life: an insider who exercises the privilege of laughter, who is simultaneously the outsider who is mocked. Against A. E. Housman's strictures on the role of the critic, we may whistle with admiration at the shrewd brilliance of this creation.

The *scurra* Sarmentus is both a *scriba* and a freedman, and he too functions as an alter ego to Horace's narrator.[17] In the second half of the poem begins a longish section describing the dinner entertainment at Cocceius's villa near Caudium. Two buffoons, Messius Cicirrus and Sarmentus, come out and do verbal combat with each other, insulting and clowning and making much of each other's shortcomings for the amusement of the company. Sarmentus is a freedman whose former mistress is living, Messius notes, and his profession is that of a *scriba*. The whole interlude is told to us in gleeful mock-epic style. Horace asks the Muse to help him recall the ancestry of the combatants, and the tale of the combat, "et quo patre natus uterque / contulerit litis." The combatants themselves seem in on the joke, and their banter is a pastiche of high-style parody. Horace concludes the tale by saying, "prorsus iucunde cenam producimus illam" (70), a line whose meter is prolonged like the dinner. Of the poem's 105 lines, the exact center is the second half of v. 53, which contains the phrase "et *quo patre natus* uterque." We have seen that the poem that follows, *Satires* 1.6, treats the issue of Horace's relationship with Maecenas, the snobbery of Roman society, and how his freedman father's status is a liability to Horace. The repeated variations on the phrase *patre natus* in 1.6 tell the story: Horace is the son of a man who was a slave, a man by definition without ancestors. The virtue instilled in him by his ex-slave father has catapulted Horace into a place next to the great Maecenas. In *Satires* 1.4 and 1.6, the qualities of Horace's heart are adduced to show he is a satirist who does no harm to others, but in 1.5 Horace also exploits the other important feature of his persona gained from his father to remind us that his own status is low and that he can therefore report this trip without threatening his powerful companions: he is not socially significant enough to be a threat. When Horace links his own persona to the clowns and specifically to the scribe-freedman Sarmentus, he recalls elements in the social position he has described for himself in the *Satires;* these are elements he shares with a figure who exists in the poem only to cause laughter, not fear.

Satires 1.5 flutters with mock-epic phrases that serve up the reliable humor inherent in casting the mundane in high diction.[18] But from a different point of view the journey *is* worthy of epic commemoration. The poem tells, and does not tell, of a journey taken that would contribute to reshaping the Western world. Great poets accompany the politicians. The men who mandate the journey will eventually divide up the world and fight each other, and one will lose. Horace is traveling, as it happens, with the winners. Every epic phrase in the poem indicates a knowledge of the gravity, the epic nature, of the mission, a knowledge at the same time denied by the comic intent with which it is evoked. When Horace says that he declares war on his belly, one may note that the journey will ultimately lead to a declaration of civil war. The poem's epic phrasing is denuded of its epic content by its low context; but the bigger context of the journey has epic/tragic proportions that the narrator cannot see. That bigger context is epic in the nature of the *Iliad,* not the *Odyssey.*

At lines 27–33 ("huc venturus erat Maecenas optimus . . ."), which describe the meeting at Anxur with Maecenas, Cocceius, and Fonteius Capito, Horace allows us to infer the larger context of the journey, a context that he does not elsewhere admit into the poem. When Horace's narrator covers his sore eyes with the black ointment, he thereby declares his own relationship to these events. His partial vision is limited to the satirist's version of reality, the immediate and physical; a deeper vision he cannot afford. He can see well enough to know that Fonteius Capito is well dressed, and he is sly enough to note that Fonteius is a great friend to Antony, the friend at odds with the unnamed Octavian. Beyond this Horace's sight cannot penetrate, for it is impaired, literally by ointment, figuratively by his satire's demands, practically by his uncertain relationship to Maecenas. Connected to the poem's other mention of Maecenas (48–49) is the other mention that Horace is *lippus.* Unable to engage in such athletic activity as playing ball, which he says is *inimicum* to him and to Vergil in their uneasy states of bodily health, the two poets withdraw to sleep. Sleep, though often embattled on this trip, here lets Horace close his eyes altogether in Vergil's company and take his distance from Maecenas.

If Maecenas is the link to the true epic stature of the journey, the satirist, the half-sighted bard, should not view him too clearly. His vision of Maecenas is fitted to his own generic orientation—not the deep internal vision of the blind epic poet Homer, but the blurry half-blindness of an epic satirist. The voice that claims our attention makes us feel the journey as his experience, and when things get too heady, Horace, satiric epic bard that he is, renders himself temporarily blind with black ointment on his eyes. He is then granted a satiric partial blindness, as total blindness is the epic poet's; the concomitant vision for the satirist is partial and low, as the epic poet's is total and high. Blindness gives Homer the figurative vision of a prophet, to see and tell the stories that give men immortality; impaired vision gives Horace the figurative vision to immortalize the story, but the wrong one as it were, his own story, of bargemen, water, sickness, jokes, fatigue. The satirist's vision is sharpened to life's tiny details, while the bigger picture, the world-shaping events, the politics, the ambition of his patron, is obscured by black ointment on his sore eyes.

A conflict of shattering proportions motivates the journey to Brundisium, while *Satires* 1.5 contains conflicts appropriate to satire's level. Just as the epic phrases throughout the poem recall the epic nature of the trip while never explicitly stating that nature, the satiric conflicts of the poem recall the poet's silence regarding the issues that would occupy Maecenas in the trip's destination. After the poet has waited with an uneasy spirit for his dining companions, he launches a small epic parody: "iam nox inducere terris / umbras et caelo diffundere signa parabat. / tum pueri nautis, pueris convicia nautae / ingerere" (9–12). Sailors and slaves yell back and forth at each other in anger, a scene the poet introduces with an allusion to the motion of the heavens. Likewise an enraged traveler, the *cerebrosus* (21), beats the boatman and the mule in his anger at the barge trip's suspension—another small conflict of the sort endemic in life, thoughtless and futile, funny in satire, devastating in epic.

The great conflict overtly allowed in this satire, which occupies nineteen lines in the middle of the poem, is the mock-epic duel of Sarmentus and Messius Cicirrus, which entertains Horace's party at the villa of Cocceius. The passage gives every indication of echoing an episode in the Lucilian model for this poem.[19] Again, the fact that Horace names the company at the dinner prompts a longing in the reader to hear an insider's account of the conversation and wit of powerful and intelligent men, but we are treated instead to the banter of two local comedians who obscure the famous guests entirely. The conflict between the buffoons parodies an epic set piece, in a poem that itself tells about a journey motivated by a harrowing conflict.[20] In the dramatic context of the poem, Horace the narrator is the epic poet of the moment who establishes his relation to the muse and tells the story according to the conventions of an epic account of battle.

The narrator mocks himself when he invokes the muse in his epic introduction of the clownish entertainment:

> nunc mihi paucis
> Sarmenti scurrae pugnam Messique Cicirri,
> Musa, velim memores, et quo patre natus uterque
> contulerit litis. Messi clarum genus Osci;
> Sarmenti domina exstat: ab his maioribus orti
> ad pugnam venere.
>   *Sat.* 1.5.51–56

Now, oh Muse, allow me to recite in a few words the battle of Sarmentus
the clown and Messius Cicirrus, and the parentage of each of these who con-
tended in this wrangle. Messius was Oscan, born of a famous clan; Sarmentus still had a mistress living: from this ancestry they sprang, to engage
the fray.

If we compare *uterque* (53) with *uterque* (28), "missi magnis de rebus
uterque / legati, aversos soliti componere amicos," then these two jokers
recall the two epic figures whom the three *legati* represent, Octavian and
Antony, undoing and reshaping the world in their anger. Sarmentus suggests to Messius that his appearance (and note that the substance of the
contest consists of trading insults on the combatants' physical shortcomings and Sarmentus's social status) makes him an apt figure for doing a
Cyclops dance (62–64), and that he would need neither mask nor tragic
buskin to perform it, nature having furnished him with these. He is fit to
perform in a tragedy and there is one at hand, but Horace, like Sarmentus,
is making the comedy.

This passage in particular has caused critics to lament Horace's focus
in this poem. A dream guest list for a dinner party yields only the great
Roman poet's account of how those guests laughed at a couple of comedians and their not very original jests. But it is hardly fair to ask our poet
to anticipate all our desires; Horace has a different task. If we take as
consistent Horace's account of his friendship with Maecenas in *Satires* 2.6,
then he will be obedient to the shape of that friendship. His role in regard
to Maecenas is to speak of trivial matters (2.6.40–46), and he fulfills that
role in *Satires* 1.5. If the conflict between Antony and Octavian motivates
the journey, it also motivates the poem, and the poem puts its own account

in the place of the journey, makes a substitution. As Horace tells us in the last line of the poem, the road and the page end at the same time: "Brundisium longae finis chartaeque viaeque est." The poem covers up the journey as the poet covers his eyes; the account allows us to see everything, the point of the trip and the principals involved, but through a satiric lens that lets us know that conflict between two men can be mocked and that beneath the subject of epic is the subject of satire, which is real life, real discomfort, and real friends.

The meeting and departing of the poet's friends, which embody the single moments of serious emotion in the poem, reflect this view and are told without the patina of epic parody. After leaving Fundi and its praetor and stopping in the city of the Mamurrae, Horace says:

> postera lux oritur multo gratissima; namque
> Plotius et Varius Sinuessae Vergiliusque
> occurrunt, animae qualis neque candidiores
> terra tulit neque quis me sit devinctior alter.
> o qui complexus et gaudia quanta fuerunt!
> nil ego contulerim iucundo sanus amico.
> *Sat.* 1.5.39–44

> The next morning dawned, the most welcome by far: for at Sinuessa Plotius and Varius and Vergil meet us—souls no brighter shine on earth, nor is there any other dearer to me than they. What a round of embracing and joy there was! So long as I'm in my right mind, there is nothing I would compare to a beloved friend.

The sudden depth of feeling is unmistakable; the day is the most favored, the souls of these friends are kinder (*candidiores*) than any on earth. There is no one to whom Horace is more tightly bound; with shining emotion the poet says that as long as he is sane, there is nothing he would compare to a congenial friend. When Varius leaves the party later, Horace says, "flentibus hinc Varius discedit maestus amicis" (93, here a sorrowful Varius leaves his weeping friends). This emphatic emotion stands out from the tone of the poem. The strongest feeling otherwise reported is a general amusement both expressed and provoked by the poet.[21] The break in tone allows the expression of a serious narrator to intrude. Elsewhere in *Satires* 1.5, friendship is political and, in the important instance of the *aversos amicos,* hostile. The friend to Antony, Fonteius Capito, is discredited by the satirist's attention to his appearance, and the friendship is subtly contrasted with the poet's, where the phrase "Antoni non ut magis alter amicus" (33) is recalled in structure by "neque quis me sit devinctior alter" (42). As to the poet's relationship with Maecenas, what he tells us in this poem is that he withdraws from him at each mention of his name; when Maecenas appears, Horace has eye trouble. Just as the satiric content of the poem simultaneously covers and reveals the political meaning of the trip to Brundisium, for example, when it puts a contest between Sarmentus and Messius in the place of the deadlier contest between Octavian and Antony, so the poet's emotion, inspired by his friendship with Vergil, Varius, and Plotius, explicates the concept of friendship in this poem and hints at the poverty of the political relationships driving the mission to Brundisium.

There is sometimes resistance among readers to believing that Horace has a view that differs from that of Maecenas.[22] The idea that Horace might disparage his patron seems a gross transgression of this famous and formal Roman relationship. But this belief both underestimates the latitude of the relationship and mistakes the nature of the criticism that *Satires* 1.5 offers. The poem is not innocent of commentary on the political and social milieu that Horace inhabited. Had the poet wanted to avoid such commentary, he could have left out the names and left the end of the trip and the poem unstated. And he could have avoided the Lucilian echoes, which inevitably link Horace to the robustly critical voice of his satiric ancestor. The criticism in 1.5 is embedded in a satiric portrait of his own experiences that is humorous and honest. Horace's aim, as he tells it, has been to write satire that does not do harm and that can tell the truth with a laugh ("quamquam ridentem dicere verum / quid vetat," 1.1.24–25). It seems to me that the criticism leveled at Maecenas here is not one Maecenas would be likely to object to nor be especially interested in. The excesses of the powerful are hard to look at and hard to bear, not for the powerful themselves, but for their witnesses. Horace can exploit the material reality of satire to express his own view, while at the same time defining his genre and himself as a satirist. Horace's friendship with the other literary figures belongs to that material reality. It is a symptom of his own *health* that he values a beloved friend above all else, in contrast to Luscus, the official at Fundi, whose unreal notion of himself prompts the poet to call him *insanus* (35): "nil ego contulerim iucundo sanus amico" (so long as I am *sanus* there is nothing I would compare to a beloved friend, 44).

Horace's persona in this poem emerges as double: as he defines himself through the experience of his body and as he links himself with characters of a low mimetic level in the poem, he makes himself laughable; as he defines himself by his friendships and makes his devotion an index of his own sanity, he offers us a serious narrator with a serious point of view. In neither instance can he be construed as a threat. We laugh when we are not afraid, and Horace practices and expresses the kind of friendship that does not contain fear. Friendship in *Satires* 1.4 proves that Horace's poetry is not *suspectum*. The dual persona of Horace here, high and low, is consistent with the figure of himself he presents to Maecenas in *Satires* 1.6. There he is low born but pure of heart, and the source of both is his father; both qualities construct a figure who, by social necessity and by nature, cannot inflict wounds with his poetry, a double security that he extends to Maecenas while writing satire, a genre known for its bite.

The persistent demand of the poem that we take the journey to Brundisium as significant only for its account of the personal experience of its narrator, who is characterized as we have seen, asks us to assess the satirist as entirely without menace, just as he has claimed he was in *Satires* 1.4. That claim is demonstrated in 1.4 by the poet's pledge that his poems will never contain the sort of backbiting sludge that constitutes the betrayal of a friend:

> hic nigrae sucus lolliginis, haec est
> aerugo mera: quod vitium procul afore chartis
> atque animo, prius ut, si quid promittere de me
> possum aliud vere, promitto. liberius si
> dixero quid, si forte iocosius, hoc mihi iuris
> cum venia dabis: insuevit pater optimus hoc me,
> ut fugerem exemplis vitiorum quaeque notando.
>   *Sat.* 1.4.100–106

This is the ink of blackest squid, pure envious bile: if I can promise anything honestly about myself, I promise this, that this vice will be far away from my pages, and before that from my heart. If I speak a little too freely, or maybe joke a bit too much, it's fair that you indulge me for this: the best

father in the world ingrained this habit in me, me so that, by noting examples of faults I might flee from them.

The questions about Horace's genre in *Satires* 1.4 are resolved in that
poem with a personal account of the poet's moral life, shaped by his
father, all pointing to the personal trustworthiness of Horace as a friend.
In similar fashion in *Satires* 1.5, the pointed emotion of the instances of
friendship (39–44, 93) illustrate the assertion Horace has made about himself in *Satires* 1.4.

In *Satires* 1.5 the same issues raised in 1.4 concerning Lucilius, satire,
fear, and friendship are not pondered in the discursive style of 1.4 but
are dramatized instead, as if to illustrate their meaning.[23] The details of
the poem contrast with the implied but ignored meaning of the journey
to Brundisium. We must assume that this meaning was well understood
by its contemporary audience, that the mention of Maecenas and Antony,
as well as the conspicuous omission of Octavian's name, articulated a
political and social situation all too obvious to anyone alive in Rome in
the last decades of the first century BCE, one that modern readers can
only reconstruct. The menace in the laconic *aversos amicos* (29) and all the
conflict inherent there stands unspoken next to the explicit preoccupations of the poem. What relief can balance the threat of civil wars, when
the "friendships" of great men threaten the lives of ordinary people and
promise terror and tragedy of genuine epic proportions? A form of relief
is perhaps found in small entertainments, in the wisdom of everyday matters, and above all in friendship, in *true* friends who make you cry for joy
when you meet (41) and weep with sorrow when you part (93). It is for
friendships like these that the poet's father, with his satirist's methods of
child rearing, fitted Horace in the previous satire and made him *sanus*.

We have seen the way in which *Satires* 1.5 enacts Horace's generic goals,
to be an unthreatening speaker of satire. But Horace is always double-
dealing with his version of satire, most obviously in the fact that, though
he claims to write against the genre by depriving it of its invective sting,
he does nonetheless like to write satire. The intimacy of the personal
details that Horace uses to make us look at this journey in 1.5 is a rhetorical device of disclosure and revelation: "I'll tell you everything, even
about my wet dream at Trivicum." But the poem is an intentional and
overt evasion. It keeps the secrets of the political meaning of the trip, of
the characters of the great politicians and poets who are on the trip, and

of the reason for Horace's presence on this trip. And, in defiance of the generic expectation for a journey poem (ὁδοπορικόν), the telos of the journey, Brundisium, is only revealed with the ending of the poem. But journey poems are always, in some sense, poems about the journey of life, and in life we do not know where and how we will end. Our vision of the ultimate goal is blurry, and we live our lives in life's material moments, only to be interrupted and cut off with the suddenness of death.

If Horace is manipulating this concept of the journey poem, with the suppression of the telos of the journey, we might evaluate again his telling of his experiences. The hidden but known purpose of the journey to Brundisium, known very well to Horace's contemporary readers, was to make a deal between Rome's powerbrokers, Antony and Octavian. Such men live in fantasies of power that break all the rules of Horace's satire. Horace's persistent punning on the word stem *sat-* (enough, satisfaction, sufficiency) is one of his generic signals in the *Satires*. The material conditions of reality, the mundane concreteness of life, provide a secure model by which we may limit and frame our imaginations, our appetites, our desires. The limit of what our stomachs can hold is the metaphor Horace uses in his first satire for the limit to our longings; if we live within our limits, we are *sanus*, and to try to live beyond those limits is to live the life of a madman. In the first four satires of his first book, Horace makes the concept of limitation a productive principle for living, for friendship, and for successful poetry; Horace's satire, as a genre of the ordinary, of the sufficient, is de facto *sanus*. This principle is articulated again in this poem, as we have seen. But the reason for the journey violates those principles of sanity. The journey is made by and for men with pretensions to power that are absurd, by men who are *insanus*, crazy—according to the precept of Horace's satire. The telos of their journey is reasonably seen as death, the end to our absorption in the reality of living. Why, indeed, would Horace want to open his eyes to look at this goal? Horace's body, vexed by travel, whose discomforts are so carefully chronicled in *Satires* 1.5, is the satiric substitute for Rome, the body politic. As this journey takes its toll on Horace's body, so too do Octavian and Antony wear down Rome. And thus the satiric bite of Horace's genre reemerges.

❋ 4 ❦

Satire as Conflict
Irresolution

Satires 1.7

If I could have found my tongue, I would not have struck him. . . . I could
say it only with a blow.

—HERMAN MELVILLE, *Billy Budd*

This chapter contends that within the satirical view of *Satires* 1.7, words
may act as the equivalent of blows, containing no more reason and giving
rise to no more justice than Billy Budd's inarticulate fist.

The seventh poem in Horace's first book of *Satires*, often slighted for its
brevity, raucous mirth, and the stupefying pun at the finish, continues
to elaborate the program for satire that Horace is constructing in that
book of poems.[1] The echoes within the poem of Lucilius and of Horace's
critical treatment of Lucilius in *Satires* 1.4 and 1.10 place 1.7 in Horace's
ongoing debate with his genre in *Satires* I. The poem's satiric frame, its
Lucilian combatants, and the dark allusion to Brutus each participates in
an elucidation of Horace's ambivalent stance toward his genre and his
model, Lucilius. Moreover, the poem's epic parodies and the implication of
the murderous proceedings of the Roman civil wars in the regicidal pun
provide a deeper commentary on the human conflict that motivates both
epic and invective combat.

Horace is concerned with conflict in the *Satires,* and I will argue that the
analysis of conflict that is visible in *Satires* 1.7 is at the heart of Horace's
objections to Lucilian satire, in regard to both its stylistic and its invective
nature. But we need to note first that the *appeal* of invective for Horace is
evident. Unlike persuasive speech, which, however manipulative or over-
bearing, must depend on the needs of the listener in order to be effective,

invective is powerful speech, a medium through which the speaker asserts himself against another and thus identifies himself positively as a separate self; as such it may serve as a defensive weapon, as Horace notes in *Satires* 2.1 when he compares his pen to Canidia's *venenum* (2.1.48).[2] Though we never see Horace use his speech, *in propria persona*, in such a way in the *Satires*, he promises us that he can. And invective has the appeal, obvious in its exposition in *Satires* 1.7, of sheer pleasure, like the explosion of fireworks, in the tumbling boisterous verbiage of invective exchange; it is a pleasure of transgression, of limitlessness, of speaking that no longer needs to hear, and is a proposition of the self unbounded by the ear's obedience to another speaker. As 1.7 will show, the invective speaker uses his speech as if it were a material weapon against another, and claims the whole verbal field with the obliterating exuberance of his assault. Invective thus provides a source of merriment for its audience, as long as the audience is not the object of its attacks. But while invective appeals to Horace as a powerful tool in the poetic arsenal, his awareness of that appeal is complicated by a consciousness of the deadly pleasures of conflict and of how invective enacts conflict.

The dangers of invective for Horace are akin to its pleasures. Those dangers have received a critical exposition in *Satires* 1.4, where Horace first addresses the problem of his satiric predecessor Lucilius. The expansiveness of invective is mirrored in Lucilius's stylistic unrestraint. In 1.4, Horace contrasts his criticism of Lucilius, that Lucilius's verses flow like a muddy stream ("flueret lutulentus," 1.4.12),[3] with a boast of his own verbal poverty: "di bene fecerunt inopis me quodque pusilli / finxerunt animi, raro et perpauca loquentis" (17–18). The gods did a good thing when they made his spirit short on resources, a wee thing, as it were, speaking a few words infrequently. It is a curiosity of *Satires* 1.4 that Horace, who might have simply established himself in the genre of his predecessor with praise and imitation of Lucilius, instead establishes a relation of conflict between himself and his satiric predecessor. He writes what amounts to a *recusatio* of satire in the genre of satire.

Where Lucilius flows muddy, Horace is spare.[4] Overtly, stylistic objections are the only ones Horace allows himself to make of his satiric model. Potential ethical objections to Lucilius's invective practice are hidden in the convoluted arguments of 1.4, concerning the status of this genre as poetry, and the fear and hatred that Horace presents as the predictable response first to satire ("hoc genus," 24), and then to poetry and to poets

(33). So in 1.4, Horace mounts a campaign against the reckless speaker and the bad friend and, as a resolution to the problem of the genre itself, establishes his own character as the surety against the danger posed by his poetry.

Satires 1.4 began with the apparent praise for Lucilius that he is the direct descendant of the Old Comic poets who marked ("notabant," 1.4.5) the criminal and the notorious. As we saw, that practice of Lucilius's poetry becomes aligned, in the course of 1.4, with the practice by which Horace's father improved his son, by marking ("notando," 1.4.106) the faults in others that he would have his son avoid. According to Horace, it is thanks to this satiric practice by his father that he is *sanus,* clean of serious faults that would bring *perniciem* (130). But Horace has further adopted the practice himself and ponders in silence ("compressis labris," 138) the behavior of others. What Lucilius did with too many words, Horace does not merely with restraint but in complete silence; satire as Lucilius practiced it is reduced to an interior monologue in Horace. In what time he has left to him, Horace says, he fools with his poetry ("illudo chartis," 139). As if to assert that he has not entirely emasculated his craft, Horace ends 1.4 with his odd boast that anyone left objecting to his now wholly benign practice of poetry will be assailed by a band of poets and forced to join their troupe (140–43). The strangeness of 1.4 is born of Horace's impossible ambivalence about the attractions and dangers of Lucilian poetic speech. If we take 1.4 as Horace's program for satire, a program based on a poetics and a social disposition that are fundamentally characterized by the same principle of verbal restraint, it is not hard to deduce the nature of Horace's critique of Lucilian invective.

Moreover, the personal and poetic restraint Horace practices, with a view to being the poet of a kind of satire that does not inspire fear and hatred, and that is therefore not under suspicion ("suspectum genus hoc scribendi," 1.4.65), is consistent with the larger theme in the *Satires* that the limits nature has imposed on our existence establish the boundaries to desire and the conditions for our happiness. To go beyond those boundaries is to court disaster; to stay within them is to live according to reason's assessment of reality and to be *sanus.*[5] *Satires* 1.1, not classified as programmatic by scholars because it doesn't mention Lucilius, nevertheless is explicit about this aspect of the Horatian program for satire: it is a genre grounded in ordinary, material reality; the limits of desire can be found in the limit of the stomach, and to demand more is to live in a wretched fantasy. Likewise in regard to social reality, the existence of other human beings and the need to live among them present a limit to our desires analogous to those material limits nature imposes.

Speech, which can be seen in terms of social desire, is enacted within the limits of a hearing audience—a hearing "other" sets the boundary to the speaking "self." If a speaker disregards the comfort of the hearer, he has failed to recognize a limit on his speech. Reasoned speech, which aims at communication, thus requires a recognition that the self is limited by other and different "selves" in the world. We have seen the satires of book 1 develop these ideas from the first poem onwards. To flood like a muddy stream is to indulge the speaking self without regard for the hearing other. Similarly, the invective impulse knows no limits and is an attempt to enact power over another, indeed, to obliterate another; its pleasure lies in the fantasy of an expanded, unlimited self, free from restraint. But to live in the world as it is truly configured is to live in accordance with reason. To recognize the limits of the self is also to permit, tolerate, and enjoy the existence of others, and, in the differences of others, to experience the real pleasures of the self. Correlative to the pleasure in the recognition of difference is the anxiety inherent in the failure to recognize difference. The "other" may present an intolerable threat if he seems to occupy the very same space as the "self." Without the distance created by differentiation, the "self" labors under the constant threat of expropriation by the all too similar "other." Speech occurring between people who recognize that the differentiation of selves permits the operation of *logos* is a use of language that makes it "the medium of exchange and the bond of union" (to quote H. W. Fowler, *Concise Oxford Dictionary* [1934, iv]), and is thus a tool for recognizing the separate identities of "self" and "other." This medium of exchange, allowing for mutual recognition between people, is the medium of friendship in the *Satires* and, as such, says Horace in *Satires* 1.5, is a symptom of his sanity.

Within the frame of Horace's satiric program, *Satires* 1.7 concerns itself with enmity, not friendship, and it is in this context that the poet focuses on the relationship between Lucilian invective and the operation of conflict. Again Horace has taken care to frame his relationship with his satiric predecessor Lucilius in *Satires* I as one of unresolved conflict, and this tension plays its part in 1.7, in company with the invective, epic, and historical conflicts it treats. Horace's introduction of his principals, Persius and Rex, is set in barbershops and pharmacies, which, as ordinary spaces where people gather to attend to their bodies, is in itself a marker of Horatian satire to open the poem:

Proscripti Regis Rupili pus atque venenum
hybrida quo pacto sit Persius ultus, opinor
omnibus et lippis notum et tonsoribus esse.
   Sat. 1.7.1–3

The pus and poison of the outlaw Rupilius Rex, how the half-breed Persius got his vengeance on it, I think is something known to every pink-eyed man and barber.

Evidence of the poet's own voice in this poem, in the mild first-person verb *opinor* (I suppose) keeps the persona of Horace at a distance from the scene he relates. "Pus atque venenum," words here describing speech, are a prominent link both to Lucilius and to Canidia, Horace's practitioner of magical invective.[6] Persius takes vengeance on the speech of Rex; as one who takes vengeance on a "king," Persius is thus made structurally parallel from the outset to the poem's final construction of Brutus, who takes vengeance on kings (Etruscan or Roman) and who is the poem's final figure of epic. Persius is carefully drawn: a rich man with big business in Clazomene and a noisome lawsuit with Rex, he is a hard character (*durus homo*)—the sort able to defeat Rex in *odium*—self-assured, swollen, and a man of keenly bitter speech (1.7.4–8). As does Rex, he bears lexical links to the Horatian Lucilius, in being *durus* and swift and sharp of tongue.[7]

His readers note that Horace is fond of having it both ways in the *Satires,* and that the act of composition removes his persona from the very scenes in which he participates. But Horace's ambivalence goes further than a contented stance of uninvolved involvement. Rudd (1966, 65–66), in speaking of 1.7, likens the poet's position to "that of a man at a party who stands on the fringe of a rather boisterous and drunken group. He stays close enough to enjoy what is being said, but for the benefit of the other guests he wears a satirical smile." It seems rather, borrowing Rudd's analogy, that Horace is simultaneously in the drunken group and outside it, that he is one of the roisterers at the same time as being a commentator; this is a more difficult position. Put another way, Horace wants to

eat his cake and not eat his cake too. There is no way to take the account
of the conflict in 1.7 away from Horace's account; he makes and tells the
poem, no matter how much distance he imaginatively tries to fabricate
between himself and the poem's matter. Similarly, Horace's relation to
Lucilius rests in part on a critique of the nature of invective speech, but
this puts him in a position of critical opposition to Lucilius. We may recognize the Horatian strategies for cobbling together a persona who can
be in two places at once, but this is not a realistic maneuver, and we are
left with the tension that always inheres in ambivalence—a disquieting,
simultaneous affiliation with two opposing stands.

With a Lucilian echo the poet says, "ad regem redeo" (1.7.9, I return to
Rex),[8] which he humorously fails to do, instead interrupting his account
of the two litigants, between whom nothing could be agreed ("nihil inter
utrumque / convenit," 9–10), to muse on epic conflict. All tiresome people
("molesti," 10) are like heroes ("fortes," 11) when they meet in battle,
says Horace. His example is that tireless pair, Hector and Achilles, who
thus function as equivalents to Persius and Rex. The epic parody mocks
and illustrates the unheroic nature of the poem's two protagonists, but it
has the equal effect of reducing Hector and Achilles to another tiresome
quarreling pair. The *summa virtus* of each allows only death as an outcome to their conflict, and that is the only reason their anger is "deadly"
("ut ultima divideret mors, / non aliam ob causam nisi quod virtus in
utroque / summa fuit" 13–15). The narrative succeeds in undermining *virtus* as a virtue; for what is its value if all it can achieve is death? The satire
portrays epic conflict solely in terms of its activity and outcome, without
a motivation whose nobility could potentially justify it. Seen in its naked
activity and deprived of motive, conflict has no purpose. There is no logic
in conflict, no valor in *virtus*.[9]

As friendship allows for productive speech shared between speakers
who recognize and tolerate their differences, enmity by contrast gives rise
to speech that serves not to link but to separate speakers whose differences
have blurred in their devotion to their conflict. Invective identifies the flaws
of the other while relying on the assumption that the speaker is blameless. Blame speech, however, encourages its return in kind, with the result
that the two parties involved in the exchange of invective conflict appear
to the outside observer to be more or less identical. Indeed, a basic feature
of violent conflict, as René Girard observes, is that the sameness of the
opposing parties inspires them both to attempt to differentiate themselves

with increasing vehemence, with the ironic result that the two appear more and more similar. There is nothing as similar to an angry man as another angry man, notes Girard (1979, 2). By displaying the similarity of the combatants, to each other and to Hector and Achilles, the poem demonstrates the implicit thesis that *molesti* and *fortes* are in the end equivalent. If conflict arises because two people fail to distinguish between self and other, each believing that the other has the power to expropriate the self (hence, as Girard [57–67] points out, the recurrent mythical theme of conflict between twins and siblings), only death can separate them, as the poem says (*ultima divideret mors*).

By characterizing his would-be heroes as Lucilian, Horace is able not only to demonstrate the essential likeness of Persius and Rex to each other but also to frame a commentary on Lucilian invective. The epic parody of 1.7 makes the verbal weapons of invective equivalent to the weapons of epic combat, with speech providing low man's spear. Both forms of conflict rely on the obliteration of the other by means of their weapons. In epic, conflict demands the exchange of a death for a life: the hero, attempting to substitute his own mortality with that of another, enacts a longing for life without limits. Homer's heroes don the armor of their slain enemies, thus signaling that the process of expropriation of the enemy "other" is complete. This procedure is most famously dramatized in the episode of Achilles' pursuit of Hector around the walls of Troy, in which Hector is wearing Achilles' armor, taken when he killed Patroclus. Visually, Achilles is chasing a second self, a Hector dressed as Achilles. The invective speaker enacts the same procedure with words; his less deadly purpose is to obtain the silence of the other.[10]

Horace's satiric program clearly countenances favoring the unheroic in this meditation on epic. The problem with Hector and Achilles, just as with Persius and Rex, is *summa virtus*. The only end to conflict is the death, in epic, or the silence, in invective, of the vanquished. By way of instructive contrast, however, Horace presents a satiric alternative to this operation of conflict:

> duo si discordia vexet inertis,
> aut si disparibus bellum incidat, ut Diomedi
> cum Lycio Glauco, discedat pigrior ultro
> muneribus missis.
>   *Sat.* 1.7.15–18

> If conflict besets two lazy men, or if a fight breaks out between unequals—
> like Diomedes and Lycian Glaucus for example—then the weaker man yields,
> and gives gifts besides.

So without the troubling business of heroic contest, conflict is resolved without fatalities and both parties survive. Another Iliadic pair, Glaucus and Diomedes, serve as Horace's exemplum of conflict resolution. But Horace has mis-told Homer's story. In book 6 of the *Iliad* (119–236) is a tale of guest friendship, discovered in the moment of battle, between the Greek Diomedes and the Trojan Glaucus. To that encounter belongs Homer's famous statement of archaic Greek realism, in which the son of Hippolochus compares the lives of men to the generations of leaves, words that epitomize the keen grace of epic. Glaucus tells the story of his family, and Diomedes, hurling his spear into the ground, declares they will do no battle, for they are bound by the guest friendship of their fathers. They leap from their horses, grip hands, and make their exchange of friendship. Then the narrative adds its little sting: Zeus stole the wits of Glaucus, who exchanged with Diomedes gold armor for bronze, armor worth a hundred oxen for the value of nine. The narrative leaves them here in characteristically mute fashion; it leaves Glaucus bested but ignorant of the fraud, and Diomedes' conquest gained not in battle but in an exchange of gifts, a betrayal in an act of friendship.

In his satirizing of epic, Horace presents Glaucus and Diomedes as unevenly matched warriors, an assumption never tested in Homer's account, and he presents the cheating of Glaucus, achieved by Zeus in an unexplained moment of Greek partisanship, as if it represented a deliberate acknowledgment by Glaucus of Diomedes' superior strength. The satiric version in 1.7 turns that exquisite and puzzling moment of the *Iliad* into a pragmatic assessment of strength and weakness, in which the mutual recognition by Glaucus and Diomedes of their dissimilarity is the grounds on which they settle a conflict. Horace rationalizes Homer's story: Glaucus is not fooled but rather strikes a deal with Diomedes to keep from getting killed. The satire puts reason over passion, denying conflict its glory and insisting on the possibility of reasonable compromise, including compensation to the stronger party, Diomedes, so that he forgo the chance of battle. All the beauty and pathos of Homer is missing: the dignity of Glaucus, the revelation of the old friendship, the careless betrayal worked by Zeus, and the arbitrary fraud. But in its place, Horace offers a resolution to a conflict that, however unheroic, is intelligible to both sides and permits life to continue. Horace's version firmly removes the epic's irrational impulse, embodied in the acts of the gods, not of humans, and grants to the mortals involved the reward of life for a reasoned resolution.

The surprising new view of epic heroes and the elimination of noble motive are good comedy. It has in addition the ring of satiric common sense, and the debunked epic material takes on a new status that questions fundamental assumptions about the value of conflict. In Horace's version of the Glaucus-Diomedes episode, the divine unreason of Zeus is converted into the ordinary unfairness of the world, and Glaucus, as *pigrior,* yields and lives. The tale is recast to demonstrate the view that the value of life lies in the mundane, and to convey the peculiarly Horatian intolerance for the unreason of conflict. In Horace's hands, satire captures the higher ground of human reason and leaves epic to glorify senseless conflict. The race in Horace's satire goes not to the swift but to the *inertis.*

Having made its point concerning heroes, epic and otherwise, the poem again takes up the conflict at hand, midline (18), midpoem, and in medias res. The similarity of the two combatants is again made evident as the pair Persius and Rex rush into court, as fit a match for each other as the gladiators Bacchius and Bithus, in Horace's words, each a splendid spectacle. Brutus, the assassin of Julius Caesar, hovers over the proceedings in an ablative absolute:

> Bruto praetore tenente
> ditem Asiam, Rupili et Persi par pugnat, uti non
> compositum melius cum Bitho Bacchius. in ius
> acres procurrunt, magnum spectaculum uterque.
>   *Sat.* 1.7.18–21

> . . . when Brutus was holding the praetorship in wealthy Asia, there's a fight between Rupilius Rex and Persius, and they're an even match—like Bithus and Bacchius. Fiercely they come roaring into court, each a grand spectacle to see.

Brutus is slyly introduced to the poem as the officiating magistrate of the trial with the remark that he was then praetor in "wealthy Asia." The mention of Brutus signals a return to the narrative, and its position in v. 18 seems to furnish information purely circumstantial to the invective spectacle that follows. We see at the end, however, that in fact Brutus is crucial to the irresolution of the poem. Consistent with the poem's strategy of taking the heroism out of conflict, Horace now likens Persius and Rex to the Greek heroes (slaves) of the Roman gladiatorial ring, using the language of gladiatorial competition. That language again makes clear the principle of conflict that those set in competition (*compositum*) are equals and alike (*par*).[11] The rest of the poem presents the competitive spectacle.

The spectators are not only those in the court, but we ourselves, the readers of the poem. What we see, in addition to the spectacle, is a shrewd agglomeration of Horace's ideas on poetic practice. Persius sets out his case, and it is greeted by the laughter of all assembled: "Persius exponit causam; ridetur ab omni / conventu" (22–23). In a reliable courtroom strategy, Persius extravagantly praises the presiding magistrate, calling Brutus "the sun of Asia" (as if Brutus were himself an inflated epic hero) and his cohort—with the exception of Rex—his "healthful stars." Rex is the dog star, hateful to farmers. Persius and Rex are both made to share the poetic faults of Lucilius, as verbal echoes of Horace's critique of Lucilius in *Satires* 1.4 and 1.10 are placed in the context of the invective exchange.

> ruebat
> flumen ut hibernum fertur quo rara securis.
> tum Praenestinus salso multoque fluenti
> expressa arbusto regerit convicia, durus
> vindemiator et invictus, cui saepe viator
> cessisset magna compellans voce cuculum.
> at Graecus, postquam est Italo perfusus aceto,
> Persius exclamat "per magnos, Brute, deos te
> oro, qui reges consueris tollere, cur non
> hunc Regem iugulas? operum hoc, mihi crede, tuorum est."
>
> *Sat.* 1.7.26–35

. . . he rushed ahead like a winter flood where it's hard to wield an ax. Then the Praenestine [Rex], in answer to this running river of wit, hurls back invective that's extract of the vineyard—he's a tough, unmoved old grape-presser, the type the traveler often has to back away from while he yells out "cuckoo" to him. But Persius the Greek, though drenched right through in

this Italian vinegar, shouts back "great gods, Brutus, I'm begging you—
you're the one who's in the habit of killing kings—why don't you murder
this King? trust me, it's a job for you."

Persius goes rushing on, Horace says, like the river in winter near which
the pruning ax is rarely borne. His speech bears not only the watery hall-
mark of Lucilian rushing (water in heedless abundance) but lacks an editor—an ax (*securis*). The *Oxford Latin Dictionary* has three definitions
for *securis*: an ax, hatchet, battle-ax; an executioner's ax, in particular one
carried in the *fasces* of a Roman magistrate (or, earlier, of kings); a part
of the blade of a vine-dresser's knife used for chopping. The *rara securis*
of v. 27 does multiple metaphorical work: Persius's speech is not cut
short by the *securis* of the magistrate, Brutus, who lets the speech run on;
nor is it interrupted by Rex, the *vindemiator*, who might also have such a
blade; and in the immediate poetic sense, the *securis* adumbrates the
pastoral context that is continued as Rex retorts from another sort of
country scene.

As if in contrast with the urbane cultivation of Horace's poetry, both
speakers in the courtroom are countrified: Persius speaks like the uncul-
tivated Italian landscape of late winter; Rex talks from the rough country
space of an Italian vintner. Whereas Persius had the Lucilian tag *durus*
and was a man unconquerable in hatred in v. 6, now Rex is *durus* (29) and
unconquered ("invictus," 30) as "the tough vintner and an invincible one."
Against the salty, abundant flooding of Persius, Rex hurls back insults
again of a liquid nature, "squeezed from the vine." The text links and dif-
ferentiates the two combatants simultaneously throughout its account of
their exchange, revealing the procedure of identification and distinction
between the participants of a conflict. The two share invective liquidity;[12]
but Persius, *hybrida* at the poem's start, is fully *Graecus* in v. 32, though he
speaks with an Italian affiliation, while Rex becomes the *Praenestinus* at
v. 28. Rex, the man from Praeneste, soaks the Greek Persius with Italian
vinegar ("aceto," 32), his return for Persius's salty wit ("salso," 28).

Thus soaked and flooded and squeezed, the invective exchange meets
its end with Persius's final appeal to the magistrate: "Great gods, Brutus,
I beseech you, who habitually overthrow kings, why don't you cut the
throat (*iugulas*) of this King (this Rex)? Believe me, it's a job for you!"
Here ends the poem: this verbal coup is the vengeance by Persius known
to the *lippi* and *tonsores* of the beginning of the poem, now revealed to

Horace's readers. Now too we have one more use suggested for the *securis* of v. 29: the magistrate's ax might execute this Rex.

Modern distaste for puns seems to have obscured from critical view Horace's gleeful daring in allowing his Persius to implicate Brutus in this last bit of word wielding.[13] Commentary on the pun has been withering, and the decorum of the allusion to the assassination of Caesar has often escaped readers, who seem to have struggled to find a date of composition for the poem that would render this reference benign.[14] Critics dislike the pun on aesthetic grounds, as a poor joke, and they dislike it on grounds of etiquette, that it is tasteless to allude to Brutus's murder of Caesar.[15] But there *is* no etiquette in the reference to Caesar's assassination. As the end to the conflict of *Satires* 1.7 is enacted, the pun, which merges the signifier "Rex" with the traditional opponent of Brutuses, is the linguistic equivalent of a deathblow; as a plunge beneath logos that defies verbal response, the pun has finished off the verbal conflict.

The pun is a verbal trick; it is like a deft move with a spear. It defeats the exchange of verbal weapons, dealing a deathblow to the argument by leaving language as communicative exchange finally dead. There is no riposte to a pun; it is a communication stopper. A pun presents a linguistic situation in which two meanings coexist in a single signifier; it is then impossible to fix the meaning, and the arbitrariness of language is revealed. One cannot choose between the two meanings; hence meaning, logos, is denied. Once invective is in operation, and the hearing part of speech exchange is denied, language forfeits its informational function; listening in 1.7 has been left to the hearing spectators, to the courtroom witnesses, to the *lippi* and *tonsores,* and to us. The pun, as the epitome of the conflict, is appropriate as a strategy and makes the verbal exchange and its sudden finish precisely equivalent to the finish of physical combat. The conflict ends with the loss of meaning in speech and the defeat of reason. The absence of reason in the pun, its smashing of signifiers, takes the logic out of speech and, as Horace has arranged it for us here, summarizes the absence of reason in conflict.

One might say that this is enough, *satis est,* that epic has been deflated, conflict mocked, and invective appreciated for its exuberance but at a safe distance from the poet and us, his audience. The laughter that the tale supplies, reproduced in those satirical spaces of barbershops and pharmacies, proves satire's work. But it is as if Horace can't leave that satirical space alone. The pun introduces its own objection when it plays with the names of Brutus and Rex and thus introduces an epic context that, unlike Homer's, cannot be retold, or un-told. If the absence of reason in the pun echoes the absence of reason in conflict, which the poem has demonstrated, then the name of Brutus as king-killer nicely makes the point. The work of the pun, as it undoes the logos of speech and undoes reason, reaffirms the un-reason of persistent conflict—its appealing "triumphs" and its whole lack of resolution. If there is a winner and a loser, the conflict itself remains. The successful removal of Julius Caesar did not end the civil wars.[16] Those puzzled by the etiquette of the pun forget what scholars, from Ronald Syme onward, have taught us about Rome in the 40s and 30s BCE, a city relentlessly drenched in the carnage of warring factions. Horace stabs us with nonsatirical reality; Brutus killed Caesar, and there was no laughter and no peace, nor did the Roman power players relinquish their dedication to heroic values. They fought on, because of their *summa virtus*. But the poem has shown the value of such *virtus*, that it temporarily stalls death, by exchanging the death of another for the inevitable death of the self; heroism exceeds reason, denies reality, life, and the limits nature supplies for our sanity.

There is an optimism inherent in Horace's treatment of conflict in 1.7, that it can be reduced from any level to be the subject of consensual laughter. But the nonsense of the pun of 1.7 itself reintroduces the problem: that conflict persists, is deadly, and, although assassination removes the tyrant, tyranny still persists.[17] The appeal of invective speech, as a tool that empowers the weak, remains tempting and unresolved for Horace in book 1 of the *Satires*. The temptation to overpower another, the longing for a self without limits, is judged by the poem to be by turns ridiculous or deadly. The pun on Brutus's name is a joke containing, not bad taste, but a small cry of pain, which is not in fact dissonant with comedy. Horace serves us an exemplum of invective speech by which he contrives his own commentary on the ambivalent pleasures of laughter, anger, and satire.

❋ 5 ❋

Talking Heads and
Canidian Poetics

Satires 1.8

In *Satires* 1.2.68–71, a man's penis speaks to him about the folly of his desires, pointing out that his own sexual requirements (the phallus's) are far more reasonable than his host's.[1] The satiric landscape in which Horace works has changed since *Satires* 1.2: the talking phallus in *Satires* 1.8 is an uneasy rendition of the philosophically assured member of *Satires* 1.2, and this is all the more surprising because this poem's phallic speaker is the god Priapus.

There are, in fact, three speakers in this poem that Priapus narrates, and Horace and Canidia are the other two. The poem undoes the power of each speaker, ambivalently in the case of the poet. *Satires* 1.8 begins with an announcement of the speaker's identity, the only poem in the *Satires* to do so, and the only poem of the first book of *Satires* that is not narrated by a figure explicitly or implicitly identified with the persona of Horace. The poem thus provides an opportunity to examine a Horatian satire that is not tempered by the poet's protestations about his own persona, and to consider the elements of this genre that the poet claims to reject as part of his repertoire. I suggest too that the poem's two speakers, Priapus and Canidia, each act as a substitute for Horace's own persona and present elements of satire that the poet has disavowed for himself, but that he also recognizes as elements fundamental to his genre, though these are problematic when spoken by his own persona. Within the triad of poems, *Satires* 1.7, 8, and 9, *Satires* 1.7 presents abusive speech and 1.9 the wearisome garrulity condemned in *Satires* 1.10. Between these two is *Satires* 1.8, treating an issue critical to the discussion of satire in *Satires* 1.4, the satirist's menace and the fearful audience.[2] *Satires* 1.8 resolves the issue of menace to an audience by insisting that our response is to laugh, which indeed we do.

The narrator of *Satires* 1.8, Priapus, is not strictly a phallus, but that is the great distinguishing feature of this god derived from a Greek fertility deity; in his Roman context he protects boundaries by threatening trespassers with punishments inflicted by his outsized phallus.[3] He is the speaker of an extant group of Latin poems, called *Priapea*, a work of uncertain date and authorship, in which Priapus relentlessly boasts and menaces and occasionally offers an assist to erotically challenged worshippers. The genre of Priapic poems was popular in the late republic and early empire in Rome, whatever the true provenance of the *Priapea* we possess.[4] Though in those poems Priapus's focus and distinguishing feature is his own exceedingly virile member, that organ plays no role in Horace's tale of Priapus; the constant threats of anal and oral penetration in the *Priapea* serve as a latent memory in the depiction of the oral and anal ineptitude of the Priapus in *Satires* 1.8.

Horace gives us a Priapic narrator markedly different from the persona of the *Priapea*. Though Priapus begins the satire with a conventional boast of his menace, he proves to be a timorous version of himself, who succeeds only inadvertently in driving the trespassers, Canidia and Sagana, out of his garden. Horace's version of a Priapic poem takes the sexual (and satiric) menace away from Priapus.[5]

The poem's beginning is a conventional Priapic opener, with Priapus's identification of himself:

Olim truncus eram ficulnus, inutile lignum,
cum faber, incertus scamnum faceretne Priapum,
maluit esse deum. deus inde ego, furum aviumque
maxima formido; nam fures dextra coercet
obscenoque ruber porrectus ab inguine palus;
ast importunas volucres in vertice harundo
terret fixa vetatque novis considere in hortis.
    Sat. 1.8.1–7

Once I was a fig tree, a worthless piece of wood, when a woodworker, unsure whether to make a footstool or a Priapus, preferred to make the god. Hence god I am, and a terrible threat to thieves and birds; for my right hand restrains thieves, along with my red rod that towers from my naughty groin;

and the reed stuck into the top of my head terrifies the marauding birds and
keeps them from settling in the new gardens.

Priapus tells us that he has been vulnerable from his very beginnings,
when the *faber* who made him debated whether to make the fig-wood log
into a god or a piece of furniture.[6] His "self" was arbitrarily determined
by the preference of the woodworker, and the claim Priapus makes to be
a *maxima formido* to thieves and birds is doubtful from the start. Nothing in the god's genesis disposes the reader to take the claim seriously, and
his happenstance existence out of *inutile lignum*, at the whim of the *faber*,
undermines the boast of his menace. The choice by the equivocal *faber*
in the opening lines prompts Priapus to speak of himself in the third person ("faber, incertus scamnum faceretne Priapum," 2) as if this god himself viewed his existence at a remove.

Horace's Priapus, focused on his scarecrow characteristics, is not the
sexually bumptious figure of the *Priapea;* but there are lexical allusions
in this opening passage that recall the sexual, menacing Priapus. In the
Priapea the god refers to his own material as *ligneus* and *lignum* (Pr. 63
and 10), and on *inutile lignum* has this to say:

> Obliquis quid me, pathicae, spectatis ocellis?
> non stat in inguinibus mentula tenta meis.
> quae tamen exanimis nunc est et *inutile lignum*
> utilis haec, aram si dederitis erit.[7]
>   *Priapea, 73*

> You randy girls, why do you look at me with that side-long glance? My prick
> isn't standing up straight from my crotch; but though now it's lifeless and a
> useless chunk of wood, useful it will be if you give it your hiding place.

The god of the *Priapea* is routinely *ruber,* as for example in Pr. 26, where
he complains that he has lost his usual ruddy look and has turned pale
(*pallidus*) from satisfying the ferocious lusts of women (he is *exfututus,*
"fucked out"). The uncertain making of Priapus in *Satires* 1.8 has its far
more emphatic equivalent in Pr. 10: "sed lignum rude vilicus dolavit /
et dixit mihi: 'tu Priapus esto'" (But the bailiff carved an unformed wooden
stump and said to me "be thou Priapus"), and Priapus refers in Pr. 63
to the "manus sine arte rusticae" (unskilled rustic hands) that fashioned

him.[8] While the surviving *Priapea* do not specify that the god is made of fig wood, there is much punning in the *Priapea* on *ficus* as both "fig" the fruit and hemorrhoid (the result of anal intercourse), which plays on the punishment a thief will take for stealing fruit.[9] In this vein there is also a play on an obscene sense of *hortus* (garden), meaning "anus," in which Priapus promises a boy that he can have whatever is in *his* garden so long as Priapus can have access to the boy's "garden" (*Pr.* 5).[10] In *Satires* 1.8, all the content of Priapus's menace is left in the poem's allusive language to recall the powerful Priapic figure who is *not* speaking here.

The voice of Priapus in *Satires* 1.8 quickly identifies him as an unwitting speaker, one who says more than he understands, who allows the reader greater insight than he himself possesses and allows the reader to be in on a joke at the speaker's expense. The gardens Priapus protects are in the Esquiline and were part of Maecenas's urban renewal project in Rome.[11] Priapus describes not the gardens but the place the gardens are meant to obliterate. The humorous sobriety of Priapus's self-description finds a startling contrast in the next lines, in which he describes the place where he stands rooted to the ground of an old burial place for the lowest levels of Roman humanity. The whitening bones that once lay on the ground, to be sadly observed by a visitor to the place, are the remains of bodies thrown out of cramped garrets, carried in poor coffins by a fellow slave to a common grave:

> huc prius angustis eiecta cadavera cellis
> conservus vili portanda locabat in arca;
> hoc miserae plebi stabat commune sepulcrum,
> Pantolabo scurrae Nomentanoque nepoti:
> mille pedes in fronte, trecentos cippus in agrum
> hic dabat: heredes monumentum ne sequeretur.
> nunc licet Esquiliis habitare salubribus atque
> aggere in aprico spatiari, quo modo tristes
> albis informem spectabant ossibus agrum.
>
> *Sat.* 1.8.8–16

It was to this place, in a time before, that the bodies of slaves, tossed from wretched quarters, were fixed by a fellow-slave to be brought in a cheap coffin; this was the common grave for impoverished common folk, for Pantolabus the taker and Nomentanus the waster: a thousand feet in the front, three hundred deep the boundary stone declared, and no one inherits the burial-ground. But now you can live in a wholesome Esquiline and stroll on its sunny rampart, where once people sadly looked at a space disfigured by whitening bones.

The intimacy of the details is a surprise in tone, a shift into pathos that is unprepared by the account by the artless Priapus. Its suddenly realistic picture of a life and a death that anyone would avoid if possible prompts compassion we do not expect from the initial lines of the poem, lines that have elicited our comfortable smile at the narrator. The new gardens have brought sunny walkways and a healthful aspect, but Priapus's account does not keep that aspect in mind, dwelling as he does on the older, sadder meaning and look of the gardens. The narration is ambivalent: the account would incline us to feel the now salubrious park as a sad place of death, but the narrator has been shown to have little authority, his power as a god and as a speaker already undermined by his account of himself. It is uncertain whether the graveyard he describes exists in fact or in his mind, whether the restored gardens really retain evidence of their past substance or the suggestible Priapus only fears they do.[12] Priapus is here an old fertility god, grown hilarious through time for his exaggerated erotic attributes and consigned to the undignified role of scarecrow, his fat red phallus as much a mark of vulnerability as of power. But he has told very well the story of the old scene on the Esquiline Hill, as if he draws out of his former Priapic identity a memory of the darker past and can paint its picture with skill. The explicit structure of his persona denies the credibility of his story, but the hint of another truth bleeds through, not enough to make that narrator authoritative but sufficient to taint the new gardens with the reality of its past. A similar narrative operation occurred in *Satires* 1.5, where the persona of Horace has told one tale of the journey to Brundisium, the satire of the uncomfortable traveler whose bodily demands shape his view, but allows the darker reality behind the trip's motivation to appear as a shadow. In both poems a dual agenda flickers: the cheerful wit of the explicit satiric program that the poet encourages lies alongside the unresolved issue of menace. We are invited to laugh at the narrator of *Satires* 1.8 and yet are placed in a real Roman space with a real Roman history, which Priapus, for all his accidental nature, happens to get right.

Having offered to us the substitute vision of the *informem agrum* for the *Esquiliis salubribus*, Priapus next makes his anxiety apparent, clearly explaining that its source is not the thieves and wild beasts that roam the place (to whom, he inadvertently tells us, he is not such a threat after all) but the females who, with songs and poisons, come to hector the human souls left here. It seems that if Priapus were the menace he originally claims to be, thieves and wild beasts would not roam the place as he says they do; in any case his Priapic accoutrements have failed to banish them.

> cum mihi non tantum furesque feraeque suetae
> hunc vexare locum curae sunt atque labori,
> quantum carminibus quae versant atque venenis
> humanos animos: has nullo perdere possum
> nec prohibere modo, simul ac vaga luna decorum
> protulit os, quin ossa legant herbasque nocentis.
>   *Sat.* 1.8.17–22

and yet the thieves, and wild beasts, that usually ravage the place aren't so much my worry and trouble as the women who work their spells and poisons and haunt the human souls: I cannot, by any means, get rid of these females, or—once the revolving moon shows forth her comely visage—keep them from coming to pick the bones and poison plants.

As if we were in doubt about his lack of impact, Priapus, in this inflated narrational turn, confesses that he has no power to prevent these women from coming here to pluck bones and deadly herbs.[13] Again, whether the bones are there to pluck and the women really take over the only partly purged gardens, or whether Priapus's imagination only would have this all occur, is not revealed by the poem. But at this point, to verify his narration, Priapus says:

> vidi egomet nigra succinctam vadere palla
> Canidiam, pedibus nudis passoque capillo,
> cum Sagana maiore ululantem: pallor utrasque
> fecerat horrendas aspectu.[14]
>   *Sat.* 1.8.23–26

I myself have seen Canidia, wrapped in her black cloak, hurry barefoot with flying hair and howling along with Sagana, the older one: their ghastly pallor made them horrifying to look at.

Priapus is eager to show the reality of what he has seen, that this was terrifying, no idle fear. His resort to inflated diction in the passage about the moon reveals his desire to be taken seriously, while simultaneously making his fear ludicrous. He has returned us to our condescension towards this narrator, that he is afraid but we aren't; the stock description of the witches orients us to the genre of narration, a spooky story that scares him more than it scares us.

Priapus proceeds with a precise and generic account of Canidia and Sagana's activities (24–35).[15] They dig the ground with their nails, and from a fetal lamb, dismembered with their teeth, they pour blood into the trench to draw out the shades of the dead (*manis*) for their responses. A woolen effigy and a smaller waxen one, used in sympathetic magic, act out a power conflict of domination and submission. These figures belong to the magic ritual in which the woolen figure represents the spell maker who wishes to fulfill a desire, and the waxen image represents the other whose will must be overcome and obliterated, as in Canidia's performance of Horace's fifth *Epode*. Here the two effigies seem thrown in for good measure, without reference to a specific magical goal (as the conquest of Varus in *Epodes* 5).[16] But they do serve to remind us that the function of Canidia and Sagana's activity is to dominate and to bind the object of their attention, and they recall once more the question of menace in satire, that the audience submits, through hearing, to the pronouncements of the satirist. One of the women calls on Hecate, the other on Tisiphone. Here Priapus speaks to his audience, telling us that "you could see" ("videres," 34) snakes and infernal dogs and (in another mock-epic flight of diction) the moon blush and hide behind the sepulchral tomb so as not to witness the witchy deeds. Priapus's address to the reader is part of the conventional narration, the ghost story that calls its hearers to participate in the scene. He asks us to participate in *his* story, the matter of concern to him. When Priapus has described the restored state of the Esquiline, he uses an impersonal construction: "licet Esquiliis habitare salubribus atque / aggere in aprico spatiari, quo modo tristes / albis informem spectabant ossibus agrum" (14–16, one can spend time in the healthful habitat of the Esquiline and stroll on its sunny ramparts, where lately people used to see a field marred by whitening bones); he makes no explicit appeal to our listening involvement in the scene. It is the fearful place that Priapus wants us to witness with him, in sympathy with his fright.

Eager still to demonstrate the reality of the tale, Priapus swears an oath that, if he lies, welcomes human and animal alike to piss and crap on him:

mentior at si quid, merdis caput inquiner albis
corvorum, atque in me veniat mictum atque cacatum
Iulius et fragilis Pediatia furque Voranus.
   Sat. 1.8.37–9

And if I am lying at all, let my head get covered with crows' crap, and Iulius and that fairy Pediata and Voranus the thief can all come and piss on me and shit too.

The joke needs little explanation: Priapus's oath is undone by his willingness to endure humiliations that park statues are likely to endure in any case, without any stipulations, and the plunge in diction to "mictum atque cacatum" has an undermining effect on the solemnity of his oath, an effect lost on the narrator but not on us. It prepares too his characterization of himself as a witness—*testis* (44)—taking its humor from the legalistic phrasing of his generally humiliated state. *Testis* too reminds us of Priapus's abnormally restrained self. The Latin pun on *testis* as "witness" and "testicle" appears in *Pr.* 15, in which Priapus tells a thief that if he thinks no one will know he's been punished (*percisum*) by Priapus, he'll be wrong: "magnis testibus ista res agetur" (the foul case will be witnessed by my huge testicles).[17]

Why recount each detail? asks Priapus, proceeding to do just that:

singula quid memorem, quo pacto alterna loquentes
umbrae cum Sagana resonarent triste et acutum,
utque lupi barbam variae cum dente colubrae
abdiderint furtim terris, et imagine cerea
largior arserit ignis, et ut non testis inultus
horruerim voces Furiarum et facta duarum?
nam displosa sonat quantum vesica pepedi
diffissa nate ficus: at illae currere in urbem.
Canidiae dentis, altum Saganae caliendrum
excidere atque herbas atque incantata lacertis
vincula cum magno risuque iocoque videres.
   Sat. 1.8.40–50

Why mention each thing, how the ghosts conversed with Sagana and echoed grim and shrill, how they buried a wolf's beard in the ground with a spotted snake's tooth, secretly, how the flame burned bigger from the image of wax, and how I bristled in terror, witness to the words and acts of these two furies, and how I got vengeance?

For a balloon bursting sounds as loud as my buttocks of fig did when they split on my fart: and those women went flying into town. You could see Canidia drop her teeth, Sagana her big wig, and the herbs and enchanted bonds fall out of their arms, and you would laugh and guffaw long and loud.

The *praeteritio* (40–45) is a prelude to Priapus's inadvertent triumph, which justifies his claim to be "non testis inultus" (a testicle/witness not unavenged). The cracking of the poor fig wood in his terrified fart sounds as loud as a burst bladder, and with this the power of the women is all undone. They scamper into town, and "you'd see" (*videres*, again involving the reader in the narrative) Canidia drop her dentures, Sagana her tall wig, and the herbs and enchanted chains fall from their arms. You would see this, Priapus says, with great mirth and laughter. The menace of Canidia and Sagana is reduced to a joke, and the narrator restored to confidence sufficient to assure us of our laughter: "cum magno risuque iocoque videres" (50). The last word of the poem speaks directly to the audience, and the last line of the poem instructs us how to respond to the story, just as Canidia and Sagana have compelled responses from the dead.

Canidian Poetics

The Priapus of the *Priapea* (lexically hinted at but thereby only inexplicitly represented in 1.8) and Canidia both present elements of power in satire that Horace denies he practices. In *Satires* 1.8, Priapus is pointedly deprived of the characteristics of menace he enjoys boasting of in his other Priapic roles, just as Horace takes the menace away from his own satiric persona in the *Satires*.

The Priapus of the *Priapea* makes verbal threats that he will use his phallus to attack the mouths and anuses of trespassers (*Pr.* 13, 22, 35, 44, 74). Oral penetration, irrumation, is in particular the most dire punishment with the greatest concomitant shame for the victim in Priapus's arsenal.[18] In *Satires* 1.8, Priapus not only makes no threats, but his boast of being "non testis inultus" (44) is undermined by his manner of vengeance, which is his loss of anal control. Vengeance itself in a situation of conflict has been put under suspicion by the previous poem, *Satires* 1.7, where Persius's revenge on Rex is achieved by a logic-defying pun.[19] Priapus's mouth, Priapus as a speaker, is deprived of his authority by being unreliable: his account of himself is wrong; his portrait of the place where he stands is ambiguous; he does not menace with a *maxima formido* but is possessed by it instead. Though he drives off Canidia and Sagana, in his flatulent revenge Priapus speaks through his anus, not his mouth, as though he were one of the victims of the *Priapea* and had lost control of his own anus—as if *he* were afflicted with figs, piles.[20] The god of the *Priapea* exercises power in raw terms of sexual domination, precisely what the Priapus of 1.8 does not do. But the poem has him "win" over Canidia, and the conquest of her and Sagana converts them into ridiculous old women, not terrifying menaces. As John Henderson points out (1989a, 61), the teeth with which they tore at the lamb fetus ("mordicus," 27) turn out to have been dentures, the loosened hair ("passo capillo," 24) a wig. They are only old women, toothless and hairless.

Toothless old women are not always a joke. In *Epodes* 8, a woman with one black tooth is the object of Horatian invective, and her menace is both revealed and contained by that invective. Her powerful sexuality, surviving beyond the years of her sexual reproductivity, is made so repulsive by the poem's art that the woman can make no claim on any reader's sympathy, nor indeed on the sympathy of the poem's speaker (which, of course, is the point). The misogyny of *Epodes* 8 (like its kin, *Epodes* 12) exposes the fear of the speaker and thereby attests to the strength of that which is feared. The parody of aging female sexuality and vanity that *Satires* 1.8 serves up is a much more efficient maneuver than the attack that the *Epodes* mount: the threat of Canidia and Sagana is told by a narrator whom we do not trust, and their posture of menace is easily undone with our laughter—the laughter that the recovered Priapus confidently predicts.

On the basis of Priapus's comic conquest over Canidia, W. S. Anderson proposes that Priapus is a version of Horace, the new unmenacing satirist, who has the power to prevail over the old dark forces on the Esquiline, that is to say Canidia and company, in the same way that Horace's benign, laughing satire triumphs over Lucilian mud and invective. But the breath of a fart is no way to win an empire or an audience, and the situation of Horace's satire is ambivalent; Anderson's thesis touches only on the positive half of that ambivalence and is unduly complacent. Like the bones that still lie in Maecenas's newly built gardens, the menace in Horace's portrait of unmenacing satire is still revealed. Priapus is drawn by Horace, his real *faber* (poet and *faber* both mean "maker"), to recall but not explicitly express his old Priapic self. This suggests to me that Priapus's old self, menacing and powerful, is appealing to Horace, just as the genre of satire in its older, Lucilian, distantly Archilochean, invective shape has enough appeal that Horace writes inside that genre, though all the while denying its nature.

The same dynamic, of attraction and denial, operates in the figure of Canidia in *Satires* 1.8. Taken out of the discrediting frame by which Canidia and Sagana are made ludicrous, not fearsome, the women's activities have a certain poetic, satiric affiliation. Anderson (1982, 81) notes the link between Horace's songs and Canidia's, between Canidia's *venenum* and Horace's pen, and there is more besides:

> vidi egomet nigra succinctum vadere palla
> Canidiam, pedibus nudis passoque capillo,
> cum Sagana maiore ululantem: pallor utrasque
> fecerat horrendas aspectu. scalpere terram
> unguibus et pullam divellere mordicus agnam
> coeperunt; cruor in fossam confusus, ut inde
> manis elicerent, animas responsa daturas.
> lanea et effigies erat, altera cerea: maior
> lanea, quae poenis compesceret inferiorem;
> cerea suppliciter stabat servilibus ut quae
> iam peritura modis. Hecaten vocat altera, saevam
> altera Tisiphonen; serpentis atque videres
> infernas errare canis, Lunamque rubentem
> ne foret his testis post magna latere sepulcra.
>   *Sat.* 1.8.23–36

I myself saw Canidia go with her black cloak tucked up at the waist and her feet bare and her hair loose and wailing with the older one, Sagana; their ghostly pallor made the two a fearsome sight to see. They began to scrape at the ground with their fingernails and to rip a young lamb with their teeth; they poured blood into a trench, so they could call forth shades of the dead to respond to them. There was a woolen doll and a waxen one too: the bigger woolen one controlled the smaller with punishments; the waxen one stood slavishly in supplication like a figure about to die. They called now on Hecate, now on brutal Tisiphon; you'd see snakes and infernal dogs, and you'd see the moon blush red and, hardly wanting to be a witness to this, hide behind the broad back of the tombstones.

Canidia and Sagana (her name means "wise") travel on *pedibus nudis* (naked feet). "Foot" (*pes*) is a shop-worn Latin pun on "meter," and the "feet" of Horatian satire are at issue in 1.4, where he says he writes in *puris verbis;* here Canidia is the satirist unbound.[21] Canidia wears a black cloak ("nigra . . . palla," 23), like the "black salt" of the *Sermones*, which Horace alludes to much later in the *Epistles* (2.20.60, in what spirit it is hard to judge). Canidia and Sagana tear at the ground with their nails and, gnawing, dismember a fetal lamb ("scalpere terram / unguinibus et pullam divellere mordicus agnam," 26–27); Horace, the proper satirist, scratches his head and bites at his nails till they bleed ("in versu faciendo / saepe caput scaberet, vivos et roderet unguis," 1.10.70–71). The satirist is a biter, recall, but Horace would turn that on himself for the sake of *his carmina.* He has done this in *Satires.* 1.4 when he turns the sharp habit of *notando* (fault-noting) by the Old Comic poets into his own self-directed, silent warnings. Dogs, the ambivalent mascot of Cynic diatribe—they are loyal and they bite—appear with snakes for the activities of Canidia and her companion (35).[22] And wax, the substance the writer scratches and molds to form letters, is here the submissive effigy, constrained with punishments in Canidia's magical ritual by the larger woolen figure (30–33).[23] Finally, what is the purpose of the ritual? To elicit responses: the women want exchange of speech ("alterna loquentes umbrae," 40–41) with the dead, who have given up their breath. Perhaps too the poet's quest for *sermo* with his silent audience is similarly impossible, and Horace must have the whole conversation without exchange, a simulacrum of *sermo.*

Between Canidia and Sagana themselves, there is a relation of unequal power; Sagana is *maior* (26), which is mirrored in their two statuettes of wool and wax. But hidden in the frame of Priapus's narration is the fundamental recollection, from the Priapic poems and scribblings, of masculine power constantly accomplished with the phallus. Priapus has lost this power in 1.8. As a version of Horace the satirist, this Priapus represents the satirist Horace has chosen to be and what he has lost in that choice— (phallic) menace.[24] In 1.8, Priapus's traditional menace is removed from him as a narrator, as he is frightened rather than frightening. The god's menace in the *Priapea* is a positive and certain enforcement of domination, which is denied to the Priapus in 1.8; but a power of equally archaic force is temporarily granted to Canidia before she is undone.

Canidia too, as a version of the satirist, is not so much the excluded Lucilian element, as Anderson suggests, but a different element that Horace does not scorn but also does not deploy; she, like the Priapus of the *Priapea,* is a denied version of the satirist (Anderson 1982, 73–74). Canidia's power derives partly from her magical speech, from her *carmina* and the *sermo* she compels, and therein lies her allure for the satirist, although the allure is denied and Canidia exposed as powerless.

Magical speech, Canidia's practice, has not been investigated much in relation to the *Satires.* But given the pervasive use of verbal magic in Roman culture, as well as the incantatory nature of Roman (and most) religious ritual, Roman poets would obviously have been well aware of this use of speech, as indeed the literary evidence shows, and it is hard to imagine that the operation of such speech would not have a fundamental appeal to a poet.[25]

In magical or any other spoken ritual, S. J. Tambiah observes, "The word is an entity able to act and produce effects in its own right" (1968, 183). In ritual the power of words derives from equating them with substance or action. Language thus deployed has the power to influence reality, has mystical and binding powers; "Language is not so much a vehicle for expressing ideas as for achieving practical effects" (184). Robert Elliott, in *The Power of Satire,* analyzes poetic satire across European, Indic, Eskimo, and Arabic traditions and relates the operation of satire and invective very closely to operations of verbal magic. His basic distinction between verbal magic and satire lies in the level of self-consciousness at work in the society: when a culture recognizes words as art, rather than procedure, magic becomes satire. "Satire as an art cannot develop so long as belief in its magical efficacy retains its hold over men's minds" (1960, 98). Elliott asserts that satire, in the broad sense, is ritual in origin, and that satire takes its effectiveness from the effectiveness of the original ritualistic formula. Of Greek phallic songs, Elliott says, the connection with ritual is unmistakable:

> In the songs, we recall, the joyous invocation of fertility is interrupted by the violent invectives of the leaders. Clearly, the motivation behind the whole ceremony is a wish of great intensity, a *demand* that life shall burgeon throughout nature. The ceremony is a bipartite enactment of that demand,

a magical representation of it: the sacred words and the sacred emblem invoke life-giving influences; the sacred mockery and invective expel blight and dearth and evil. No doubt the individuals who were satirized by name in the ceremony somehow represented what was to be driven out. How they were affected by the verbal assaults, we do not know, but the association of satirical attack with magical efficacy is very strong. It would be strong even outside a ritual contest. It would be overwhelming at a sacred occasion which was dominated by the personality and the charismatic power of utterance of a poet like Archilochus. In those circumstances personal satire might well drive a victim to death. . . . Archilochus' verses against Lycambes were, in fact, part of a fertility rite. (Elliott 1960, 58–59)

Horace's *Satires* would seem to occupy a middle ground in Elliott's conception of cultural development, between words as art and words as procedure. Disbelief in the power of magic allows satire to exist, in Elliott's terms, in the Roman republic, but belief allows magic to be widely practiced. Magical speech, in its link to invective, is persuasive speech gone past persuasion, with the similar aim of controlling an audience but abandoning logos in favor of pure coercion; it goes past the reason of the hearer and uses speech as a weapon, relying on the extra power of magical belief in symbols (like the "effigies" in 1.8) and in incantation, where words are instruments. In a sense, it is easier to reject Lucilius, another literary satirist, than to forego the temptations of the magical speaker's primal power, though Horace is, of course, a sophisticated Roman and a Callimachean poet—despite his fondness for visiting fortune-tellers in *Satires* 1.6.114. For a poet working in satire, an invective genre, the attraction of the kind of powerful speech that Canidia represents seems obvious.

John Henderson reads this satire, in the context of his discussion of gender issues in Roman satire, as "standing up for" the male hierarchy by reducing the feminine power of Canidia, exposing her and Sagana as "silly old hags."[26] But the satirist expresses a certain fascination with that power, even when carefully degraded and disavowed. It would not come up so often otherwise. And this would not have so strong a point if Canidia did not appear twice more in the *Satires*, at the beginning of the second book, in 2.1 as mentioned (where *venenum* is Canidia's weapon in the same way that the pen must be Horace's weapon), and with particular significance at the end of 2.8, where she takes the last line of the work. Canidia has, in a sense, the last word (or the last gasp) of the *Satires*. In the final poem of book 2, an account of a dinner party related to Horace by one Fundanius concludes (as do both the meal and the poem) with the snobbish and abrupt departure of the guests, who are appalled at the host's ostentation. Maecenas was at this dinner; we think we know where he sat. Fundanius says that he and unnamed companions fled the untasted meal "as if Canidia had breathed on the meal with breath more foul than African snakes" ("velut illis / Canidia adflasset peior serpentibus Afris," 2.8.94–95). Indeed, Canidia breathes her last here, never to reappear in Horace's work. Nor does Horace ever again write satires or epodes and so will never grapple again with the potential flight of a reader from his satire. Such is the power Horace grants to Canidia.[27]

Horace is interested in both the Priapic power to menace and Canidia's power to coerce (the control of a hearer afforded by magical speech has attractions), elements denied but not ignored. Satire has the potential for the menace of invective and the power of magical speech. But Canidia *is* finally excluded from *Satires* 1.8. Tambiah describes the essential problem in speech that acts instrumentally, which is the problem in both invective and magical speech:

> The role of language in ritual immediately confronts problems if placed in relation to a primary function of language which is that it is a *vehicle of communication between persons*. By definition, the persons in communication must understand one another. In ritual, language appears to be used in ways that violate the communication function. (Tambiah 1968, 179; my italics)

Horace's *Satires*, which he only calls *sermones* in book 1, are keenly conscious of their audience.[28] The satires of book 1 do what Tambiah calls the primary function of language; they communicate, and furthermore they express overt and covert anxiety about the effect on a listener of menacing speech and invective. *Satires* 1.7 has demonstrated the purposelessness of invective and conflict, and Canidia's power-speech in 1.8 has been undone by a strategy that itself seems to suggest the hopelessness, for communication (the "primary function of language"), of coercive speaking. Priapus's breath, impotent in speech against the coercive power of Canidia's speech, takes another route and frees him from her power; speech has no counteractive power over magical speech, and its defeat requires a strategy beneath logos (here, beneath the mouth). *Satires* 1.8 powerfully denies coercive speech by demonstrating that its speakers remove logos. (Farting is the appropriate response.)

Does the narrative of *Satires* 1.8 belong to Priapus or to the poet-*faber* Horace? Who has recovered his power of speech from the forces of magic? Priapus makes his escape from the frightening women (who, thanks to his narration, never menaced us, the listeners) not by means of speech but by breath rerouted, yet the poem's final moment returns the narrative authority to Priapus, to dictate to us our response. He says we would laugh if we had *seen* "cum magno risuque iocoque videres" (as if we would have been like the spectators to the battle between Persius and Rex, 1.7.22: "ridetur ab omni"). So too do Canidia and Sagana compel responses from the dead, "alterna loquentes / umbrae" (40–41).

Horace's personal statements, or those of his persona, about laughter in the *Satires* are ambivalent, at once cautionary and approving:

praeterea ne sic ut qui iocularia ridens
percurram: quamquam ridentem dicere verum
quid vetat?
   Sat. 1.1.23–25

Besides, not to rush on, laughing like a joke maker—although what is to prevent one from telling the truth with a laugh?

❧ ❧

          longe fuge: dummodo risum
excutiat, sibi non, non cuiquam parcet amico;
   Sat. 1.4.34–35

Steer clear of him: he'll go after anyone, even himself, even a friend, so long as he gets a laugh;

❧ ❧

ergo non satis est risu diducere rictum
auditoris.
   Sat. 1.10.7–8

So it isn't enough to pull a laugh out of the reader.

➤ ◄

ridiculum acri
fortius et melius magnas plerumque secat res.
   Sat. 1.10.14–15

A joke often cuts through important matters more sharply and keenly than
serious analysis.

In *Satires* 1.5 there is much laughter; three times (1.5.35, 57, 98) the travelers laugh at the people and sites they visit. Progressively drawing the reader
into the operation of the poems, *Satires* I has you, the reader, watch the
laughter in 1.5, whereas you do the laughing yourself in 1.8, as the narrator instructs you in how to contribute to the poem's action. Laughter is a
friend to the truth in Horace's satiric universe, yet laughter is not sufficient and may be banal, may be a menace.
   In *Priapea* 41, Priapus gives these instructions to passersby:

quisquis venerit huc, poeta fiat
et versus mihi dedicet iocosos.
qui non fecerit, inter eruditos
ficossissimus ambulet poetas.

Let whoever comes this way be a poet and offer funny poems to me. Let
the one who doesn't do this go off with piles and a very itchy walk with the
intellectual poets.

Priapus will inflict his usual punishment if he doesn't get laughter from
a poet, with the curious note that the punishment will include enforced
association with learned poets. Horace, certainly *eruditus,* nevertheless
writes a funny poem for Priapus, telling *us* to laugh. As the *faber* of the
poem, Horace has the power to deflect fear with laughter, but a measure
of uncertainty persists about the relationship between the speaker of satire
and his audience, and about the extent to which the speaker wishes to
retain the power to menace. Priapus in 1.8 boasts that he is a *maxima
formido,* a great menace, but is then denied such a power. Horace denies
his own persona that power, yet as a poet seems drawn to its capacity to
take control of its listener.

One final curiosity, borrowed from the historical record and far away from Horace's text: Suetonius records in his *Vita Horati* that Augustus called Horace (*inter alios iocos*) *purissimum penem* (my blameless little pecker?). Is the speaking phallus a speaker we should trust? In the next poem, *Satires* 1.9, the audience will be invited to practice the invective, as well as the laughter, for Horace the sly satirist.

→ 6 ←

Auditor—Adiutor

Satires 1.9

Horace knows the name of his interlocutor in *Satires* 1.9, but we don't.[1]
What we do know of this famously disliked figure in 1.9, we know from
Horace, and though we may observe that Horace treats him less than gal-
lantly, no one wants anything to do with him. In not permitting the reader
to like the interlocutor, the poem achieves one of its evident ends: to
deny the interlocutor the position he hopes to attain with Maecenas, with
Horace, and with us. Horace's desire to have a quiet and solitary walk
through the streets of Rome is obviously thwarted, but another desire of
the poem, for Horace to be rid of his companion once and for all, to take
him out of the literary competition, is brilliantly achieved. The interlocutor, a poet who wants a place like Horace's with Maecenas, is consigned
to nameless ignominy for as long as Horace will have an audience. We
the listeners to *Satires* 1.9 do for Horace what the interlocutor does not
do, which is to keep quiet and listen, and in so doing we become the very
thing the interlocutor says he will be, Horace's backer, his *adiutor*. The
poem invites the reader to practice the very invective against the interlocutor that Horace's own character in the poem refuses to practice. Although
Satires 1.9 has enticed its readers to blame the figure whom Horace meets
on the Sacred Way, the figure of Horace in the poem is no blame speaker;
it is the readers of the poem who become Horace's avengers.

The drama of *Satires* 1.9 is based on the curious premise that Horace
does not possess the power to verbally defeat his talkative companion on
the Via Sacra. This poet, embraced by Maecenas against all social odds
on the strength of his poetic gifts, cannot deploy his verbal skill to get a
morning's walk by himself in this poem.[2] Horace is again illustrating his

satirist's character, as manifested in his speech; he prefers that his persona should submit to verbal tyranny rather than engage in it. In the verbal combat described in *Satires* 1.7, the speech exchange occurs between two coercive speakers who do not hear each other, and even the listeners within the drama are spectators, as if watching, not hearing, the exchange of speech. In the drama of 1.9, because Horace chooses not to use speech to fight back, a one-way speech "exchange" occurs between one speaker and one hearer. There is an abuse of the idea of exchange in both the instances of *Satires* 1.7 and 1.9, since in speech the term "exchange" implies an alternation of the role of speaker and hearer on each side, giving words (speaking) and receiving them (hearing). In neither satire does successful exchange occur because hearing fails in both: Persius and Rex only speak and do not hear; the interlocutor of 1.9 speaks much and cannot hear Horace.

Early in the poem, in his polite misery Horace envies the angry nature of one Bolanus, which, could he adopt this figure's abusive speech, would presumably rid him of his companion: "o te, Bolane, cerebri / felicem!" (1.9.11–12, You lucky man, Bolanus, for your hot temper). But Horace has previously (in *Sat.* 1.4.100–103) disclaimed the character of one who practices harmful, combative speech. The only choice Horace allows his own persona is to hear and be conquered by the interlocutor's abundant, irresponsive speech. By creating this drama in 1.9, Horace can again illustrate the claims he made in *Satires* 1.4, that indeed he does not indulge in speech harmful to his listener, in the sort of abuse he would have to adopt to force the interlocutor to go away. Further, he has the opportunity to demonstrate the effects of verbal tyranny by being its object and, by so doing, to point out its dangers, its attack on the listener, and the listener's consequent impulse to reject the speaker. His poetic convictions pose as servant to this goal: his genius is such that he cannot produce cumbrous quantities of verse ("di bene fecerunt inopis me quodque pusilli / finxerunt animi, raro et perpauca loquentis," 1.4.17–18), and his aesthetic is such that it dictates a spare, gentle style. Most of all, the narrative poem Horace gives us in *Satires* 1.9 enlists his silent hearers' sympathy in such a way that we are acutely eager to render Horace the service of hearing, which his persona is denied in the drama. By rendering that service, we remove the interlocutor from the competition for Maecenas; our judgment against the interlocutor is severe. What we hear in the poem instructs us that the interlocutor deserves his exclusion, and we learn from this example that

what Horace the poet wants from us is our silence so that the poet may
speak. The dramatic silence of Horace's persona in the poem, his thwarted
desire to be heard, and the wholly discredited status of the interlocutor,
all dispose the hearer of the poem to side with Horace, to be his *adiutor*
by being his *auditor*, in what proves to be (non)verbal combat with the
interlocutor for the favor of Maecenas. The interlocutor will never get
another hearing.

The beginning of 1.9 makes a poetic announcement:

Ibam forte Via Sacra, sicut meus est mos,
nescio quid meditans nugarum, totus in illis.
   Sat. 1.9.1–2

> I happened to be going along on the Sacred Way, mulling over this and that,
> as is my habit, completely absorbed.

The opening is a statement of self-sufficiency, Lucilian refraction, poetic
involvement ("meditans . . . totus"), a Catullan echo, and the ultimately
Horatian note that such activity was his habit.[3] Alongside the Catullan
sound of *nugae*, and Horace's own use of the word referring to poetic
triflings (*Epp.* 1.19.42), *nugae* also connote the satiric realm, the mundane
and small. The singular *mos* (habit) becomes in the plural *mores* (character, the collective habits), the entity that gives rise to the poetic activity of
the satires for Horace, to his particular version of this genre.[4]

Lucilius haunts this poem, as he does other satires in book 1, serv-
ing again to help Horace define himself as a satirist. Critics have sensed
this without explicitly noting the process of self-articulation that occurs
in *Satires* 1.9. George Converse Fiske posited a model for this poem in
Lucilius's sixth book of *Satires*, in which, Fiske suggested, a follower who
refuses to detach himself from Scipio's suite hangs on tenaciously even
after being abused by Scipio, who attempts to evade him.[5] The evidence
for the existence of the Lucilian model is as usual inconclusive, but in its
support Fiske adduced the opening and closing lines of Horace's poem.
Horace's "Ibam forte" (1) recalls two instances of "ibat forte" in the Lucilian fragments we possess, one of which is relevant to Fiske's hypothesized
Lucilian model for 1.9.[6] Horace's closing line to 1.9, "sic me servavit Apollo"
(78), recalls a Lucilian line in which he quotes Homer, *Iliad* 20.443: "nil ut
discrepat ac τὸν δ' ἐξήρπαξεν Ἀπόλλων, / fiat."[7] It seems likely that Horace

is alluding to the Lucilian line, and having translated the Greek into Latin, Horace can also illustrate his stricture against Lucilian hybrid versifying, a stricture explicitly expressed in *Satires* 1.10.20–30.[8] And, as I will later demonstrate, in 1.9 it is dramatically important that Apollo has saved the poem's narrator: τόν has become *me*. Lucilius's direct quotation of Homer has become Horace's own line, and the god's action in 1.9 directly embraces the poet.

Porphyrio recognizes the Homeric echo in the Horatian instance and notes Lucilius's use of the quotation from Homer in his sixth book, but he ventures no suggestion of a Lucilian model poem for 1.9. Whether or not such a prototype poem existed in the Lucilian corpus, the lines clearly echo Horace's satiric predecessor and, since they are significantly placed at the beginning and end of 1.9, provide evidence that Horace continues to use the *inventor* of satire to define his own satiric activity. The reader who responds by hypothesizing a Lucilian prototype poem cooperates with Horace's intent: Horace prepares us to imagine how different that poem would have been from 1.9; how differently Lucilius would have treated the interlocutor had it been he rather than Horace on the Sacra Via; how, from what Horace has made us believe, Lucilius would have rained invective on the talker of 1.9. The Horatian persona, in contrast, behaves submissively, does not drive the man off with harsh ridicule but rather endures and prevails, patient with him as he is with his writing. A hypothesized Lucilian original simply elaborates the set of self-defining contrasts that Horace has already formulated for his readers between himself and Lucilius.[9]

The wistful opening lines of the poem shift abruptly at the hasty approach of Horace's interlocutor:

accurrit quidam notus mihi nomine tantum,
arreptaque manu "quid agis, dulcissime rerum?"
  Sat. 1.9.3–4

This character, known to me only by name, comes rushing up, grabs my hand, and says, "What's up with you, my good friend?"

The style of the interlocutor's approach itself presents a contrast between the two figures: Horace strolls along in leisurely, solitary, and silent contemplation of a kind perhaps connected to poetic composition, while the unnamed (but known-only-by-name) interrupter rushes up to Horace with

a chatty address. It emerges as their interaction proceeds that the interlocutor has Lucilian traits, and not only that Lucilius is a literary recollection in the adumbration of Horace's poetic theory, but also that Lucilian
poetics have a dramatic exponent in the figure of Horace's interlocutor
while Horace's character dramatizes Horatian poetics. "Noris nos . . . docti
sumus" (7, you know me, I'm an educated man), says the interlocutor,
prompting the keen wish in Horace to take flight and his confession to us
that he envies the hot temper of Bolanus.[10] *Tacitus* and *garriret* make the
point of the contrast:

> "o te, Bolanus, cerebri
> felicem!" aiebam *tacitus*, cum quidlibet ille
> *garriret*, vicos, urbem laudaret.
>   *Sat.* 1.9.11–13

"Bolanus, lucky you for your hot temper," I murmured *silently*, while the
man *chattered* on at will, admiring the neighborhoods, the city.

As a result of the poet's continuing silence, the interlocutor recognizes
that Horace longs to get away ("'misere cupis' inquit 'abire; / iamdudum
video: sed nil agis; usque tenebo'" 14–15) but nevertheless tells Horace that
he is there for the duration. Horace, in response, conjures an imaginary
sick friend, one whom the interlocutor does not know, whom he plans to
visit across the Tiber, a long way off near Caesar's gardens, too far for his
companion to follow. The strategy Horace employs here—"I'm going a
long way to visit someone you don't know"—is designed to draw attention to the interlocutor's distance from the circles Horace travels in, literally and literarily. Unsurprisingly, the interlocutor fails to take the cue
by acknowledging that he is an outsider; he takes no notice, and, resem-
bling the combatants of *Satires* 1.7, declares with ominous persistence:
"non sum piger" (19, I'm not lazy).[11] At this Horace says to us: "demitto
auriculas, ut iniquae mentis asellus, / cum gravius dorso subiit onus"
(20–21, I lay down my ears like an unhappy ass when the load on his back
is too heavy).

The onslaught of the interlocutor's speech is here the onus that, through
his exhausted ears, converts Horace into a beast of burden. The poem that
follows this one, *Satires* 1.10, provides a poetic handbook against which to
measure the verbal disposition of the interlocutor in 1.9. Using Lucilius as

his springboard, Horace will articulate what a poet should and should not do. In contrast to Lucilius's much-noted poetic loquacity, he says:

> est brevitate opus, ut currat sententia, neu se
> impediat verbis *lassas onerantibus auris;*
>   *Sat.* 1.10.9–10

> Brevity is necessary, so that the idea runs along smoothly and doesn't trip itself with words that *burden exhausted ears.*

The figure of the interlocutor continues to make the reader recall the Horace-defined faults of Lucilius. When Horace resigns himself to his "burden," the interlocutor takes up the business of his pursuit, declaring his poetic fitness for friendship with Horace:

> "si bene me novi non Viscum pluris amicum,
> non Varium facies: nam quis me scribere pluris
> aut citius possit versus? quis membra movere
> mollius? invideat quod et Hermogenes ego canto."
>   *Sat.* 1.9.22–25

> "If I know myself, not Viscus, Varius, or anyone will be a better friend to you than I will; for who could write more poetry, or do it faster than I can? Who could dance (move his limbs) more smoothly? Even Hermogenes would envy what I can sing."

The interlocutor owns up to possessing, as a virtue, the capacity for that very abundance and speed in writing which Horace laments in Lucilius's writing (*Sat.* 1.4 and 1.10).[12] In *Satires* 1.4, Horace calls Lucilius *garrulus;* the interlocutor practices the speech of a *garrulus* in *garriret* (13). The poetic traits that the interlocutor boasts of as virtues, traits on the basis of which he declares boldly that he will successfully compete with Viscus and Varius for Horace's friendship, are what Horace calls faults in Lucilius. That the interlocutor believes reference to syrupy (*mollius*) dancing (or the effeminate manipulation of verses?) or to the envy of the scorned Hermogenes (1.4.72) will gain him favor further marks his vast distance from Horace's sphere.[13]

As if the interlocutor's grievous errors in assessing both himself and

Horace provided the narrator with just cause for extracting himself, Horace responds with a query about the man's family (25–26): "Don't you have a mother, relatives, who need your help?" But the interlocutor is a man alone in the world and replies with apparent good cheer that he has no one, that he's buried them all. Now it is no longer Bolanus whom Horace envies but these relatives; "felices," he says, "nunc ego resto" (now I am left).

In the verses of the Sabine *anus* that Horace confides to us, following the interlocutor's disclosure that he has buried all his relatives, the interlocutor is alluded to as *garrulus*, as the agent of death to Horace:

> confice! namque instat fatum mihi triste, Sabella
> quod puero cecinit divina mota anus urna:
> "hunc neque dira venena, nec hosticus auferet ensis,
> nec laterum dolor aut tussis, nec tarda podagra:
> *garrulus* hunc quando consumet cumque. loquaces,
> si sapiat, vitet, simul atque adoleverit aetas."
>   *Sat.* 1.9.29–34[14]

Do me in! For the grim prediction is at hand, the one the Sabine crone chanted to me when I was a boy a boy, as she turned her divining-urn: "It won't be deadly poison, nor an enemy's sword that carries this one off, nor affliction in the lungs nor cough, nor the slow-moving gout; a chatterbox, when the time comes, will kill him off. If he's wise, he'll stay away from talkers once he's become a man."

The association between the portrait of the interlocutor in 1.9 and the poetic shortcomings of Lucilius adumbrated in 1.4 establishes the interlocutor as an outsider, as one unaware of Horace's well-articulated poetic program, which scorns quickly produced, abundant verse. It also dramatically demonstrates the effect of this prolixity in *sermo:* Horace's ears are loaded down with the burden of the interlocutor's speech, so that Horace is converted to a beast, to the point where it will kill him. Heard speech enters through the ears and has an internal, invasive power, a power like poison, a sword, or disease to disrupt the body from within. There are dangers, though these are posed humorously, for the listener. These speech characteristics are combined in the interlocutor with a personality that steadfastly denies the desire of his hearer; consistent with his speech, the personality of the interlocutor overwhelms Horace, his listener. As Persius and Rex did in 1.7, the figure of the interlocutor dramatizes the dangers of Lucilian speech (justifying Horace's poetic claims against his predecessor and his own practice of satire), but unlike Persius and Rex, he does this in interaction with a listener, the figure of Horace. Again, if Horace's character in the poem were to defeat the interlocutor in the drama of 1.9 by means of his own verbal powers, he would not be able to illustrate the silencing, deadly effects of Lucilian speech. Horace's choice is situated against both invective and garrulity, since both may be lethal to the listener.

Horace's allusive literary competition with Lucilius in 1.9 is not, however, the poem's primary competitive arena. At the conclusion of the revelation to the reader that the Sabine folk-muse predicted his death by talk to Horace in his boyhood, we find our walkers at the temple of Vesta. It so happens ("casu," 36) that here the interlocutor must decide whether or not to appear in a court case, and, finding Horace unwilling to cooperate in promoting his suit, he gives it up and determines to stick with Horace (35–42).[15] The interlocutor here indicates that the goal of his association with Horace is to become a member of Maecenas's group. He proposes to be Horace's backer (*adiutor*); he will help take out the competition if Horace is only willing to introduce him to Maecenas:

> "haberes
> magnum adiutorem, posset qui ferre secundas,
> hunc hominem velles si tradere: dispeream ni
> summosses omnis."
>   *Sat.* 1.9.45–48

"You'd have a great backer, someone who could be your second player, if you'd introduce your man here, yours truly: I'll be damned if you didn't clear them all away."

We see here a hint of the densely competitive world that gave rise in *Satires* 1.6 to Horace's protestations against those who envy him. The interlocutor is evidently hopeful for a place with Maecenas; he is in some sense, therefore, putting himself in competition with Horace for the favor of Maecenas, while proposing to be on Horace's side against the rest of the competition. Horace's reply is curious. It is his longest speech to the interlocutor, his only address to the interlocutor that seems free of irony or deceit, and the only utterance to which the interlocutor seems to attend. Horace does not mention Maecenas himself, only the place, the house:

> "non isto vivimus illic
> quo tu rere modo; domus hac nec purior ulla est
> nec magis his aliena malis; nil mi officit" inquam
> "ditior hic aut est quia doctior; est locus uni
> cuique suus." "magnum narras, vix credibile." "atqui
> sic habet." "accendis, quare cupiam magis illi
> proximus esse."
> *Sat.* 1.9.48–54

"We don't live that way there, it's not how you imagine; no house is freer [recall 'puris verbis,' 1.4] nor more different from such vices; it doesn't matter," I tell him, "that this one is richer or that one more learned; the house belongs to each one alike." "Quite a story you tell, scarcely believable." "And yet it is so." "You fire me all the more with a desire to be near that place."

There is no competition in this place, and the interlocutor has quite the wrong idea of life under the aegis of Maecenas—no place could be more free of the evils (*his malis*) he imagines.[16] Indeed, the very imaginings of the interlocutor show his unfitness for the place. Horace speaks not of Maecenas but of his house, a place, and thereby gives a concrete location, as it were, to the interlocutor's exclusion. A household excludes those outside the family, and the interlocutor plainly doesn't belong inside this household; he is not a member of the family. Horace then ironically suggests to the interlocutor the terms for his pursuit of Maecenas (54–60); fired by Horace's words, the interlocutor imagines epiclike penetration of Maecenas's sanctuary.[17] Horace toys with the interlocutor, encouraging his plans to lay siege to Maecenas (56–60), and the interlocutor tops off his enthusiasm with an epic-sounding tag line: "'nil sine magno / vita labore dedit mortalibus'" (59–60). These are the last lines of this famously talkative interlocutor who, with eighteen lines, nearly a quarter of the poem, yet to go, is henceforth silent.

It *is* a wonderful story Horace tells and hard to believe, and perhaps it is captious to wonder if poets in Horace's day were so very different a breed from their modern counterparts, and whether even Maecenas could have fostered such harmony in his house. We may nevertheless feel skeptical about the context of the drama itself. At least one member of the house-hold of Maecenas, Horace, is jealous enough of his place in that *domus* to do in this poem precisely what the interlocutor promises help Horace do: clear away the competition (48). Horace so thoroughly discredits the interlocutor in *Satires* 1.9 that, though he claims to know nothing more of him than his name, even that is suppressed, and the man is known only as a demonstrative pronoun, *ille*.[18] The poem is an utter victory for Horace the writer of the poem, if not for the persona Horace in the poem.

Does your stomach clench up a little when Horace says "non isto vivimus illic"? Do the words evoke a sadness at all the exclusions *you've* been dealt, the hopes you learned were foolish, the weaknesses you felt suddenly exposed? Do you feel a mixture of revulsion and sympathy as the poor fellow, whom English critics are pleased to call the Bore, says, "magnum narras, vix credibile," as he tries to strike the right tone, tries to belong by expressing his admiration? Does the exchange make you squirm? The poem is full of desire and longings that go thwarted and unfulfilled, longings that the speaker believed and heard and most of all approved. We all say: "Let me be the one," and some of us succeed better than others in the illusion of being the one. Maecenas is the one in this poem; Horace is momentarily the one because his troublesome compan-ion believes it. The companion—whom we call the Bore because we want to believe that *we* are the one, because we believe that Horace is the one—furnishes us all with the welcome outsider to define the rest. He is hope-lessly outside; his every shrug and nuance yells out his fumbling exclusion and relieves us of our fears. Thankfully, we are not he, so we name him Bore. How good for us all to be inside for a moment, with Horace, with Maecenas, with Augustus, making all the old rules new. A child's wish for power drives us to such logical incongruities, with the result that we line up alongside the murderers and proscribers of the Roman world, sitting next to Horace at the dinner party he ultimately wouldn't attend (*Sat.* 2.8), trying to find *auctoritas* in an unsteady world where we can never have what we want.

Apollo, the Ear, and Saving Horace

The arrival of Aristius Fuscus (60) silences the interlocutor but does not rescue Horace. The ensuing speech between Horace and Fuscus concerns a promise of speech that Fuscus refuses to make good on. Horace is hop-ing for rescue by conversation with him, and Fuscus claims that religious scruples prevent this conversation: he will speak with Horace another time. Ironically, an *adversarius* (an opponent of the interlocutor in a lawsuit) is directly responsible for removing Horace's adversary by bringing him to court; but it is Apollo, as a remotely presiding *numen* of the law court, to whom Horace ultimately expresses his thanks:

> "alias loquar." huncine solem
> tam nigrum surrexe mihi! fugit improbus ac me
> sub cultro linquit. casu venit obvius illi
> adversarius et "quo tu, turpissime?" magna
> inclamat voce, et "licet antestari?" ego vero
> oppono auriculam. rapit in ius: clamor utrimque:
> undique concursus. sic me servavit Apollo.
>
>   *Sat.* 1.9.72–78

"I'll talk with you another time." This is as black a day as ever dawned for me! The scoundrel escapes and leaves me under the sacrificial knife. By chance, the litigating opponent comes up to him, and shouting at the top of his lungs, he cries, "Where are you off to, you vermin?" and to me, "Can you be a witness?" I do indeed offer my ear. He hustles him to court: there is yelling on both sides and rushing all about. That's how Apollo saved me.

The final two lines contain the allusion to Lucilius's lines that describe Apollo's snatching of Hector out of battle to face Achilles and death another day: τὸν δ' ἐξήρπαξεν Ἀπόλλων. The *rapit* of v. 77 is a better Latin translation for ἐξήρπαξεν of the Homeric/Lucilian line than *servavit*. The interlocutor, not Horace, is removed, to face the defamed anonymity of this poem. Apollo is the Callimachean poetic deity apposite to the poetic principles articulated in this poem.[19] The Homeric line Horace borrows from Lucilius is translated and altered and packed with wit. Apollo, the Callimachean god, saves Horace, the figure of the poem, by allowing Horace to write a poem such as this one and which fulfills his poetic principles. Poetic principles have allowed Horace to discriminate against the interlocutor and have contributed discrediting elements to the portrait of the interlocutor. It is thanks to Apollo that Horace has the place he does with Maecenas. Insofar as he represents the removing agent of the interlocutor, the law court, and furnishes Horace with the wit and the poetry to remove the interlocutor from the esteem of all who read the poem (a readership that includes Maecenas), Apollo performs a saving action that is dual. The *adversarius* who touches Horace's ear, a robust Roman gesture (which here reverberates with Callimachean meaning), exploits the only resource remaining to Horace's burdened, exhausted, ass's ear.[20] Horace now can speak, and reach our ears.

In my discussion of *Satires* 1.9, I have called Horace's unwelcome companion on the Sacra Via the "interlocutor." English-speaking critics have referred to this character as the Bore, or, in a flourish of subtlety, the Pest.[21] But the poem does not name the interlocutor and, as I noted earlier, designates him throughout with only the demonstrative pronoun *ille*.[22] Even Aristius Fuscus, to flesh out his character, gains a couple of invective-style epithets from Horace in the poem, *male salsus* and *improbus* (65 and 73). The anonymity of the interlocutor (as if the poem were saying "he is no one") represents one of the poem's strategies for drawing the reader's sympathy toward the poem's narrator. In a critical discussion of the poem, to assign to the interlocutor a designation such as the Bore presupposes a reading of the poem that fails to consider its consequences. The nickname Bore (or any other) assumes a particular assessment of the interlocutor. That assessment, while it aligns the reader in cozy kinship with the beleaguered Horace, may blunt a perception of the various tensions that the poet Horace is carefully revealing in the poem's drama, though his own character on the Sacred Way would deny those tensions and would have us do likewise.

Horace has taken some pains to depict his social insecurity in the heady world of Roman sociopoetics and Maecenas's coterie (*Sat.* 1.6). The interlocutor of 1.9 commits social and poetic solecisms with childish and hopeful innocence. A poetic naïf, he lunges into an enthusiastic boast of his verse-making prowess, hitting every unfashionable poetic note with great efficiency (22–25). The common ground of character and poetic skill has already been well established in *Satires* I, so the interlocutor's poetic gaffe is no surprise after his clumsy introduction of himself and his inability to act on Horace's wish for solitude, which he does perceive: "'misere cupis' inquit 'abire'" (14). The problem of the drama in *Satires* 1.9 lies in the uncertainty of Horace's own social position as he describes it in the *Satires*. As he tells it, it was the victory of his character, his heart, that won him a place with Maecenas. He does not say that it was his poetry that won him this place, though that was surely the basis on which Vergil and Varius have recommended him to Maecenas. In *Satires* 1.6, we learned that Vergil and

Varius have told Maecenas "what Horace was" ("dixere quid essem," 55), and that Horace, on meeting Maecenas, does likewise: "quod eram narro" (60). He says little, overcome with gulping modesty: "ut veni coram, singultim pauca locutus, / infans namque pudor prohibebat plura profari" (56–57). Maecenas responds equally laconically: "respondes, ut tuus est mos, / pauca" (60–61). Horace goes away (*abeo*). There is a long gestation, nine months of waiting on Maecenas's silence before the acceptance into his friendship came for Horace. Horace is born again in this acceptance but does not forget his first birth, which made him the manner of man he is (*quod eram, quid essem*) and fitted him for this second birth. His father made him *purus* (1.6.69), ready for this household than which none is *purior:* "domus hac nec purior ulla est / nec magis his aliena malis" (1.9.49–50).

The description of Horace's entry into Maecenas's company (1.6.52–64) is the text against which the interlocutor's desire for inclusion is measured. Even without our own instincts for social rules, which we see the interlocutor break, we have the particular rules for this situation laid down in 1.6. The interlocutor's overabundant speech (*garrulus, loquaces,* etc.) contrasts explicitly with the terseness of Horace's successful interview: Horace and Maecenas both say *pauca* (56 and 61). Horace's declaration about himself to Maecenas is painfully free of any boast. It is the conceit of Horace's whole relation with Maecenas in the *Satires* that his writing plays no role. If Horace is the successful model, then the interlocutor does everything wrong: his approach is bold and talkative; he boasts of his accomplishments (he is *doctus*) and his poetry (23–25); he cannot go away and he cannot wait. Nor, unlike Horace in 1.6, does he appear to know what sort of person he is: "'si bene me novi, non Viscum pluris amicum, / non Varium facies'" (22–23); he is devastatingly wrong in this, and his reward is *Satires* 1.9.

The poem is Horace's opportunity to be the insider who maintains the rules of the house. The loss of a walk by himself is a small price to pay for the reward the poem gives the poet. Such is his security too that he endures the interlocutor very ill, portrays him with humorous extremity. The interlocutor's talk is *killing* Horace ("sub cultro," 27), and only Apollo can "save" him. But there is still a problem; why does Horace write a poem in which he depicts himself as verbally powerless? Horace has taught us about his social vulnerability, a vulnerability counteracted by the powerful influence of his father's purity, but not about his verbal helplessness.

Why is nonspeech the great feature of his encounters with Maecenas? How is silence converted by the poem, and why?

It conforms with the character Horace has drawn for himself in *Satires* I that he should not engage in hostile speech, seemingly the only kind of speech his interlocutor in 1.9 might notice. But furthermore, Horace's readers are silent. If there is a place for poets, there must be a place for silent hearers, but they must be willing, and Horace has made us willing, silent hearers. We do far better by Horace than Maecenas does; we ask for only what he gives us, and we gratify his desire to be heard. We do not ask him to play ball, we do not complicate his life with the burdens of greatness or envy, we admire his status as a freedman's son, and we take him at his word that his virtue is perfect within the realm of human expectations. *Satires* 1.9 is a great persuasive speech to gratify the poet's desire, certainly at the expense of one hopeful petitioner to the house of Maecenas, but the poet has arranged it so that this does not cost those who matter: we are sure that we are included in that group. The poem flatters the reader shamelessly, and we are easily suborned. We are won over as silent listeners, pleased not to be cursed ourselves with the interlocutor's terrible tastes, character, and talkativeness.

Horace has convinced us, by revealing his own situation as the interlocutor's victim, that we win more by identifying with him, by making the poet's voice our own, than by identifying with the interlocutor. Our silence is justified because Horace speaks for us—we have a more capable speaker than we ourselves could be on our own, and the poet gratifies our desire by speaking for us. We do, in fact, as readers, go further and practice hostile speech ourselves, calling the interlocutor not *ille,* but "the Bore," "shameless social climber," and so forth. Horace persuades us to practice the type of satire that he withholds from his own persona.

If Horace handily dismissed the interlocutor in 1.9, there would be no need for us, the readers, to gratify Horace's wish to be heard, since he would have been heard. Given the nature of the interlocutor, this would require a kind of speech from Horace foreign to his persona in the *Satires.* Horace says himself he isn't *cerebrosus* (11), though in the stress of the manufactured moment he claims to wish that *were* his nature. To be the agent himself of rejecting the interlocutor, Horace would have to be a different character from the one he has presented—he would have to undermine the version of the harmless satirist he has been at pains to depict for himself—and he would also need to practice a type of speech he has denied himself, something like invective. This is poetically and ethically not a possible choice for him if he is to remain persuasive as the unthreatening satirist. Moreover, though his readers might take pleasure in seeing Horace get rid of this awful character, we would not have a poem that so fully enlists our sympathy for the poet's persona and for his desire to be heard. Horace would have made himself heard, and our second hearing would only be a witnessing, like the spectators in the courtroom for the battle of Persius and Rex in *Satires* 1.7. We, the readers, would not be the crucial factor in gratifying Horace's need to be heard, and thus we would not be so necessary a part of the poem. We would be outsiders, not stigmatized the way the interlocutor is as an outsider, but not the insiders we become by being the only figures in the drama (insofar as the reading puts us into it) who listen, attend, and are the true, solicited *adiutores* such as the interlocutor only hopes to be (46). Unlike the interlocutor, we are not denied. Aristius Fuscus, as a nonlistener (60–72), acts as the model that we readers of the poem avoid being; Fuscus has the opportunity to protect Horace by exchanging speech with him, but he rejects that opportunity. As readers of or listeners to the poem, however, we hear the unheard poet of the satire's drama and are willingly silent while Horace speaks to us. Just as Priapus recovers his power over the women in the gardens in 1.8 by means of his narrative, making us laugh (showing that they are laughable, not menacing), the figure of the poet in 1.9 recovers his power to be heard with his narrative by engaging us; and unlike Fuscus, we stay and listen. We even practice satire for the poet, calling the interlocutor unflattering names when Horace will only call him *ille*.

There is nothing unique to satire in the process of forging the speaker-hearer relationship; every poet must do this to have an audience, must make the listener's silence justifiable to the listener, must gratify the desires of the hearer along with his own. But Horace has an extra burden in the *Satires* for two reasons. One is that satire has a kinship with listener-hostile genres such as diatribe, invective, and Greek Old Comedy (1.4.1 ff.), the practice of satire by Lucilius, as Horace tells it. The lurking presence of Canidia and the speech of magical coercion in *Satires* 1.8 testify to this kinship. Another reason is that by designating his genre as *sermo*, Horace invites a natural comparison with everyday speech, which invariably belongs to dialogue. The exchange of speech in conversation gratifies the participants by requiring each to speak and respond, to share the roles of hearer and speaker. *Sermo* is not a speech practiced by a solitary speaker,

and yet a poet is a solitary speaker. Both of these circumstances complicate things for Horace the satirist. He rejects diatribe after *Satires* 1.4 and
rejects much of the Lucilian component in his own practice of satire. His
disposition toward coercive speech is one of fascination, but he locates his
fascination in the figure of Canidia; he is careful to reject its weapons
from his repertoire. His statement in 1.4 that people hate verses and fear
poets makes diatribe, invective, and coercion impossible for the satirist
who argues against such emotions in his reader as relentlessly as Horace
does in *Satires* 1.4.

But the solution of *sermo* is hardly satisfactory because conversation
can only be artificially reproduced by a poet in dialogue: the speaker for
both parts is still the poet; he has the only voice. It seems significant that
in *Satires* 1.9 (the first poem of the *Satires* that represents *sermo* in dialogue) the positive feature of conversation, whereby two people interact
in an exchange of the roles of speaker and hearer, is represented as not
occurring. *Satires* 1.9 is a stunning failure as effective conversation: one
of the speakers longs only for solitude throughout the conversation, and
the other can only speak, failing wholly to respond to the spoken desires
of Horace's dramatic character. The situation depicted is one that everyone has been in, though readers prefer to identify with Horace rather than
with his interlocutor. It is indeed the poem's invitation, to sympathize in
rueful recollection of the instances in which we too have failed to escape
the needs of another, another whom we consider innocent but beneath our
attention, and there are few figures more attractive to identify with than
Horace. He is, after all, a success in our eyes, and we are not reluctant to
align ourselves with a discomfited genius. But the fondness for our poet
and the self-flattering light in which our sympathy casts us obscure the
questions of the drama's improbability.

It is easy to object that the poem is only about what it looks like it is
about: the good nature of Horace abused by an insensitive companion
and the humorous turns that ensue.[23] The traditional readings of *Satires*
1.9 variously condemn the interlocutor, depending on the temperament of
the critic, as a bore, a pest, a careerist, a vulgar place-hunter.[24] These readings focus our attention on the givens of the poem and in particular on
the interlocutor's status as an outsider. They leave the reader safely within
the comfort of Horace's circle.[25] It is my instinct, however, to question a
reading of the poem that gives such comfort to its readers, when the poem
is written by a poet elsewhere so overtly dubious, certainly choosy, about

his readers.[26] I suggest that the desire the poet expresses in the drama of
1.9, that he be heard and that the listener attend, a desire so easily granted
by the reader of the poem, has the beguiling effect of putting the reader
in the position of fulfilling the wishes of the poet and seduces us away
from a greater comprehension of the poem's issues. It is too easy to be
content with the image of ourselves as Horace's ideal readers, the Plotius
and Varius of the moment, and in our contentment to stop short of con-
templating the power that a speaker may exercise over an unwilling hearer,
the power that speech has to deprive the hearer of the fulfillment of his
desires, and the impotence of the hearer to protect himself by means of
speech in return.[27] One mirror of the relation between Horace and his
interlocutor is the relation between the poet and the reader; Horace speaks,
we listen. We pinpoint the difference between our silence and the silence
of Horace's persona in 1.9 in our willingness, eagerness, to hear. But structurally the poet of any poem occupies the same position as the interlocutor of 1.9, a speaker who does not hear the returned speech.

We know that magical speech can coerce the hearer against his will;
while speech is voluntary, hearing is not. In the verses of the Sabine *anus*
who told him that a *garrulus* would kill him one day, Horace articulates
the relation of speaker to hearer.[28]

> "hunc neque dira venena, nec hosticus auferet ensis,
> nec laterum dolor aut tussis, nec tarda podagra:
> garrulus hunc quando consumet cumque. loquaces,
> si sapiat, vitet, simul atque adoleverit aetas."
>   *Sat.* 1.9.31–34

> "It won't be deadly poison, nor an enemy's sword that carries this one off,
> nor affliction in the lungs nor cough, nor the slow-moving gout; a chatter-
> box, when the time comes, will kill him off. If he's wise, he'll stay away from
> talkers once he's become a man."

Horace is not vulnerable, according to this prediction, to the usual
penetrating weapons of poison, a sword, or disease, all killing entities that
internally disrupt the body; the threat to him comes rather from the penetration of words through his ears. Speech has this external, invasive power
over the hearer. The interlocutor of 1.9 is no magician; all speech, not just
magical, has the power to coerce the hearer against his will, as the poem

demonstrates. We cannot ascribe intent to kill to the interlocutor here, only intent that his desire prevail over the poet's. Perhaps it is the same thing. What then is the situation of speech for a poet and his hearing audience? Is the willingness to listen the crucial factor in making speech deadly or benign? The benign relationship that Horace establishes with his readers in 1.9 suggests that this is indeed the case. But we should not in our willingness to listen overlook the fact that we thereby put ourselves in the satirist's power. And Horace, after all, by writing *Satires* 1.9, shows that he has the last word.

There are two problems in satire for Horace that emerge in *Satires* 1.9. Horace's Callimachean sensibilities disdain the overabundant speech of Lucilius and Lucilius's stylistic echo, the interlocutor (not to mention the poetic outcast Hermogenes). And the verbal hostility that Horace might use to drive off the interlocutor is satire's other problem, already disavowed by Horace thoroughly in 1.4; this disavowal is enacted by Horace's own character in 1.9. Both problems in the satiric genre, as Horace inherits it from Lucilius, are problems of the relation between the speaker and the hearer, poet and audience. The speaker exercises power over the hearer with undesirable results: no communicative relationship is formed between the speaker and the hearer.

Speech can dominate, a speaker can dominate a hearer, and, as the instance of the Sabine *anus* illustrates, the hearer obliterated by the invasion of words has no self: words kill. The interlocutor's words in 1.9 are going to kill Horace, who is left "under the knife" by Aristius Fuscus. But the outcome of Horace's storytelling in 1.9 is that we readers love Horace; Horace successfully makes a relationship with his audience. The success of 1.9 is underarticulated by critics, because it is hard to look at oneself as a reader. The popularity of the poem is the result of Horace's successful embrace of his reader. In no other poem in the *Satires* do we feel so fully a part of the poet's program, and for good reason. Horace invites the reader to play a part in the drama and does so with such consummate skill that we never look at that part; we merely play it. We like the poem without ever recognizing that we like being part of the poem. Seeming to do no harm, we indulge our impulses and fail to see that what we indulge is the pleasure of condemning and excluding. The pleasures of domination are hard to examine.

Satires 1.9 is a poem about exclusive relations between people. It is unpleasant to note that the timeless popularity of 1.9 rests on the pleasure the reader takes from cooperating with Horace's exclusionary tactics. The poem makes anger safe, and from a certain ethical point of view, *Satires* 1.9 is a rather nasty poem. Readers universally comply with Horace's invitation to scorn and exclude the poem's primary figure, take pleasure in the invitation, and take pleasure in their own compliance. We *like* to scorn people as long as we are given sufficient justification. Shrewd readers (Johnson, John Henderson, Oliensis) observe that Horace has portrayed himself as every bit as vulnerable to the scorn saved for the interlocutor as the interlocutor is. And they have observed that Horace saves himself by turning the same knife on the interlocutor. But I would like to draw our attention to the pleasure readers experience in doing that knife-turning, which *is* the pleasure of invective/satiric speech. We may view Horace as hypocritical; we have a choice between full compliance with Horace and disdain for Horace for stooping to use the very tools that he so much does not want used on him. But it is Horace who has given us the information with which to disdain him, and we can't observe the entire operation until we observe ourselves. Our difficulty is that we like to practice invective; we like to exclude. Horace presents the appeal of satire, the satire he wants to both reject and practice.

Unsatisfying Fulfillments

Satires 1.10 and the End of Satires 1

Horace's last poem of the first book of *Satires*, 1.10, needs to do the work of finishing off the book. Horace does this finishing work partly by summarizing what his genre is and how he has done satire. This summarizing takes the shape of a poetic theory consistent with the poetics we find in all of Horace's oeuvre, but in 1.10 it is done specifically in the terms of satire's poetic theory. The last poem is an *ars satirica* of sorts. Crucial to this *ars satirica* (reprising what he has said and demonstrated in the first book) is the pun that Horace makes on the name of his genre, *satura*. Horace never calls this poetry *satura* in the first book of *Satires*, referring instead to *hoc genus* (this genre, 1.4.24, 65) or to *sermo* (conversation, speech, 1.4.42, 48). But throughout book 1, Horace puns on *satis/satura* when he is speaking of his genre either as an ethical medium or as an aesthetic/poetic medium.[1] Horace's idea of what is sufficient is fundamental to his theoretical formulation of his satire; this satiric formulation of fulfillment applies to the technical definition of satire, but it also applies beyond that to a larger ethical-poetic outlook. What is *satis,* what is enough, is defined by the *fines*—the boundaries and limits—on the other side of which lie excess and violence. Horace's moral and poetic formulations in book 1 may be seen as belonging to the map of what is within and without *satis:* health and unhealth, reason and madness, good poetry and bad, even the right and the wrong relation between a poet and his audience.[2] So satire itself becomes a genre of boundary markers in Horace's hands. To know what is enough is also to recognize when you have reached the end. If the last poem of *Satires* I has the role any final poem in a book has, to finish and let the performance end, then this is a particularly significant task in a book of poems whose theoretical principle has consistently adverted to the need for finitude and boundaries. *Satires* 1.10, constituting the outside boundary of the book, is itself a speech act of completion.

Each poem in the first book of the *Satires* provides a different context for satiric sufficiency, but 1.10 has a double task: to develop the idea of satiric limits, and to provide a satisfactory terminus to his book of poems. *Satires* 1.10 must limit and fulfill both programmatically and structurally. Like each of the other poems in *Satires* I, this one needs to limit the genre's invective impulse; but in addition it needs to limit the desire for more poems and, by so doing, end the book.

Let us begin with the end of the ending poem of *Satires* I. The first-person narrator of the poem (whom I call Horace) has spoken for ninety-one lines about Lucilius, Roman poetry, his poetic competitors, and related issues. He stops short suddenly and says, "Go, boy (slave), and quick write all this down in my little book"—"i, puer, atque meo citus haec subscribe libello" (92). Here ends book 1. This final line has an ironic, undermining effect; it seems a reversal of the poetics that Horace has presented with care and craft throughout the first book of *Satires* and especially in this poem. In 1.10, Horace gives aid and comfort to every writer then or since, by noting that good poets scratch their heads, bite their nails to the quick, and erase a lot (70–73). But the final line of 1.10 suggests that this poem wasn't written at all, that it is not a poem but rather transcribed speech, a harangue delivered to an unidentified addressee for a slave to get down on a *charta* before the speaker changes his mind, or loses the thought, or perhaps something else. So the book ends mendaciously: Horace did write this poem and he probably did turn over his stylus as he composed it. The final line is also anticlosural in nature. The boundary of this poem and this book is made to seem equivocal and arbitrary. Just as in *Satires* 1.5 (the final poem for the first half of the ten poems of book 1), there is no narrative premonition that the end is approaching, and the indeterminacy of 1.5 is echoed here too. *Satires* 1.5 ended with an allusion in the last line to the poem's page (*chartae*), 1.10 ends by alluding to the book, *libello;* this is the last word of the poem and of the book. It is as if the naming of the object *libellus* will finish the poem, and as if this is as much of a limit the poet can muster. Neither 1.5 nor 1.10 has plot or argument to prepare the listener for the apparently arbitrary end; there is no moment that concludes the progress, but instead simply a stopping. The poet who writes little and slowly finishes off *Satires* 1.10 (and the book) by feigning a great rush when he tells his slave to go quickly and write down the poem he has just dictated.

Furthermore, if the poetic haste of the last line is inconsistent with every other poetic precept Horace has expressed in this book of satires and hence confounds closure, likewise the persona of the satirist here is at odds with the figure he has maintained elsewhere in book 1 and seems to open up doubt where clarity and consistency would close. Whereas Horace has been the poet who cannot do harm (1.4), will speak only benign trivialities (1.5), or cannot summon the verbal force to drive away an annoying companion (1.9), in *Satires* 1.10 he speaks invective freely against other poets. Horace reprises the poetic stance of 1.4, that restraint is the necessary element of good poetry, but he fails to restrain his own attacks on certain of his poetic competitors. For all the overt suspicion he has cast on invective speech in *Satires* I, Horace leaves the field of poetry open for invective conflict. Here he is not able, or pretends not to be able, to contain his own impulse toward invective.

I have suggested that in *Satires* I Horace views the invective impulse as one of many boundary-breaking impulses that characterize, or are akin to, madness. The poetic theory emerging in 1.10 is a crucible of madness and reason: when the poem speaks of the tightly crafted poetry that Horace says is worth reading again ("iterum quae digna legi sint," 1.10.72), this stimulates the poet's longing for an audience. Yet those who undeservingly do gain a big audience (a "turba," 73) with sloppy, runny poetry rouse the poet's competitive anger, his invective, and his madness—if we take it that invective signals a loss of reason.

We have seen repeatedly in *Satires* I that desire poses this danger: it leads us to imagine ourselves beyond the borders of reality. These are the borders of satire as well. *Satires* 1.1 observes that "though your threshing floor pound out a hundred thousand bushels of grain, despite this your stomach will hold no more than mine" ("milia frumenti tua triverit area centum, / non tuus hoc capiet venter plus ac meus," 1.1.45–46). Wealth bespeaks greed, and greed's desire remains forever unfulfilled; but the belly is easily filled. So when Horace reaches the end of this first poem of the *Satires,* he reprises the poem's opening—that no one lives content with his lot ("nemo . . . illa / contentus vivat," 1.1.1–3)—with a Lucretian allusion to a satisfied dinner guest. Just as Lucretius had written:

Cur non ut *plenus* vitae conviva recedis,
Aequo animoque capis securam, stulte, quietem?
   DRN 3.938–39

Why don't you withdraw from life, like a full dinner guest, and take your
rest you fool, carefree with a tranquil heart?

so Horace finishes his first satire:

inde fit ut raro qui se vixisse beatum
dicat, et exacto *contentus* tempore vita
cedat uti conviva *satur*, reperire queamus.
iam *satis est.* ne me Crispini scrinia lippi
compilasse putes, verbum non amplius addam.
   Sat. 1.1.117–21

And so it is that rarely do we find one to say that he has lived well, and,
content with his span of time, takes leave of life like a filled-up dinner guest.
Now this is enough (full). So that you won't think I've rummaged through
the desk of half-blind Crispinus, I'll add not one word more.

In this programmatic moment in Horace's first satire, Lucretius's *plenus*
becomes *satur*, and then the poem itself is full, enough, *satis*. The limit
of the stomach is a border that can't be breached, and that border is
deployed, further, to adumbrate Horace's satiric principle and to toy with
his genre's name. The limit of the stomach is coterminus with life's limit:
leave when you are full, satisfied, and *contentus* inside the limits of both
your stomach and your mortality. The desire to live forever is the paradigm desire of those who cannot live within their mortal means, and this
desire may as well define madness. Sane human beings live within the limits, recognize they are not gods, and, filled up, accept the end. Sane poets
know their limits and know when to end a poem.

Excess can go in both directions, however. You can refuse to accept
boundaries, or you can insist on rigid and unreal boundaries. Either path
refuses satire's vision of nature and health; either path makes for madness.
There is a mean in all things, as Horace says in the first poem: "est modus
in rebus, sunt certi denique fines, quos ultra citraque nequit consistere rectum" (1.106–7, There is a mean in things; there are, in fine, sure borders

beyond which and short of which one cannot stand). But in the last poem of book 1, the confident moralist of 1.1 has become an uneasy, competition-bound poet with a penchant for calling other poets names, a poet struggling to be *contentus* within increasingly severe limits. The poised finish of the first poem has no counterpart in the ending of last poem, with its final snipe at poetic competitors and the worried instruction to the slave to get this down on paper. The satirist is not sure now how to end a poem.

The principle of *satis* in this book has somehow failed, and the progress from 1.1 to 1.10 seems negative. The demanding stylist speaking in 1.10 twice describes a poet as *contentus* (1.10.60 and 74), but in neither circumstance does the word connote fulfillment. The first instance concerns Lucilius, where *contentus* describes a hypothetical poet whose compositional failings are likened to those of Lucilius. *Satires* 1.10 is marked as programmatic by the appearance of Lucilius in the second line, and the poem's evaluation of Lucilius opens up a critique of both style and the genre of satire, just as it did in 1.4:

> quid vetat et nosmet Lucili scripta legentis
> quaerere, num illius, num rerum dura negarit
> versiculos natura magis factos et euntis
> mollius, ac si quis pedibus quid claudere senis,
> hoc tantum *contentus*, amet scripsisse ducentos
> ante cibum versus, totidem cenatus, Etrusci
> quale fuit Cassi rapido ferventius amni
> ingenium, capsis quem fama est esse librisque
> ambustum propriis?
>   *Sat.* 1.10.56–64

What's to stop us, too, from reading what Lucilius wrote and wondering whether it was the toughness of the man, or of his material, that denied him poetry better fashioned and flowing more smoothly, than what you get when you slap on a meter of six feet, and are content that you wrote a couple hundred lines before your dinner, and as many when you've eaten—like Cassius the Etruscan, whose genius ran faster than a boiling stream (and the story goes he died in a pyre made of his own bookshelves)?

The circumstances of contentment in v. 60 define Lucilius's inadequacy as a poet. Contentment here means bad style, unfulfillment, and a disposition that puts poetry second to a good meal. This poet is content to produce a lot of poor poetry, and he is satisfied with bad poetic food. His poetry and his contentment are grotesquely linked to gross matters of life and death; such a one was Cassius, and his own prodigious output consumed him.

In the first poem of *Satires* I, the limit of the stomach served as Horace's metaphor for a limit on desire, forcing longings of the heart and the imagination into an equation with hunger: you can gratify your desires in the same way that you gratify hunger and fill up the container of longing if you observe those metaphorical boundaries.[3] In the course of book 1, beginning with the fourth satire's exploration of satire, invective, and Horace's relation to his genre, Horace appears to examine fullness and longing with increasing anxiety and to come to 1.10 far more unsatisfied than he ended in 1.1. Having explored the turf of satire, the poet seems clouded by his inquiry. The ideal of satisfaction modeled on a material paradigm has come to seem increasingly unstable as Horace negotiates between a theory of an ideal and actual desires as they emerge in practice. Most of all, poetic theory, as Horace expresses it, is a theory of perfection not possible in the world. In reality endings are not perfections; poems are finished in the same way that lives are finished, with imperfections and incomplete actions. Horace's theory of satire, as an arrangement of borders and limits, becomes unreal: *Satires* 1.10 is equivocal, nonbounded, and includes invective. A breakdown of satire's theoretical clarity occurs in the very act of making claims for methods of achieving poetic perfection; living within the limits of the stomach makes for bad poetry.

Horace continues, from the example of the unfortunate Cassius, to ponder Lucilius (67–68). He has more than hinted, here and in 1.4, that Lucilius is too poetically unbound to produce good poetry. Lucilius does, however, earn the epithets *comis et urbanus;*[4] and he is more polished than an unskilled author of song untouched by Greeks, is more polished than the *turba,* the throng, of older Latin writers. Horace appears to be attempting to rescue Lucilius from the crypto-invective he has cast Lucilius's way. As to his poetic failings, the poem suggests that if you were to put Lucilius in a time machine, he would meet the demanding standards of Horace's day (67–71).

The demanding standards of Horace's day, however, have a certain satiric darkness about them. What kind of completion are we looking for in *perfectum* (70)? The poet turns satiric biting against the hand that feeds him ("vivos et roderet unguis," 71), while he carves out this *perfectum*, this achieved and perfect thing. Had Lucilius been born in Horace's time some editorial impulse would direct him to trim the ragged edges of his verses according to perfection's boundary, the boundary of desire whose metaphor is the stomach's physical limit.[5] No more eating and composing, composing and eating—what led to Cassius decomposing—and very little, it would seem, of that magisterial contentment that accompanied the diner of *Satires* 1.1 as he pushed himself away from the board of life. There is instead, Horace continues, a certain starvation in this post-Lucilian poetry that has the poet eating at himself (not a good meal) if he wants to write poetry that gets read more than once (72–77).[6]

As if the food weren't poor enough, contentment next is found in your audience of a few readers. The *turba*, that throng that haunted Horace's other programmatic satire of the first book—the timorous *turba* in *Sat.* 1.4 that fears poets but becomes the band of poets who proselytize like Jews—undergoes a new transformation in 1.10. The crowd of older Latin poets make Lucilius look polished:

> fuerit Lucilius, inquam,
> comis et urbanus, fuerit limatior idem
> quam rudis et Graecis intacti carminis auctor,
> quamque poetarum seniorum turba:
>   *Sat.* 1.10.64–67

I say I grant that Lucilius was genial and urbane, grant that he was also more polished than an author of rough verse untouched by the Greeks, and more polished than the throng of older [Roman] poets:

But the unbounded throng of older Latin poets becomes (73) the unbounded audience. The *turba* you would toil to please, if you were a madman, is a borderless crowd that fills up on bad poetry, and their satisfaction defines the poetry: if you please them, you have failed to observe the stern boundaries of this *ars satirica*. While the *turba* at the end of 1.4 was made up of poets themselves, a group in that poem whose restraint had been much articulated by Horace, here the *turba* is the audience whose pleasure has the frightening power to define the quality of your poetry. Though the poet's desire may make him yearn for a great crowd to hear him, he must trim that desire and, sane, not *demens,* live inside the limits of this *ars;* he must be content with just a few readers.

What poet longs to be heard by just a few readers? What poet longs to be unknown to the world? This is limiting desire indeed. Singing and poetry are born of the impulse to name and know and live beyond the body's narrow limits. Horace's metaphorical boundary of the stomach and the body, the material limits of life within which we gain our contentment, does violence to the impulse of song. Unbounded desire in satire has had two dangers in Horace's account: one is bad, uncut poetry; another is invective. Horace's poetic limits have made his satire harmless and spare, no burden to the listener's ears (1.10.10). But as those limits are articulated in *Satires* 1.10, the excess of rigidity begins to endanger poetry itself. In 1.4, Horace ambivalently boasts that he is no blowhard like Crispinus is, and his poetic talent is *rara et perpauca.*[7] That modest talent finds its match in *paucis lectoribus* (the few readers); but how few the words and how tiny the audience, before the limits are too tight to endure, desire too harrowed, for the poet to write poetry at all?

The audience Horace names in 1.10 are the denizens of Maecenas's house, or a near-identical bunch. The audience that Horace wants for his *lectores pauci* is housed in 1.10 inside an invective frame. We will return to that frame, but we should look first at how the poem articulates the poetic good and bad before it states its desire for an audience and expresses its rage at the poets who have a listening *turba.*

The Boundaries of Poetry: Praise and Blame

Horace's invective against his fellow poets smacks of the anger of frustration. From the invective in 1.10, we deduce a state of competition between Horace and some of his fellow poets that has been well presaged in the denials of the previous poem, 1.9, during Horace's exchange with the excluded interlocutor of that poem. The intemperance in 1.10 suggests that Horace is feeling the pinch of his artistic principles, and that envy, more than disinterested critique, is the engine of his blame. But what poetry *is* the poetry that avoids Horace's poetic invective? Lucilius gets praise for his bracing content, but only after he has walked into 1.10 on his ill-shod foot, with Latin poetry's fond pun on the foot, metrical and human:

Nempe *incomposito* dixi *pede* currere versus
Lucili. quis tam Lucili fautor inepte est

ut non hoc fateatur? at idem, quod sale multo
urbem defricuit, charta laudatur eadem.
nec tamen hoc tribuens dederim quoque cetera: nam sic
et Laberi mimos ut pulchra poemata mirer.
    Sat. 1.10.1–6

Yes, I said that his verses run on an ill-formed foot, Lucilius's do. Who is
so blundering a fan of Lucilius that wouldn't admit this? But, the same
Lucilius, for girding at the city with deep wit, is praised in the same poem.
Nevertheless, because I grant him this, I don't give him everything: if I did,
I should have to admire the mimes of Laberius as being great poetry.

We may recall too that Lucilius stood on one foot in 1.4, at that poem's
outset, and was accused of being harsh in his poetic composition: "durus
componere versus" (8). But Lucilius has always been double, as Horace
allows, blamed and praised in the selfsame poem (*eadem charta*, 4).
Lucilius rubbed down the city with his great wit, but Horace is quick
to say he is not going to be caught without his critical faculties for that
and give Lucilius other credit—that would be like calling pantomime
great art.

Wit is good, laughter is good, but not without more than that; that is
not enough, *non satis est* (7). It is not satire; we need more. And yet, here
Horace switches again: wit offers the virtue of brevity and thus the poet's
expression runs and does not trip itself ("se / impediat," 9–10) with words
that burden, not the way Horace (like a pack animal) in 1.9 took on the
burden of his interlocutor's words through his ears (7–10). Wit furnishes
the same result as Horace's own poetic soul does, that soul in 1.4 which
he says speaks but few words.

The recollection of the genealogy of satire in 1.4 brings the poem to its
first bit of invective:

                    ridiculum acri
    fortius et melius magnas plerumque secat res.
    illi scripta quibus comoedia prisca viris est
    hoc stabant, hoc sunt imitandi: quos neque pulcher
    Hermogenes umquam legit, neque simius iste
    nil praeter Calvum et doctus cantare Catullum.
        Sat. 1.10.14–19

A bit of foolery can frequently cut serious matter more sharply, better than a
blade. It's because of this those men who wrote Old Comedy still stand, still
call for imitation: I mean the ones your lovely Hermogenes never reads, and
neither does that ape who can't do anything but recite Calvus and Catullus.

Good Latin poets, those who aren't fakes, know their Greek literature. The
(sarcastically) handsome Hermogenes ("pulcher," 17) and that unnamed ape
("simius iste," 18) are *doctus* only enough to know Roman poets. But strictures follow: no mixing Greek and Latin, and no Romans writing Greek.
The first prohibition condemns Lucilius's boisterous hybrid language-
play of Latin and Greek, the second condemns the young Horace. In his
youthful zeal, Horace wrote in Greek (31–35), but Quirinus, doing a turn
on Ennius's dream of Homer, appears to Horace in a dream and tells him
he'd be crazy to write Greek poetry.[8] "Coals to Newcastle" says Quirinus,
who turns out to be something of a wit as well as a literary critic: "'in
silvam non ligna feras insanius ac si / magnas Graecorum malis inplere
catervas'" (34–35, It wouldn't be any more insane to carry wood into the
forest than for you to decide to fill out the massive troops of the Greeks).
The purity of the language provides another boundary to restrain poetic
language, another means of satiric control that Lucilius did not practice,
but Horace does. The sea is one more poetic/material boundary.

Desiring This Man's Gift and That Man's Scope: Comparatives

The most difficult boundary to negotiate, however, may be the one that
other poets constitute. When the poet of *Satires* I was still striking a confident tone, he said in *Satires* 1.3 that happiness lies in indulging the other
as you do yourself: see his faults with the same bleary short-sightedness
("oculis . . . lippus inunctis," 25) with which you view your own. The stakes
in this poem, however, seem to be far higher. You, the *te* (and the sub-
jects of the second-person verbs) of the poem, are a poet; you compete
with your predecessors and with your contemporaries—this competition
is your literary criticism. The precept of the first three satires in book 1,
that competitive striving makes misery and that happiness is only found
within the borders, seems lost. The abundance of comparative words and
constructions in vv. 47–67, where Horace speaks of his choice to write
satire, manifests the idea that poetry is as competitive an endeavor as the
interlocutor in *Satires* 1.9 supposed; and this time we do not face Horace's
prim denials.

At the poem's midpoint (46), and in a prime example of Horace's reality-based poetics, the poet explains very oddly that he chose to write satire because the generic slot was open (40–49). If he did not want to compete with his contemporaries Fundanius, Varius, Vergil, and Pollio, who had effectively mastered the genres of New Comedy, epic, pastoral, and tragedy, then Horace had remaining to him only "this"—"hoc erat" (46)—that is, satire (he refers to his genre with only the demonstrative pronoun, just as he did in 1.4). Varro of Atax and others have tried but not succeeded at "this"; he can write it better than they ("melius," 47), though he is *one* lesser ("minor," 48) than the genre's *inventor* (Lucilius). Piously, Horace says that he wouldn't dream of tearing Lucilius's crown off his head,[9] although he can't help quoting himself (1.4.11) again to note that in Lucilius's muddy stream there is more (*plura*) you would want to take out than leave in: "at dixi fluere hunc lutulentum, saepe ferentem / plura quidem tollenda relinquendis" (50–50). Look, says Horace, nobody is perfect: Homer nods (52) and Lucilius himself parodied Accius and laughed about Ennius's less-weighty verses ("versus Enni gravitate *minores*," 54), though Lucilius never claimed he was better than those criticized ("*maiore reprensis*," 55). The poem's mysterious addressee, called *doctus* in v. 52 when he is being indignantly interrogated as to whether he finds nothing to criticize in Homer, seems to be implied in the query that follows about the cause (the themes or the man?) of Lucilius's hard verses (56–57). Those verses could have been better formed ("*magis* factos," 58) and moved more silkily ("euntis *mollius*," 58–59) had Lucilius been somewhat less like that Cassius whose genius was more ebullient (*ferventius*) than a roaring stream; had he lived in his time, Lucilius would have been more like Horace. The addressee, who does live in Horace's time, will be bidden soon to edit remorselessly, if he wants to write anything worth reading twice.

The last comparative of this section, and the penultimate one of the poem, is *seniorum*, modifying *poetarum*—that throng of older Latin poets whom Lucilius excels in polish (*limatior*), since he is acquainted with Greek lyric. Lucilius is exempted from this *turba* of old Latin poets with no polish, no *finishing* touch—they are themselves borderless in composition and style.

> fuerit Lucilius, inquam,
> comis et urbanus, fuerit limatior idem

quam rudis et Graecis intacti carminis auctor,
quamque poetarum seniorum turba: sed ille,
   Sat. 1.10.64–67

I say I grant that Lucilius was genial and urbane, grant that he was also
more polished than an author of rough verse untouched by the Greeks, and
more polished than the throng of older [Roman] poets: on the other hand,
Lucilius . . .

The dense array of comparative words and constructions starts at the
poem's second half, when Horace ponders his choice of genre and strug-
gles with his relation to its founder (as he dubs Lucilius). Horace made
Lucilius the offspring of Greek Old Comic poets in *Satires* 1.4. Here Horace
grants a link with Greeks to Lucilius, in order to take another potshot at
his own unlettered contemporary poets (cf. 16–19). And he saves Lucilius
from the crude mob of early Roman poets. The thicket of comparatives
ends here, with the time-travel gambit—Horace's condescending resolution to his psuedo-unease over Lucilius's poetic failings.

In his queer, posthumous, crypto-competition with Lucilius, Horace
blames and praises Lucilius at once, wanting, he makes it appear, to blame
Lucilius without himself being blamed. The result is a competitive disposition both muted and condescending, and Horace seems to compete
even more successfully with this predecessor than if he had simply attacked
him or, as Lucilius did with Ennius and Accius, gleeful parodied him.
Lucilius instead is reinvented in Horace's own image, as a head-scratching
nail-biter.

In Horace's account here, poetry belongs to competition; this view is
not unique—rather, it is the account in 1.9 of Maecenas's uncompetitive
domus, which Horace expresses to his interlocutor, that is the unusual one.
Simply because, in some sense, poets need audiences to exist, there is
always a contest for an audience. Horace cannot bear the anxiety of competing with Fundanius, Pollio, Varius, and Vergil in their poetic genres,
possibly because to Horace poetic competition is near lethal, not the boisterous business that it seems to have been for Lucilius. Poetic competition
in Horace's satire is an agonistic invitation to invective, or, more broadly,
it is an invitation to the kind of anger that undermines the obedience to
reality's limitations, which Horace's principle of satire advocates. Horace
has tried in each poem of the first book to construct boundaries or to

deconstruct unbounded behavior. Yet embedded within the very nature of the poetic enterprise, in the composition of poetry and the longing for the audience that will hear and listen, is a desire to go beyond human boundaries, a beckoning toward perfection and being something more than human.

The Audience in the Frame

saepe stilum vertas, iterum quae digna legi sint
scripturus, neque te ut miretur turba labores,
contentus paucis lectoribus. an tua demens
vilibus in ludis dictari carmina malis?
non ego: nam satis est equitem mihi plaudere, ut audax
contemptis aliis explosa Arbuscula dixit.
men moveat cimex Pantilius, aut cruciet quod
vellicet absentem Demetrius, aut quod ineptus
Fannius Hermogenis laedat conviva Tigelli?
Plotius et Varius, Maecenas Vergiliusque,
Valgius, et probet haec Octavius, optimus atque
Fuscus, et haec utinam Viscorum laudet uterque!
ambitione relegata te dicere possum,
Pollio, te, Messalla, tuo cum fratre, simulque
vos, Bibule et Servi, simul his te, candide Furni,
conpluris alios, doctos ego quos et amicos
prudens praetereo; quibus haec, sint qualiacumque,
adridere velim, doliturus si placeant spe
deterius nostra. Demetri, teque, Tigelli,
discipularum inter iubeo plorare cathedras.
i, puer, atque meo citus haec subscribe libello.

    Sat. 1.10.72–92

Up-end your pencil often, if you want to write things worth reading more than once, and, content with a few readers, don't work to make the throng admire you; or would you be a lunatic, and prefer that your poems were read aloud for dictation in bad schools? Not I: it's enough if the knights applaud, as the brassy Arbuscula said when she'd been hissed—the rest she scorned. What do I care about that bug Pantilius, why should I feel agony because Demetrius mocks me when I'm not there, or because Fannius, Hermogenes Tigellius' hopeless hanger-on, puts me down? Plotius and Varius,

Maecenas and Vergil, Valgius and Octavius—let them like my verses, and splendid Fuscus, and I hope both the Visci can praise them! Free of any self-interest I can name you, Pollio, you Messalla, and your brother, and at the same time you, Bibulus and Servius, and along with them you too, marvelous Furnius, and some number of others, learned men and friends whom I discreetly do not mention; I wish these verses, such as they are, to delight these men, and I will grieve if they please them less than I had hoped. Demetrius, and you Tigellius, go and whine among the girls sitting in school. Go, boy, quick, and write this down in my little book.

In book 1 of the *Satires*, Horace strives to limit the desire to go beyond boundaries, and to demonstrate the merit of living within them. Maecenas's *domus* comes, in 1.10, to be for Horace the audience of *pauci lectores* that the poem advised its addressee to be content with. This contentment, this limitation, contrasts with the madness associated with toiling to please a *turba* (73–75). (Similarly, in *Sat.* 1.6 madness is associated with the crowd, which may judge Horace to be *demens* for eschewing the rewards [and the burden—*onus*] of high social status in favor of the simple, satiric life that his birth gave him, while Maecenas may judge him *sanus* [1.6.93–99]. Maecenas is in the hand-picked audience of 1.10.) But what sort of contented poet is Horace here as he ostentatiously shrugs off the wounds that Pantilius the louse, Demetrius, et al., deal to him?

The contentment rings hollow. Horace has remonstrated with the addressee "an tua demens / vilibus in ludis dictari carmina malis?" (74–75, Or would you, madman [*demens*], like a lunatic, rather your poems read out for dictation in bad public schools?), in a manner reminiscent of Quirinus's address to himself in his dream, and then puts in his second statement in the poem of what is enough, *satis est* (76), and makes his emphatic satiric statement again, bringing his own poetic principle out for contrast: "non ego, nam satis est." His quotation of the unknown but appealing mime Arbuscula has her announce what is *satis*,[10] and it recalls his testy statement early in the poem that wholly to approve of Lucilius's poetry would be like calling Laberius's mimes great poetry. Now Horace mimes the mime Arbuscula and does so at the most important moment of the poem. She tells what is enough, what is *sat*-ire; what is enough is to have Maecenas's *domus* as an audience. The audience of the *turba* makes for bad poetry. In *Satires* 1.4, the poet's own constitution was the cause of his poetry; the poet himself, not as artist but as ethical figure, defined and limited the satire: Horace, raised in satire by his father, could not write poetry to do harm or to frighten an audience. His character was the surety for the poem. Here, very curiously, it is the audience that defines the poetry: you have failed if you please a crowd, succeeded if you please just a few readers.

The menace of the *turba* now is now quite different from its threat in *Satires* 1.4. The hate and fear that the throng has for poets who note their faults is now moot; far worse for the poet is the admiration of the throng, whose borderless nature stigmatizes the poetry it favors. The threat, in turn, would be no problem if the throng's admiration were not attractive, did not in fact stimulate a longing that this most fiercely restrained of poets has to keep in check. The attraction for the unbounded audience we can only infer, reliably, from the invective, which betrays the sting of envy, or it would otherwise have no purpose in the poem. So when Horace chooses an audience that is not big but best, its borders will confine and restrain the poet. This defined audience protects Horace's poetry to the same extent as it defines the poem's value.

Horace's desired audience is defined by being named. The first line that names the audience, v. 81, echoes v. 40 of *Satires* 1.5: "Plotius et Varius, Sinuessae Vergiliusque"; in 1.10 it becomes "Plotius et Varius, Maecenas Vergiliusque." The Maecenas whom Horace was unable to look at in 1.5 is readily embraced here, and the self-referential quotation characterizes Horace as having an abiding relationship with his chosen audience. It is impossible, therefore, to avoid the suggestion that the audience of 1.10 is made up of the members of Maecenas's household that Horace has praised in the previous poem for having no competitive spirit. *Satires* 1.9 gave its audience the most detailed and persuasive instructions about its response that any poet could give, and that poem is a brilliant success, a perfect satire. It uses satire's anger with shrewd skill; the persona of the satirist in the poem gives all his anger to the audience for it to enact, for the audience to condemn the "Bore," and for the audience to freely approve of its own anger. The anger in 1.10 seems by contrast badly managed, leaky, spilling onto the poetic competitors who make Horace feel insecure. The poised control of 1.9, as a result of which the exclusion the poem performs on the interlocutor conversely embraces the audience of the poem, gives way in 1.10 to messy anxiety and the blatantly exclusive act of naming the audience the poet would please and blaming those he scorns.

The audience named in 1.10 will protect Horace from the dangers of competition, they are defined in such a way as to ensure the virtue of the poet's verse, and finally they are themselves strong speakers, poets, friends, and the literary luminaries of the late republic. Insofar as they are strong speakers, they are invulnerable to even the inadvertent coercive speech that may dwell in Horace's satire. In this sense the audience Horace wishes to please is one capable of the exchange between equals that furnishes true communication free of the operation of domination, and a kind of poetry, then, that can belong to Horace's hopeful definition of satire: the conversation, *sermo*, of sane human beings, a poetry of reason, reality, and fulfillment.

But the act of naming is also an act of poetic dominion. However delicate, humble, and eager with longing Horace's final list is, it nonetheless lays claim to authority, like an epic catalog, that again breaks satire's rules and touches on the divine. To name is to fix—as Canidia would know—not in the toils of an incantation here but in a poet's immortal words. Such naming shares in the longing to live forever. The closing half of the invective frame, in addition to setting a chill clamp on the genial safety of the invocation of Maecenas's *domus* and the appeal to the audience, brings us back to the competitive situation of the poem and the failure of the satire to be *satis*. Horace in fact (if fact is relevant) does have this audience yet is not fulfilled, and the poetic longing to please an audience is by its nature more permanent, more ever-hungry, than the poet's real ability to please. Horace mastered satiric fullness in book 1 of the *Satires* (the *satur* of 1.1) in terms of material pleasure and social ambition, and he presented poetic desire as a type of the same madness that he so easily mocked in others. He lampoons the insanity of Luscus in 1.5, the mad sexual appetites in 1.2, the crazed intemperance of the politically hopeful in 1.6, and the incontinent anger of a Persius and a Rex in 1.7, but he also portrays himself as vulnerable to the same kind of unbalance in his poetic longings. The end of 1.10 pries open the full ambivalence of Horace's poetic situation in satire, to expose for the reader the multilayered problem of his genre. The great strangeness, its radical disposition, is to portray the very longings that violate the ethic of satire by participating in those longings, in a satire. He talks about a kind of madness while engaging in it. When Horace spits it out that he bids Demetrius and Tigellius to go whine among the seats of schoolgirls, he engages in speech that he has categorized as *insanus*, while also having just marked out the audience who will hear this poem to exclude Demetrius and Tigellius. He demonstrates the anger that these fifth-rate poets arouse in him and resorts to power-based speech, pointing out thereby that poetry, and he himself as a poet, cannot adopt the principles of satire that he has given us, those principles that would otherwise keep him sane.

There is no way to end this conundrum. Two unsatiric gestures end the poem. First the epic catalog takes a leap toward immortality; then the invective frame reveals the psychic rupture of satire's bounded, limited sanity. Horace deals with this satirically in the final line of the poem, by taking flight from the logos of speech while giving instructions to the slave to record that speech: "Go write this down in my little book."

The anxiety in the poet's speech seems not quite quelled, nor, despite the explicitly chosen audience, can the poet be free from having to resort to power-based speech; Pantilius and Tigellius remain a threat. In *Satires* 1.10, Horace leaves us with a final reservation about the situation of the reader in the *Satires*. There is an inherent irony in the concept of a conversational genre of poetry. *Sermo*, ordinary speech, finds its usual place in conversation between two parties; it is a kind of speech we do not practice in solitude. When rendered in writing, it is up to the poet either to enlist and assume the response of the listener, as in *Satires* 1.8 and 1.9, or to reproduce dialogue, as Horace does in the second book of the *Satires*. In either case, however, it is a simulacrum of conversation, and the poet's is still the only voice. In the genre of satire, where the strong voices of incantation and invective that disempower the listener are part of the genre's generic inheritance, there is a special danger for the poet who, as Horace does, wants willing and acute listeners. In dialogue Horace can retreat from the pose of a single poetic speaker who has the ability, even if he chooses not to use it, to menace his audience; in dialogue the listener becomes witness to a conversation in which she or he is not addressed—the possibility for direct address and hence threat to the hearer is removed. But the breath of Canidia still has life in the last line of the *Satires*, and I think Horace bids farewell to his *Sermones* with that in mind. When Horace next turns to hexameter poetry, some fifteen years later he chooses the safely enclosed genre of the epistle, and there he need not tangle with either of his satiric ghosts, Lucilius and Canidia. And in the *Epistles* he avoids eye contact with his reader altogether and directs his poetic gaze to a known and named reader, his (fictional) correspondent.

NOTES
BIBLIOGRAPHY
INDEX

Notes

Introduction

1. *Institutio Oratoria,* 10.1.93. See Coffey (1976, 207n2) for bibliography on this famous *mot* of Quintilian. The possible range of Quintilian's *quidem* here might travel from utter clarity to ironic deprecation: "We know for certain that satire is our own genre," or "Satire is, whatever else, at least ours" (and this hardly exhausts the possible nuances of the particle here). Gratwick offers two possibilities for the phrase: *quidem* is adversative—"by contrast to other genres with Greek roots, satire is all ours," or, "but in satire we Romans win easily" (1982, 160–61).

2. Diomedes' *Ars Grammatica,* 3, from the fourth c. CE, is the *locus classicus* that supplies the etymological fuel for modern suggestions about the derivation of the term *satura.* Van Rooy (1965) gives a thorough account and exploration of the question of satire's literary roots and the proposed etymologies; see also Coffey (1976, 3–23) and Gratwick (1982). Hendrickson's two articles (1911 and 1927) are still fundamental to the discussion of Roman satire's genesis; see too Ullman's response to Hendrickson (1913). Gowers (1993b, 110–11), whose interest is in the culinary and digestive nature of satire's origins, reprises and deftly elaborates Diomedes' four proposed etymologies for satire.

3. Nagy investigates the binary opposition of praise and blame, showing how they "reflect two antithetical social functions expressed in two formal modes of discourse" in the archaic Greek community; "Indo-european society operated on the principle of counterbalancing praise and blame, primarily through the medium of poetry" (1979, 221–22).

4. See Nagy (1979, 223–32) on how blame speech in turn attracts ridicule and blame to its speaker.

5. Lejay (1911), for instance: "qui dit satire Latine, dit mélange," lix. Lucilius (ca. 180–102 BCE) and Juvenal (ca. 60–140 CE; see Coffey [1976] and Ferguson [1979, xv–xix]) are the historical bookends of Roman satire. The temper of satire that survives into European literature is Juvenal's.

6. See Oliensis (1991) for a full exploration of the unease of this relationship.

7. For example, figures such as Rupilius Rex in 1.7 or the talker of 1.9 are getting their comeuppance from Horace for insulting him. Rex, the reading goes, mocked Horace for his low birth during the time Horace was a tribune, and this has caused the poet to write 1.7. This suggestion is repeated by Wickham (1903) and Gow (1901) following the scholiast. The suggestion by Vulpius (see Palmer 1893, 219) that the talkative figure of 1.9 is Propertius is roundly discounted by commentators as chronologically impossible, but the existence of the suggestion indicates the modern wish to paint a clearer picture of the ancient world than is possible. Apropos such suggestions, Fraenkel comments: "In matters concerning Horace I know of no *fable convenue* that was ever killed for good" (1957, 118). Charles Martindale (1993) gives the subtlest and most inclusive account of the slipperiness of Horace's own image in his poetry, the lenses through which readers see him, and the consequent impressions of admiration and betrayal that this image of Horace inspires in his readers.

8. A. Parker observes about *Sat.* 1.4: "Even in the 1970's, when biographical criticism was very unfashionable, this poem still inspired speculation on the inner life of Horace" (1986, 168).

9. See, for example, Hare, who in an endearing preface to his translation of Horace, says, "I have tried to make my Author look somewhat like Himself in an English Dress" (1737); consider the unlikely prospect of performing the same sartorial transformation on Juvenal.

10. Richlin 1992, 185. Richlin alludes to *Sat.* 2.1.30–34, in which Horace states that Lucilius confided his secrets to his books, so that his whole life is there revealed as if laid out on votive tablets.

11. Bowditch 2001, 10. In remarking that two recent works on Horace "rest their interpretations on reconstructed versions of a 'historical' Horace," Bowditch admits disarmingly in a footnote that while one of these, W. R. Johnson (1993), "betrays a willingness to fall under the spell of Horace's seeming accessibility if not candor . . . my own argument is, no doubt, similarly vulnerable."

12. Coffey (1976, 232) quotes Hodgart (*Satire,* London, 1969, 134): "Just as the Sabine farm foreshadowed the English country house, so Horace's image of himself foreshadowed and helped to mould the English idea of the gentleman." Cary, for example (in the revealingly titled book *Horace: His Life, Friendships and Philosophy, as Told by Himself* [1904]), quotes the preface to Lonsdale's and Lee's *Works of Horace* (1873): "'The man Horace is more interesting than his writings, or, to speak more correctly, the main interest of his writings is in himself. We might call his works "Horace's Autobiography." To use his own expression about Lucilius, his whole life stands out before us as in a picture. . . . Almost what Boswell is to Johnson, Horace is to himself. We can see him, as he really was, both body and soul.'" Cary's summary of Horace, though quaint, hardly differs in substance from the assessments of scholars such as Wickham, Fraenkel, or Rudd.

Freudenburg, on the other hand, says Horace "chose to stress his father's humble station in life even though it is obvious that he grew up in the most privileged circumstances" (1993, 5); likewise, Freudenburg notes, Horace's portrait of himself in *Sat.* 1.5 "though conventionally accurate and certainly humorous, bears little resemblance to the poet Horace or to the actual status he enjoyed in the circle of Maecenas's friends" (205). As Zetzel remarks: "Need it be pointed out that that poor freedman, who seems to have had to struggle to put his son through school, was wealthy enough to leave his son the census of a Roman *eques*?" (1980, 62). Zetzel's argument about Horace's persona, linked to his argument for seeing the artistry of the poems and rescuing Horace from the grip of autobiographical interpretation, sees an artfully incompetent narrator whose statements are largely untrustworthy. Hendrickson (1900) first suggested there were fictional elements in Horace's autobiography, in order to distinguish his satire from that of Lucilius, but, as Leach notes, "his idea of Horatian fiction-making has not been widely accepted" (1971, 622).

13. For instance Coffey maintains that "Horace understood the power of Lucilius's political and personal attacks on individuals who were denounced or ridiculed by name. But in the 30s it would have been dangerous, especially for a freedman's son, to write political lampoons" (1976, 90–91). Freudenburg (2001, 7, and 15–124 passim) goes further and incorporates the loss of republican free speech in Rome into the timorous low-status persona of Horace's satirist, thus rendering Horace fully the "loser" to Lucilius in the satire sweepstakes.

14. Cf. Archilochus fr. 296W, that his mother was a slave; discussed in Nagy (1979, 247). On the low status of Bion of Borysthenes, the Cynic (to whose *Sermones* Horace refers in *Epistles* 2.2.60) cf. Kiessling and Heinz (1961, 107) and Freudenburg (1993, 205).

15. Quotations from the *Satires* in this volume are taken from Wickham 1901. All translations are mine unless otherwise noted.

16. Strubbe, speaking of imprecations on funerary stones in the Greek and Roman ancient world, says, "The force of a curse is based on a more general belief in the efficacy of the word. This power is increased if the word is spoken by a person of higher status, such as a king, a priest, parents, the dying, or the dead" (1991, 41). Note, again in light of this observation, the mitigating effect of Horace's construction of his low-status persona in the *Satires*.

17. Elliott (1960) sees the roots of satire, his definition of which is extremely broad, in all forms of abusive and invective speech, including elements of Greek Old Comedy, Archilochean iambics, Eskimo ridicule duels, and archaic Irish satire, to name a few. Henderson, speaking of the power of iambic speech, comments: "[P]ublic attacks on individuals relied for their forcefulness . . . upon the belief that words, especially words sung by a poet, had magical and even lethal power. The malefic individual *will* of the iambic poet could, through his words, become sovereign over the powers of nature" (1991, 17–18).

18. Romilly quotes Baudelaire's contention that to use a language well is to practice a sort of magic, "une espèce de sorcellerie évocatoire" (1975, 85).

19. See Kotansky (1991, 107), who remarks that nearly everyone in Rome would have had resort at some point in his or her life to the work of magic for gaining some practical end (involving illness, lovers, legal disputes, etc.).

20. See Rudd (1966, 154–59) for a clear discussion of the two genres and the extent to which they are like and unlike each other.

Chapter 1. The Limits of Satire, *Iam satis est*

The epigraphs are taken from Long and Sedley 1987, 1:150 (2:155).

1. Freudenburg (1993) has sensitive readings of *Sat.* 1.1–3 in terms of Callimachean aesthetics and their contemporary philosophical context, but these poems are still not seen as a part of the whole book. In a later work Freudenburg is less patient with these poems, whose speaker, he says, "is not much of a philosopher at all. But neither is he much of a satirist" (2001, 7).

2. *DRN* 1.936–37. The commentaries note that *praeterea* is a favorite Lucretian conjunction.

3. The popular ethical stance Horace conveys in the *Satires* is so overwhelmingly masculine in aim and interest that I make no attempt to produce generalizing pronouns that are gender neutral; the insights of Horace's philosophical moralizing may be useful to any human being, but his own application is to the humans known as men.

4. In its closing, *Sat.* 1.1 remarks: "When I'm asking you not to be a miser I'm not ordering you to be a spendthrift" (103–4). The opening of 1.2 concerns the irony of one extremely wealthy usurer, Fufidius, whose fear of being thought a spendthrift drives him to extremes of torment, first of his clients, then of himself (1.2.12–22).

5. Cf. expressions such as "he's led around by his dick," or from the German, "when the penis stands up, the mind goes to sleep."

6. See Fraenkel on "the magnificence of the obsolete *prognatum*" (1957, 82).

7. See, for example, Cantarella (1992), Habinek (1997), and much else.

8. What Epicureans would call "natural" desires. Natural desires are good and can be satisfied, unlike those deformed by false or empty belief, which do not obey the limits of nature, and which cause misery.

Chapter 2. Horace and His Fathers

1. *Sat.* 2.1.30–34, where Horace implicitly identifies his own habit with that of Lucilius, who, says Horace, confided his secrets to his books, so that his whole life is there revealed as if laid out on votive tablets. Of the centuries of readers who have reported that they have found "a kind of friend," Charles Martindale (1993, 11) remarks: "So striking an inscribing of the self is not found commonly in literature."

2. *Sat.* 2.6.17: "quid prius illustrem satiris musaque pedestri?" Freudenburg (1993, 153) notes the Stoic precept that speech ought to reflect and be consistent with life, and to favor a rough-hewn, authentic style of speech (and person) over "smooth-fitting words," which suggest dishonesty, "flash versus substance," and he contrasts this with the careful style of Horace. My view is that Horace does present that type of consistency in this poem, by rendering his life in such a way as to make it seem as carefully wrought as his speech.

3. Gowers says of the genre's name: "*[S]atura* was originally some kind of mixed dish named by analogy with a person or his stomach, mixed with a great variety of things and bursting at the seams" (1993b, 110).

4. The sincerity, and the meaning, of the opening lines to 1.4 is a scholarly crux on the Horatian literary stance in the *Satires*. See Anderson (1963, 1–37); for an account of the views and their partisans, see Freudenburg (1993, 96–105) and A. Parker (1986, 44 and 155).

5. A. Parker comments: "Lucilius's nature and that of his subject matter is ultimately referred to as *dura,* an adjective often used to express the lack of literary cultivation" (1986, 49). Cf. *Sat.* 1.10.56ff. For Horace's poetic generation, the adjective *durus* of course holds great ambivalence, containing as it does the fully positive charge of masculinity but working against the modernizing impulses of first-century BCE poetics.

6. See introduction; blame speech in turn attracts blame and ridicule to its speaker.

7. On the literary theory at issue in the mock debate of vv. 38–62, see Freudenburg (1993, 119–52).

8. Freudenburg (1993, 119–50) is illuminating on the dismemberment of Ennius (for whom Horace's regard is elsewhere not high), noting Aristotle's comparison in the *Poetics* (7.1450b34–51a6; also 8.1451a30–35) of a "beautiful tragedy to a living creature, whose limbs, though reckoned separately, are integrally connected to one another and in perfect proportion to the whole. To alter this arrangement, he [Aristotle] suggests, is equivalent to severing the limbs of a living creature and, thus, destroying or disfiguring the whole. . . . The double significance of τὰ μέρη, 'parts,' or 'limbs,' coupled with the surgical metaphors that conclude the passage (διαφέρεσθαι καὶ κινεῖσθαι) makes clear that Aristotle again has in mind the analogy between a poem and a living body" (121).

9. On Lucilian parodies of Accius and Pacuvius, see Lejay (1911, 139) and Fiske (1920, 456).

10. The epic diction and the portentous future imperative *caveto* have a wholly undermining effect on the seriousness of the poet here.

11. Leach (1971, 630) notes that the comparative *liberius,* "rather free," tones down the *multa cum libertate* (5) of Old Comedy and Lucilius. Anderson (1963, 4–5) sees a portrait of Lucilius in the drunken dinner guest.

12. Leach (1971, 619) notes that Horace Sr., having been a slave, has no ancestors

of his own, so refers to the whole tradition of Roman virtue for pedagogic use with his son. I would go further and note that Horace suggests in this poem that he has no *literary* ancestors; while Lucilius is descended from Greek Old Comedy, Horace is the product of a biological/material influence that he himself makes into a literary one.

13. The phrase recalls too the compressed Horatian poetic style. As Bramble says, Horace implies "that his virtuous self-questioning leaves a desirable mark on his style" (1974, 22).

14. As Leach says, "Horace has constructed a purely literary background for Lucilius, but attributes his own artistry to a non-literary source" (1971, 618). Leach's fine article on this poem demonstrates the similarity of the portrait of Horace's father in 1.4 to Demea, the father in Terence's *Adelphoe*. Leach argues, however, that because Demea is proved foolish in Terence's play, the similarity to Horace's father indicates irony in Horace's *pietas* toward his father, and that the self-irony thus implied allows Horace to apologize for Lucilian elements in his own work. While I agree with Leach that the portrait of Horace's father operates to divide Horace from Lucilius, and that Horace is never entirely free of irony, I think that the *pietas* of the portrait is sincere; the *pater ardens* provides a foil to the "real" father in the satire, giving Horace an ethical edge over Lucilius in his satiric practice.

15. *Sat.* 1.10.46–48: "hoc erat, experto frustra Varrone Atacino / atque quibusdam aliis, melius quod scribere possem, / inventore minor" (this [the genre of satire], which Varro of Atax tried in vain, as did some others, was what I might write with more success, though lesser than its inventor).

16. Most mythic representations of sons killing fathers seem to reflect not the offspring's defiance but the parent's fear, the fear of the one who feels his authority diminish as the child's strength increases.

The infuriating and elegiac (elegiac in the sense of lament) work by Harold Bloom, on the issue of poetic fathers and sons was not, I confess, either an influence or an anxiety in my thinking on *Sat.* 1.4 and 1.6, but *The Anxiety of Influence* (1973) is a book well worth reading for anyone who has ever wondered about anything. I find intriguing, for example, Bloom's recurrent use of "flowing" and "flooding" metaphors to describe the activity of a precursor's poetic influence on the poet, precisely the metaphor Horace deploys to criticize Lucilius ("cum flueret lutulentus, erat quod tollere velles," 1.4.11; "dixi fluere hunc lutulentum, saepe ferentem / plura quidem tollenda relinquendis," 1.10.50–51). "The word 'influence'," Bloom writes, "had received the sense of 'having a power over another' as early as the Scholastic Latin of Aquinas, but not for centuries was it to lose its root meaning of 'inflow'" (26) and, again, "The anxiety of influence is an anxiety in expectation of *being flooded*. . . . The ephebe [Bloom's term for the younger, influenced poet] who fears his precursors as he might fear a flood is taking a vital part for a whole, the whole being everything that constitutes his creative anxiety, the spectral blocking agent in every poet. Yet this metonymy is hardly to be avoided; every good reader properly *desires* to drown, but if the poet drowns, he will become *only a reader*" (57). Horace has traditions of his own (see, e.g., Scodel 1987, 204; Freudenburg 1993, 189) for the tradition of speaking of poetic "flooding" in reference to overabundant words, but it is interesting to note, in light of Bloom's thesis, that the poetic father is a block to the poet's creativity, that Bloom speaks, as Horace does, of what needs to be removed.

17. On the phrase "naso suspendis adunco," Wickham says, "the suggestion that the purpose of curling the nose is to hang on it the object of contempt is a comic touch of Horace's" (1903, ad loc.); there is, however, the modern (derived from Yiddish?) taunt, "it should hang from your nose." See too John Henderson's remark on the nose, "that favourite organ of Satire" (1989b, 91).

18. The phrase appears three times in 1.6, vv. 6, 45, and 46, and in variant forms: "quali sit quisque parente natus" (6–7); "ingenuo . . . non . . . patre natus" (21); "'quo patre natus?'" (29); "quo patre sit natus" (36); "non ego me claro natum patre" (58); "non patre praeclaro" (64). Gordon Williams's argument that the label for Horace's father of *libertinus* is deeply misleading—that Horace's father was in fact a well-heeled and well-connected member of the Sabine aristocracy who got into political trouble and briefly suffered the customary punishment of enslavement—makes Horace's choice of his father's portrait in 1.6 all the more interesting. Although Williams suggests that the "essential falsity" of the portrait in 1.6 "would be immediately apparent" (1995, 312), Horace has successfully fooled most of his readers, as the need for Williams's reconstruction demonstrates.

19. *Sat.* 1.6.46: "rodunt omnes libertino patre natum" (they all carp at me because I am a freedman's son). Horace uses the term *rodunt*, "biting" or "gnawing," which is also the verb describing the activity of the faithless friend in 1.4.81, "absentem qui rodit amicum," who serves to demonstrate that Horace is, by contrast, a satirist who does no harm. Nagy points out that in archaic Greek "blaming is made parallel to biting," and that the language of blame is correlated to the language of devouring meat (1979, 225). Horace, liking to have it both ways, is here the victim of satire, as well as its practitioner.

20. See White (1978, 85) on the role of the literary *amicus* as providing a readership for the poet and the far greater importance of that over material support, which in most cases was not necessary—certainly not in Horace's—despite the generically useful notion of his poor background.

21. Rudd (1966, 43) links *pudicum* to the previous lines (81–82), which describe how Horace's father chaperoned his son on his school rounds, and suggests that the word refers specifically to protecting the boy from the sort of sexual naughtiness that Juvenal and Quintilian allude to as a danger in classrooms. The word *pudicus*, however, can also denote a more general sense of modesty, decency, or bashfulness (s.v. Lewis and Short, *pudicus;* and *OLD* second entry), and I suspect Horace exploits here both senses.

22. See Rudd (1966, 41), Williams (1995, 298), and Oliensis (1998, 30–36). Horace elsewhere has no trouble confessing his poetic excellence—for example, "exegi monumentum aere perennius" (*Odes* 3.30.1), or, within the first book of the *Satires*, the unconvincing modesty of Horace's hopes for his poetic audience, 1.10.81–91, from which audience he explicitly excludes those whom he scorns.

23. See Lacey (1986, 121–44), who notes: "An acceptance of this idea [the inequality of citizens] lies at the root of the patron-client relationship, since this relationship also illustrates the Romans' acceptance of inequalities between free men, and relationships in which one man has a claim on another inherited from a paterfamilias by his *heres* or *heredes*. This hereditability of the relationship, based though it was on *fides*, and not on the total subservience in property matters of those in *postestas*, nevertheless shows the Roman notion that inequality was acceptable" (124).

24. *OLD* s.v. *patronus*—[*pater* . . .]; the suffix -*nus* (-*onus*) indicating "enlargement," cf. *colonus*.

25. See Lacey: "It was also perhaps because of *patria potestas* that the Romans acknowledged the fact that all citizens were not equal" (1986, 133).

26. On the satirist as an excluded figure, see, for instance, Witke (1965, 135–37), in his review of *St. Jerome the Satirist* by David S. Wiesen, who notes the characteristic solitude of the satirist in his praise for Wiesen's portrait of "one of the world's most lonely and learned men" (Wiesen 1964, 19).

27. Bramble links Horace's Callimacheanism to his depiction of his material world in 2.6: "[T]he satirist's modest Callimachean professions are matched by similarly modest social and economic conditions" (1974, 22). In this view Callimacheanism puts the low genre of satire on high poetic ground. See too, for Horace's satiric Callimacheanism, Zetzel (2002, 41).

28. Bramble notes: "[S]tylistic ideology is now tailored to βίος, most notably in Horace" (1974, 163).

29. And, as Oliensis (1998, 34) points out, the starkness of the father's social ambition for his son is cloaked in the most moral desire that Horace have a good education. Johnson (1993, 28–31) perceives fissures in Horace's portrait of his life and his father and considers the psychological effect on the young Horace of the father's vaulting ambition, the son's resentment at being made a tool of his father's ambition, and the consequent unmitigated, authentic yearning for freedom that Johnson sees informing Horace's poetic life and work.

30. See Duckworth (1952, 243–45) for summarizing notes on fathers and sons in Terence and Plautus. Segal (1968, 15–21) sets the Plautine treatment of fathers and sons succinctly in both its Roman sociological and Freudian context. Konstan says: "In ancient Rome, paternal power was very great, and could extend well into the adult life of the sons and daughters. This authority doubtless caused the children some anxiety, which may have been relieved in some measure by the spectacle of stern old men tweaked and outwitted by youths and slaves and marginal members of society" (1983, 19).

Chapter 3. Practicing Theory, or, Perils of the Open Road

1. For a summary of the debate concerning the date and historical context of this poem's events, see Rudd (1966, 54 and 280–81). Current opinion favors the spring of 37, but another meeting of Antony and Octavian, in the autumn of 38, is also a candidate. Musurillo (1955, 159–62) describes the scholarly debate on this point, noting that Palmer (1893) favors the autumn of 38 on the evidence of the gnats in the satire, Gow (1901) the spring of 37 on the evidence of the frogs. DuQuesnay (1984, 19–58), arguing in general for a consideration of the political dimension of *Sermones* I, says of the time: "The administration of politics was in chaos and Italy was infested with brigands, its ports blockaded and afflicted with famine" (39–40).

2. Critical irritation at the "substitution" of important historical and cultural evidence with travel trivia in this poem is notable. Palmer (1893) assesses the poem as "interesting but on the whole disappointing"; Morris (1909) notes: "The satire has a certain accidental interest from the glimpses it gives of the manner of traveling in the year 38 BC [*sic*] and it contains a few interesting personal allusions . . . , but it is for the most part made up of trivialities. It falls short to a surprising degree of the account which *we should expect* [my italics] Horace to give of a fortnight's association with a group of men so cultivated and so eminent"; Gibbon: "'The maxim that every thing in great men is interesting applies only to their minds and ought not to be extended to their bodies'" (Rudd 1966, 57, quotes Gibbon); Freudenburg notes: "We might expect some rather deep reflection from the satirist on the gravity of the situation, a description of Sextus Pompey's menacing fleet or an account of the serious counsel he offered Maecenas along the way" (1993, 203). DuQuesnay, who is not irritated, justifies Horace's material on diplomatic, not literary, grounds: "Horace is notoriously reticent about the political context and his account is noticeably free of all tensions . . . he transforms a recent moment of threat and crisis into something familiar, ordinary, and amusing" (1984, 40).

3. See Ehlers (1985, 69–83) on the poem as *recusatio*, its recollection of the *Odyssey,* and Horace's acquaintance with the structure of the *Aeneid,* the work of another companion on the journey.

4. Nonius is the great source for the fragments of Lucilius, but other writers of a literary bent quote Lucilius until the end of the empire. For great clarity and good sense on the fragments of Lucilius, see E. H. Warmington (1938). The collection of Lucilius's fragments by Marx (1904) is the other standard text for Lucilius; Krenkel's 1970 edition, ill-treated by reviewers, attempts to assemble and translate the fragments with more coherence than they perhaps justify.

5. Quoted by Fiske (1920, 306). Fiske notes the sense of "rivalry" contained in *aemulatur* and the inadequacy of the word "model" to convey the whole meaning of this type of ancient literary imitation, which contains aspects both of competition with, and tribute to, the older poet, elaborating and refining the tradition

in which the younger poet is working. Knoche notes: "With the *Iter Brundisium* in the fifth satire he entered into competition with the *Iter Siculum* of Lucilius" (1975, 79). The poem about the trip to Sicily is believed to belong to Lucilius's *Satires*, book 3, fragments 94–148, in Warmington (Marx 1904, 97–146). Concerning the whole genre of journey poem, before and after Lucilius and Horace, cf. Lejay (1911, 140–43), Rudd (1966, 281n4), Gowers (1993a, 48–66, 62n9).

6. Note that the poem's opening announces the trip's starting point but only the destination of its first day, Aricia.

7. Gowers suggests that Horace's companion was a book: "At *Sat.* 2.3.11–12 he names four Greek writers as his 'companions' on a writing-trip: *quorsum pertinuit stipare Platona Menandro, / Eupolin, Archilochum, comites educere tantos?* Cf. Martial 14.188 on a parchment volume of Cicero: *si comes ista tibi fuerit membrana, putato / carpere te longas cum Cicerone vias*" (1993a, 63n32); this would explain the subsequent absence of Heliodorus from the action in 1.5.

8. See Fiske (1920, 306–16) for a full, if adventuresome, account of Lucilian echoes in this poem. Some appear to belong to the journey to Sicily satire, others, by Fiske's reckoning, seem borrowed from elsewhere in Lucilius's work. It is obviously never possible to be sure, given the random condition of Lucilius's transmission. See Rudd (1966, 54ff.) for some of the arguments with Fiske and in general with the methods of discovering Lucilius through Horace.

9. Just as *amicus*, "friend," can describe a patron or a client, similarly the word also describes public, political "friends," in which case other senses of the word that connote intimate attachments are not relevant.

10. Of the condition of the *lippus*, Gow says that the condition was "a form of ophthalmia which was very common in Rome. . . . Probably the purblind condition of the *lippus* made him ridiculous" (1901, ad loc.).

11. Gowers, speaking of the epic that is missing from the poem, notes: "Meanwhile, the only explicit treaty of the poem is a tryst made with a girl who lets Horace down and causes him to have a wet dream" (1993a, 56).

12. Contrast Catullus 32.10–11, where the satisfaction the poet wants and anticipates matches his desire, *satur*, in other ways already: "nam pransus iaceo et satur supinus / pertundo tunicamque palliumque" (for I am full of lunch lying here on my back, and my boner is poking at my tunic and my cloak).

13. See Brink for clarification of the town's identity (1995, 296–313).

14. See Hopkinson (1988) on Theocritus *Idyll* IX, where he notes that Philoxenus (400 BCE) wrote a satirical dithyramb in which Dionysius I of Syracuse is depicted as "the unperceptive monster Polyphemus." It is the first literary appearance of the Cyclops in love.

15. Suetonius tells us in his *Vita* of Horace that Horace regretted his allegiance to the republicans after Philippi and received a post as a [quaestor] *scriba*. Horace alludes to this in *Sat.* 2.6. See Armstrong (1986) for a full and interesting discussion of Horace's status as an *eques* and the significance of the post of *scriba*. Armstrong

indicates, as does White (1993), that the friendship with Maecenas would not have much altered the poet's already materially comfortable circumstances.

16. This is Palmer's guess (1891). Wickham (1903) suggests an array of meanings, none of them contradicting the idea of inappropriate pretensions to status by Aufidius.

17. *scurra*, s.v. *OLD*: "A fashionable city idler, man about town; (the term came to be used mainly with ref. to the offensive wit affected by such a person, and from Augustan times denoted a professional buffoon or sim.)."

18. Satire had a predisposition to epic parody in Lucilius, and Horace makes full use of it in this poem. Some commentators have suggested that fitness for epic parody was in fact a motive for Lucilius to settle on hexameters as the meter for his satire. Horace takes up the hexameter verse of Lucilius for satire, and it is henceforward Roman satire's meter. See Fiske (1920, 156) and Richlin (1992, 172).

19. Lucilius 109–14 Warmington / 117–20 Marx are the fragmentary lines believed to belong to a similar entertainment in Lucilius's satire. See Fiske (1920, 308), but also see the remarks of Coffey (1976, 230n55).

20. Rome knew much about civil wars by this time; see Rudd (1966, 36–37) and DuQuesnay (1984, passim).

21. Discounting hunger and fatigue as physical rather than emotional states, the only other emotions are exhibited among the hapless attendants to the journey—the anger of the slaves, boatmen, and travelers; the mock anger of the buffoons; and the fear of the slaves as they try to escape Vulcan's tongue with dinner (75–76). Gowers notes: "The real peak of the poem is Horace's reunion with his poetic friends: on such a footloose journey, friendship is the only bond" (1993a, 58).

22. Cf., e.g., DuQuesnay (1984), who considers it virtually impossible that Horace would be critical of Maecenas and Octavian, even in the context of satire. Henderson, in the opposite corner but equally skeptical that Horace is capable of dissent in this, thinks the same: "he [Horace] is the exemplum of the world being fashioned by Maecenas, which is to say by Octavian Caesar" (184, 1999).

23. As Freudenburg says, "This is the critique of *Satires* 1.4 made real. Talk about satire has become the genuine article" (1993, 202–3).

Chapter 4. Satire as Conflict Irresolution

1. Rudd (1966, 64–67) provides a representative of the impulse to discount the poem. Others, however, have seen various serious purposes at work in it. Schröter (1967), Buchheit (1968), and Van Rooy (1971) see articulations of literary critical theory in the Homeric parodies and the arrangement of the satire in its book; DuQuesnay (1984, 34) views the poem's litigants as identified with a republicanism that Horace, as *amicus Maecenatis*, now mocks. John Henderson's compelling and disequilibrating essay on 1.7 is salutary for any tempted to overlook the lack

of innocence in either the poem or its critical reception: "[M]ost commentary has obediently taken up the work of be-littling that the poem represents and in its work of representation incites" (1994, 148).

2. For Horace's ongoing relationship with the magical-invective figure of Canidia, see Oliensis: "Horace alludes to Canidia *en passant* as if to establish her as a fixture in his poetic world" (1991, 109); Canidia appears in *Epodes* 3, 5, 17, *Sat.* 1.8, 2.1, and she provides the last breath of the *Satires* in 2.8 (see ch. 5).

3. This criticism is reprised at 1.10.50, in self-justification.

4. Horace's spare style slips into a whole disposition of restraint in 1.4: he doesn't recite in the forum, but only to friends and only when compelled; nor does he make careless attacks on others.

5. *Sat.* 1.2, which applies this satirical program to sexuality, argues that the body's needs are simple and that it is immoderate desires that get people in trouble. At 1.2.68–71, a man's penis is the speaker of reason, noting the limits of its wishes; the body provides the natural, and right, limits to desire. For Horace in general, indulgence of desire leaps past the boundaries of the body, for instance, greed in 1.1, sexual ambition in 1.2; what we can imagine will make us happier, less mortal, larger in life, has the opposite effect. Freudenburg, in discussing the philosophical disposition Horace adopts in *Satires* I, notes that *iam satis est*, at 1.1.120, "links the satirist's stylistic principles . . . to the traditional moral values he has preached throughout" (1993, 192). Horace's recurrent puns on *sat-* reinforce the point that satire is a genre driven by the concept of "sufficiency."

6. *Venenum* is the stuff of Canidia's troublesome work in *Sat.* 1.8.19, and in *Sat.* 2.1.48 *venenum* is Canidia's defensive weapon, favorably compared to Horace's *stilus* (2.1.39); *pus*, the festering matter of a sore, is found in Lucilius, who says that Lucius Trebellius calls it up, along with fevers and debility and vomit ("in numero quorum nunc primus Trebellius multost / Lucius, nam arcessit febris senium vomitum pus," 494–95 Marx / 531–32 Warmington).

7. Lucilius, in Horace's account, is *durus componere versus*, 1.4.8; at 1.10.57, Horace calls the nature of Lucilius's material *dura*.

8. Lucilius frag. 1227 Marx / 1076 Warmington: "nunc ad te redeo." See Fiske (1919). Fraenkel (1957, 121 and 103) notes this particular allusion and its partner in *Sat.* 1.6.45.

9. While it is sorely tempting to construct a parodic connection between Horace's critique of heroic *virtus* here and our long fragment of Lucilius, the so-called *virtus* fragment (1326–38 Marx / 1196–208 Warmington), I am wary of such an impulse. Horace had some thirty thousand more verses of Lucilius to play off of and be influenced by than we do, and what we have in the *virtus* fragment from Lucilius seems to explore a very different strain of the semantic range in *virtus* from that which Horace is exploring in 1.7.

10. The iambic tradition, beginning with Archilochus, did, of course, contain the idea that words could be lethal, a tradition that Horace and the Romans knew

well. For a discussion of the movement from magical invective to satire in the course of the development of culture and literature, see Elliott 1960.

11. On *par pugnat* and *compositum*, see, e.g., *Sat.* 1.1.102–3: "pergis pugnantia secum / frontibus adversis componere"; at 2.6.44, Maecenas asks the poet: "Thraex est Gallina Syro par?" The technical language of gladiatorial conflict is frequently deployed by Roman writers metaphorically for both epic and political contexts. Barton (1992) discusses the growth of the significance of the gladiatorial arena in the late republic and early empire as a metaphor for civil war (see p. 38, on Lucan in the *Bellum Civile* 4.705–10, for a conjunction of the epic and the political). See too Barton's remarks on the necessity of equal opponents: "[T]here was, quite literally, no triumph without equality" (182).

12. "flumen," 27; "fluenti," 29; "expressa," 28; "perfusus," 32; Parker remarks of the relation between Horace and Lucilius in *Sat.* 1.5: "We are meant to compare the two satirists, and Horace ensures that we do by invoking over and over the imagery of mud and water with which he had damned Lucilius in the poem before" (1986, 73). The process continues in 1.7.

13. DuQuesnay (1984, 37) recognizes the political nature of Horace's "word act" here but denies it any daring by situating Horace snugly under Maecenas's wing at his writing of the poem. DuQuesnay's view of the poem as a send-up of republican pretensions to *libertas* and *virtus* and written, as he suggests were all ten satires of Horace's first book, for the poet's friend Maecenas goes against the view that 1.7 must have been written before Philippi in 42 BCE.

14. One argument for the early composition of *Sat.* 1.7 is based on the assumption that the joke involving Brutus would be tasteless to make *after* his death; but as Rudd (1966, 66) wonders, why publish it at all in that case? The secondary argument is that the poem's style and construction are immature, i.e., not to the liking of the editor in question. Palmer remarks: "[T]hough the poor pun celebrated might at the time it was uttered be deemed worthy of a poetic address . . . to recur to it after years would show weakness and silliness of mind" (1893, 208). Dryden hated the poem and, speaking of the conclusion, says: "[A] miserable clench, in my opinion, for Horace to record. I have heard honest Mr. Swan make many a better, and yet have had the grace to hold my countenance" (quoted by Anthon [1860, 466]). Rudd considers the poem a failure (66–67). Fraenkel (1957, 118–21), succinct and wise on the question of dating *Sat.* 1.7 (there is no cause to think it is early), is delighted by it, though he classes it among the poems that Horace pulled from his portfolio to round up the number of poems in the first book of *Satires* to ten, in emulation of Vergil's *Eclogues* (along with 1.8 and 1.9); cf. Zetzel (1980, 73n3) on the relation between the *Eclogues* and the *Satires*. Coffey thinks the final pun "lacks civilized decorum" and sees the poem as "an inept make-weight" (1976, 78). John Henderson (1994, 154) revises a similar catalog of annoyance.

15. The very evident Roman fondness for puns in their literature makes moot the critical rejection of *Sat.* 1.7 on the grounds of not liking puns. Porphyrio calls

the pun on Rex "urbanissimus iocus." See Van Rooy on "the Roman love for word-play, including puns on names" (1971, 81n54).

16. John Henderson calls this moment "the *sparagmos* of the Signifier, our glimpse of the body politic lynching Language" (1994, 163).

17. This is (part of) John Henderson's point, "there is always unfinished business with Caesars" (1994, 151), and, "Horace won't get rid of Brutus's memory, of Brutuses, of the replicability of '*Brutus*', so easily as the *ultio* got rid of Brutus" (167).

Chapter 5. Talking Heads and Canidian Poetics

1. "huic si mutonis verbis mala tanta videnti / diceret haec animus: 'quid vis tibi? numquid ego a te / magno prognatum deposco consule cunnum / vela-tumque stola mea cum conferbuit ira?'" (*Sat.* 1.2.68–71, If the brain of this man who's seen so much trouble were to speak to him with the words of his prick, he'd say this: "what do you want? am *I* asking for a daughter of a famous man, pussy dressed in pearls, when my blood is up?").

For another example of this conversational genre, see the sixteenth-century *Lullaby* of George Gascoigne, where the host instructs his organ. On Priapus as a talking artifact, see Fraenkel (1957, 121–22) and O'Connor (1989, passim).

2. Anderson considers the likeness of the persona of Horace to his narrator, Priapus, in this poem, the similarities between the encounter of Priapus and the two women (Anderson calls them witches) and that of Persius and Rex in 1.7, and the dramatically similar situations of Priapus in 1.8 and Horace in 1.9, in which both narrators escape a Lucilian force; Horace's escape in 1.9 is, Anderson remarks obviously, "less gross" (1982).

3. Richlin notes: "The god himself can be construed as a talking phallus" (1992, 116).

4. For the Greek origins of Priapus, his development as a Roman deity, and the *Priapea*, see Rudd (1966, 68–70), Buchheit (1962), Richlin (1992), and W. H. Parker (1988). I have used Parker's text for references to the *Priapea*.

5. Anderson remarks that Priapus "seems devoid of the salty lust normally exhibited and boasted about by the god of the *Priapea* and familiar myths" (1982, 79).

6. Priapus's substance is a poor wood, easily split and associated with little substance; cf. Theoc. *Id.* 10.45, ἀνὴρ σύκινος, and S. S. Ingallina (1974, 181). Rudd (1966, 283n27) notes the association of fig wood with amulets, with triviality and contempt (English: "I don't care a fig"), and with fertility. Kiessling and Heinze (1961, ad loc.) cite Pliny, *N.H.* 16.209, for the value of fig wood.

7. This text taken from Hooper (1999). On the possible orifices suggested by *ara*, "altar," see O'Connor (1989, 157). On *ara* for female genitalia, see Adams (1982, 87).

8. The positive identification of the wood god in Pr. 10 is actually a joke about

how badly he is carved: he has to announce that he is a Priapus because he is otherwise unrecognizable.

9. A fig-wood Priapus does not appear in the Hellenistic epigrams. For Horace's other literary sources for Sat. 1.8, see O'Connor (1989, 83).

10. See Adams (1982) for *hortus = culus* (*anus*) (84) and for *ficus*, "anal sore" (113).

11. Anderson says of 1.8 that it "records one of the first topographical changes that anticipate those of Augustan Rome" (1982, 74); see too his citation of Lugli, *I monumenti antichi di Roma e Suburbio*, III (Rome, 1938), 456 ff. Cf. Steinby (1996, 3:74–75) on the topography, and Bodel (1994, 38–59) for a full examination of the legal and physical relation between the graveyard and the gardens. For a more ironic view of the satire, the gardens, and Horace, see John Henderson: "As Agrippa tackled the sewers of Rome and Maecenas transformed inner-city mass-graves into pleasure-gardens where culture could flower, the poet's eye could see a start to the development of the *Urbs*. . . . As Octavian's friend Maecenas saved Italy from war (with Antony), so Maecenas's friend Horace saved the *horti* from sliding back into darkness" (1989a, 62). Henderson, like Anderson, views Horace in his poetic activity as a partner with Maecenas in the project of creating a "new" Rome, but he is critical, presenting Horace as a feeble player in a corrupt game of masculine hegemony. But as I see it, the poem admits too much dissenting material from the "old" Rome and "old" satire to allow us take Horace as an unambivalent backer of "new" power. The exercise of power in any form seems too much under suspicion in *Satires I* to completely justify this view.

12. Rudd (1966, 70) seems to suggest that the gardens envisaged were mid-construction at the writing of the poem, so perhaps vestiges of the old graveyard were still visible. But the poem does not say this and it presents the graveyard as a thing of the past, supplanted by what is now visible (*nunc licet . . .*). Priapus's focus on the former appearance of the gardens somewhat undermines the idea expressed by Anderson and others that Horace is presenting the place where he joins Maecenas and his friends for relaxation (first suggested by Porphyrio, ad loc. 1.8.7). The "new" versus the "old" garden is used by Anderson to support the idea that associates Horace, Maecenas, and this desexed Priapus with confidence in the new order coming to Rome. I regard this idea with suspicion.

13. The English translation "witch" for *quae* (19), and generally for Canidia and Sagana in this poem, is somewhat misleading, to the extent that the Latin only designates them as females, in fact a more disquieting representation. "Witch" makes them a special subset of the class of women, a refinement the Latin does not offer: it is potential in the nature of female to be menacing.

14. Lewis and Short, s.v. *pallor*, notes it is in contrast to *ruber*.

15. For details of the magical activities, representative of their type, see Ingallina (1974, 79–108, 181–93), Lejay (1911, intro. to *Sat.* 1.8 and ad loc.), and Rudd (1966, 283nn29–34).

16. Some commentators assume that Varus is involved in this ritual and is represented by the waxen image, that the presence of Canidia in this satire automatically connects somehow to the drama of *Epodes* 5, but nothing in this poem supports that assumption.

17. See Adams (1982, 67, 212, 227) on the enduring nature in Latin of this metaphor.

18. See Richlin (1992, 26) on invective and the *os impurum*.

19. See Anderson (1982, 79–80) on the link formed by *venenum* and *ultus* (1.7.1–2) between *Sat*. 1.7 and 1.8.

20. See Hallett (1981, 341–47) on Priapus's piles as a result of being a pathic, and O'Connor (1989, 154 and passim).

21. Regarding the pun, see Hinds (1987, 16–17): "Few word-plays are more familiar in Latin poetry than the one between the bodily and metrical senses of the word *pes*." The unknotted hair of the women is part of the magical scene, which forbids any "binding" to allow for the flow of magical influence (see Ingallina [1974, 91–95] and Kiessling and Heinze [1961, ad loc.]); but see too John Henderson (1989a, 61) on the women "unleashed," alluding to their potential sexual menace.

22. Cf. Freudenburg (1993, 79); see too Oliensis (1991, esp. 110–17) on the dual implications of dogs for Canidia and Horace.

23. Cf. Rudd (1966, 71), Kiessling and Heinze (1961, ad loc.), and Ingallina (1974, 101–3).

24. *Flaccus* (limp) as John Henderson notes: "Priapus becomes the spent force of H *Flaccus*, unbecomingly unmanned, impotent before the (ch)arms of Woman" (1989a, 60).

25. On the pervasive use of magic in daily life in antiquity, see Kotansky (1991, 107–37) and Graf (1997, 1–2). For evidence of magic in literature, cf. Lowe (1929) and Tavenner (1916), a useful but somewhat more naive account than Lowe's.

26. This is Rudd (1966, 72), whom Henderson quotes, pointing out that Rudd's locution itself has an allegiance to masculine hierarchy: "The *telling* of the story *does* metamorphose the frightening witches into 'a pair of silly old hags.' The male voice uses its monopoly of language to do so" (1989b, 111).

27. Oliensis notes that Canidia closes both the *Satires* and the *Epodes* and "is thus a structural counterpart to Maecenas, who is invoked at the beginnings of both collections" (1991, 110). Oliensis suggests that the origins of invective are in impotence, and that both Canidia and Maecenas are a drain on Horace's resources (Canidia supplies the otherwise absent mother to Horace, and she is an unfit one).

28. The genre's name as *satura* appears in *Sat*. 2.1.1, interestingly, to open the second book, and at 2.6.17.

Chapter 6. Auditor—Adiutor

1. I refer to the talkative figure whom the poet encounters in 1.9 with the neutral designation "interlocutor," for reasons I describe later in the discussion

(despite the fact that "interlocutor" suggests a more successful exchange of speech than in fact occurs in the poem between Horace and his unwelcome companion).

2. Regarding the relationship with Maecenas, see *Sat.* 1.6; Horace, of course, will not say that his poetry was the cause of his inclusion in Maecenas's house.

3. Catullus 1.3–4, "namque tu solebas / meas esse aliquid putare nugas."

4. Note Horace's use of *mos* as a comprehensive assessment of character in "defendas ut tuus est mos" (you defend him in your way, 1.4.95), where Horace defends his own satiric practice by exposing the poverty of his accuser's character. His accuser's "way" reveals insufficient character to defend his friend unambivalently, and he cannot resist an arch comment on his friend's misdeeds. In the same poem, *mos* was the basis of the satirical Horace Sr.'s education of his son (1.4.117). The phrase summarizes Maecenas's laconic response on his first meeting of Horace, 1.6.60–61: "respondes, ut tuus est mos, / pauca."

5. See Fiske (1920, 330–36) and Anderson's discussion of his hypothesis (1956, 148–66). Rudd (1961) argues persuasively against the existence of the Lucilian prototype and those who would adopt it on Fiske's reconstruction of the Lucilian fragments; see esp. 90–96.

6. Lucilius fragments 1142 Marx / 258 Warmington: "Ibat forte domum. Sequimur multi atque frequentes." The other instance of the phrase in our fragments is 534 Marx / 559 Warmington: "Ibat forte aries," whose context the preservation makes much easier to construe; it is an amusing fragment concerning the great dangling weight (*onus*) of a ram's testicles: "'Ibat forte aries,' inquit, 'iam quod genus, quantis / testibus! vix uno filo hosce haerere putares, / pellicula extrema exaptum pendere onus ingens'" (534–36 Marx / 559–61 Warmington, "A ram happened to be going along," he said, "—now there's a species, what testicles! you'd think they clung by a single slender thread, this huge weight that dangled, attached to the edge of his fleece").

I am sorely tempted to connect *this* fragment to our satire, to have Horace jokingly recall the grotesque portrait of Lucilius's ram as he strolls the Sacred Way, informing the clinging weight of the interlocutor, affixed to himself, with the raunchy cheer of those Lucilian gonads; but this is, as Lucilius would say, a slender thread. Fraenkel (1957, 112–13) notes that the *ibat forte* formula is a common and old beginning to an anecdotal tale (αἶνος) going back to Archilochus.

7. 231–32 Marx / 267–68 Warmington: "So that it may be all the same and become a case of 'and him Apollo rescued'" (Warmington's translation).

8. As Fiske observes, "in keeping with his aversion to the mixture of Greek and Latin" (1920, 335). Anderson notes: "Horace is implicitly criticizing Lucilius for citing the original Greek" (1956, 148).

9. The hope too for the Lucilian model may reflect the reader's wish to see the interlocutor get the treatment he doesn't get in 1.9; a few loud words of abuse would be preferable to the mean slow-kill that *Sat.* 1.9 delivers to the nameless interlocutor.

10. Recall that the *cerebrosus* figure in *Sat.* 1.5.21 contrasts with the enduring suffering of Horace on the barge trip, evidence again that the overt angry response is not available to Horace.

11. Recall that in 1.7.17 it is the quality of being *pigrior* that allows for resolution to conflict.

12. To reprise the familiar lines: "nam fuit hoc vitiosus: *in hora saepe ducentos, / ut magnum, versus dictabat* stans pede in uno: / cum flueret lutulentus, erat quod tollere velles: / *garrulus* atque piger scribendi ferre laborem, / scribendi recti" (*Sat.* 1.4.9–13, for his failing was in this: as if it were a great achievement he would often dictate, in an hour, a couple hundred lines, and do it standing on one foot, so to say; in this muddy stream of verse there was some you would remove; he was chatty, and lazy at the work of writing—of writing rightly; as to how much he wrote, I won't waste time on that.).

"quid vetat et nosmet Lucili scripta legentis / quaerere, num illius, num rerum dura negarit / versiculos natura magis factos et euntis / mollius, ac si quis pedibus quid claudere senis, / hoc tantum contentus, *amet scripsisse ducentos / ante cibum versus, totidem cenatus*" (*Sat.* 1.10.56–61, What's to stop us, too, from reading what Lucilius wrote and wondering whether it was the toughness of the man, or of his material, that denied him poetry better fashioned and flowing more smoothly, than what you get when you slap on a meter of six feet, and are content that you wrote a couple hundred lines before your dinner, and as many when you've eaten?).

13. On Hermogenes as a poet without restraint or taste, see *Sat.* 1.3.129, 1.10.18, and 1.10.80.

14. I follow editors (here Borzsàk 1984) who punctuate the text to read vv. 29–34 as Horace's silent thought, rather than as words spoken out loud to the interlocutor, as Wickham's *OCT* text does.

15. The interlocutor's circumstances in the satire are ruled by chance ("casu," 36 and 74); contrast Horace's statement that it was no accident that he was befriended by Maecenas: "felicem dicere non hoc / me possim, casu quod te sortitus amicum" (1.6.52–53). Horace, who until this point has been pursued by the interlocutor, now says of himself: "ego, ut contendere durum est / cum victore, sequor" (42–43). Recall that Lucilius is *durus* (1.4.8). Horace, consistent with his conquered state, now is the follower. On the martial elements of the interlocutor, see Anderson (1956).

16. See White (1993, 37–38) on the unrealism of Horace's depiction in 1.9 of the associates of Maecenas and the likelihood of dissent among them. Of the interlocutor in 1.9, he comments: "Though his sentiments are meant to be repugnant, they cannot be dismissed as naive" (38).

17. Horace's imagined house of Maecenas also serves as a utopian opposite to the open, unregulated spaces of the Roman street, where he is vulnerable to such incursions on his mental peace as the one here. This is much in keeping with the general persona Horace promotes for himself, a poet of the elite whose ideal life

is quiet, countrified, cheered by select friends under his own roof; out on the democratic street, life is urban, noisy, and undifferentiated.

18. Curiously, the interlocutor refers to himself with a demonstrative pronoun: in his own speech *ille* becomes *hic* (44).

19. On Horace's Callimacheanism, see, e.g., Scodel (1987) and Zetzel (2002).

20. *Hymn to Apollo*, 105–7; Horace is surely alluding to the role of Envy in this hymn. See John Henderson (1999, 206). Tadeusz Mazurek (1997) makes a crucial corrective to the traditional reading of the dramatic outcome to *Satires* 1.9, whereby the "saving" Apollo performs is nothing of the kind for the poet. Mazurek persuasively shows that the practice in "antestari," to call someone as witness (a practice well known to any contemporary audience), would mean that the satirist, having offered his ear, is immediately dragged off to court *along with* his interlocutor, and has not escaped at all. Aristius Fuscus is then the Apollo who has *failed* to save Horace, and Mazurek interprets the final lines of the satire this way: "'Will you testify as a witness?' Alas, I offered my ear. He dragged him to court. Shouts everywhere; gawkers all around. You call this salvation, Apollo?" (vv. 76–78). Mazurek's reading only increases the impulse to pity the (self-ironizing) satirist whose vicitimization finishes the poem.

21. Anderson (1956) calls him the *garrulus*, borrowing from the verses of the Sabine *anus* that Horace recalls as he contemplates his inability to escape his companion and imminent death. For his other designations by critics affronted by the interlocutor's importuning, see Rudd (1966, 74). Coffey, who calls the character "a scheming social climber" (1976, 79) says, "Horace's importunate man is often referred to as 'the bore' but Rudd's label 'the pest' is perhaps the most *helpful* succinct designation" (230n69, my italics). Helpful to whom? Shackleton-Bailey has "a vulgar place-hunter" (1982, 20); John Henderson (1993) offers "careerist," with irony. Freudenburg (1993) has as an index entry: "bore, the."

22. Apart from the introductory *quidam*, the interlocutor is called *ille* in the poem, referred to seven times, four in the nominative, two in the dative, once in the accusative. Each instance falls at line end, as if to add syntactic exclusion to the rest.

23. That the poem is, for instance, a character sketch of a *garrulus* based on Theophrastus and Lucilius, cf. Theophrastus 3 and 7, Lucilius fragments 1138, 1142, 234, 230?, 236?, 228, 231–32 (Marx 1904–5); see Anderson (1956) and Rudd (1966, 74 and 284).

24. Although see John Henderson's frolicsome account of this satire (1993 and 1999, 202–27) for a dissenting and subversive view.

25. As if we too were in the newly built Esquiline gardens of Maecenas in the scenario Porphyrio envisages for 1.8.

26. See, e.g., 1.4.33, "omnes hi metuunt versus, odere poetas"; and the astonishing list of the readers Horace *chooses* (1.10.81–90), the great poets who are his contemporaries.

27. On Plotius and Varius, see 1.10.81 ff. and the discussion of this passage in chapter 7.

28. The *Sabella anus*, the old Sabine woman who is Horace's fortune-teller here, is at least kin, if not identical, to the *sagae* (wise women, cf. Sagana in *Sat.* 1.8) who chant spells, communicate with the dead, and are in general party to knowledge beyond the "masculine" Roman world of logos (Dickie 2001, 15, 131, 176).

Chapter 7. Unsatisfying Fulfillments

1. See especially *Sat.* 1.1.62, 119–20; 1.4.41, 54, 116.

2. On the poet and his audience, in 1.10: "rictum auditoris" (7–8); "legentes" (56); "paucis lectoribus" (74).

3. Gowers notes, "Horace uses the human appetite in Book I as his model for the proper recognition of limits, moral and literary" (1993b, 129).

4. Cf. *urbani* (13)—one of the styles for a satirist to imitate; *comis* of Fundanius (41); of Lucilius (53).

5. Again: "est modus in rebus, sunt certi denique fines, / quos ultra citraque nequit consistere rectum" (*Sat.* 1.1.106–7).

6. Striking quite a different poetic posture in the Epistle to Florus: "praetulerim scriptor delirus inersque videri, / dum mea delectent mala me vel denique fallant, / quam sapere et ringi" (*Epistles* 2.2.126–28, I'd rather be thought a witless and lazy writer, so long as my poor writings please—or I don't notice—than to be clever and snarling).

7. "di bene fecerunt, inopis me quodque pusilli / finxerunt animi, raro et perpauca loquentis" (1.4.17–18, the gods did well when they fashioned in me a spirit that's poor and short, that talks little and but rarely).

8. In Ennius's invocation to the Muses at the beginning of his *Annales* he recounts his dream that Homer appeared to him to say that his spirit was reincarnated in Ennius.

9. Note the similar wording in *Sat.* 2.1.62–64, with Lucilius tearing off skin: "cum *est* Lucilius *ausus* / primus in hunc operis componere carmina morem, / *detrahere* et pellem, nitidus qua quisque per ora / cederet, introrsum turpis" (*Sat.* 2.1.62–65, when Lucilius first dared to put together songs in this genre, and to tear off the skin that people wear for looking glamorous in public, while inside vile).

10. If we trust the scholiast on the figure of Arbuscula.

Bibliography

Adams, J. N. 1982. *The Latin Sexual Vocabulary.* Baltimore: Johns Hopkins University Press.

Anderson, W. S. 1955–56. "Poetic Fiction—Horace *Serm.* 1.5." *CW* 49:57–59.

———. 1956. "Horace, the Unwilling Warrior: Satire 1,9." *AJP* 77:148–66.

———. 1963. "The Roman Socrates: Horace and His *Satires.*" In *Critical Essays on Roman Literature,* vol. 2: *Satire,* ed. John P. Sullivan, 1–37. London: Routledge Kegan Paul.

———. 1974. "Autobiography and Art in Horace." In *Perspectives of Roman Poetry,* ed. G. Karl Galinsky, 33–56. Austin: University of Texas Press.

———. 1982. "The Form, Purpose, and Position of Horace's Satire 1,8." In *Essays on Roman Satire,* 74–83. Princeton, N.J.: Princeton University Press. Reprinted from *AJP* 93 (1972): 4–13.

Anthon, Charles. 1860. *The Works of Horace.* New York: Harper Brothers.

Armstrong, David. 1986. "*Horatius Eques et Scriba: Satires* 1.6 and 2.7." *TAPA* 116: 255–88.

———. 1989. *Horace.* New Haven, Conn.: Yale University Press.

Barton, Carlin. 1992. *Sorrows of the Ancient Romans.* Princeton, N.J.: Princeton University Press.

Bettini, Maurizio. 1991. *Anthropology and Roman Culture: Kinship, Time, Images of the Soul.* Baltimore: Johns Hopkins University Press.

Bloom, Harold. 1973. *The Anxiety of Influence: A Theory of Poetry.* Oxford: Oxford University Press.

Bodel, John. 1994. *Graveyards and Groves: A Study of the Lex Lucerina.* American Journal of Ancient History 11. Cambridge, Mass.: Harvard University Press.

Borzsàk, Stephan. 1984. *Q. Horati Flacci Opera.* Leipzig: Teubner.

Bowditch, Phebe Lowell. 2001. *Horace and the Gift Economy of Patronage.* Berkeley: University of California Press.

Bramble, John C. 1974. *Persius and the Programmatic Satire: A Study in Form and Imagery.* Cambridge: Cambridge University Press.

Brink, C. O. 1995. "Second Thoughts on Three Horatian Puzzles." In *Homage to Horace: A Bimillenary Celebration*, ed. S. J. Harrison, 296–313. Oxford: Clarendon Press.

Brown, P. M. 1993. *Horace Satires* I. Warminster: Aris and Phillips.

Buchheit, Vinzenz. 1962. *Studien zum Corpus Priapeorum*. Zetemata 28. Munich: Beck.

———. 1968. "Homerparodie und Literaturkritik in Horazens Sat. I.7 und I.9." *Gymnasium* 75:519–55.

Cantarella, Eva. 1992. *Bisexuality in the Ancient World*. Trans. Cormac Ó Cuilleanáin. New Haven, Conn.: Yale University Press. Originally published as *Secondo natura* (Rome: Editori Riuniti, 1988).

———. 2003. "Fathers and Sons in Rome." *CW* 96:281–98.

Cary, Clarence. 1904. *Horace: His Life, Friendships and Philosophy, as Told by Himself*. New York: Privately printed.

Cloud, Duncan. 1989. "Satirists and the Law." In *Satire and Society in Ancient Rome*, ed. by Susan H. Braund, 89–125. Exeter: Exeter University Publications.

Coffey, Michael. 1976. *Roman Satire*. London: Methuen.

Corbeill, Anthony. 1998. "Dining Deviants in Roman Political Invective." In *Roman Sexualities*, ed. by J. P. Hallett and M. Skinner, 99–128. Princeton, N.J.: Princeton University Press.

Crook, J. A. 1967. "*Patria Potestas*." *CQ* 61:113–22.

Cucchiarelli, Andrea. 2001. *La satira e il poeta: Orazio tra Epodi e Sermones*. Pisa: Giardini.

Davis, Gregson. 1991. *Polyhymnia: The Rhetoric of Horatian Lyric Discourse*. Berkeley: University of California Press.

Derrida, J. 1981. *Dissemination*. Trans. Barbara Johnson. Chicago: University Press. Originally published as *Dissémination* (Paris: Éditions du Seuill, 1972).

Dickie, Matthew W. 2001. *Magic and Magicians in the Greco-Roman World*. London and New York: Routledge.

Duckworth, George E. 1952. *The Nature of Roman Comedy: A Study in Popular Entertainment*. Princeton, N.J.: Princeton University Press.

DuQuesnay, I. M. leM. 1984. "Horace and Maecenas: The Propaganda Value of Sermones I." In *Poetry and Politics in the Age of Augustus*, ed. Tony Woodman and David West, 19–58. Cambridge: Cambridge University Press.

Ehlers, W. 1985. "Das 'Iter Brundisium' des Horaz (Serm. 1,5)." *Hermes* 113:69–83.

Eitrem, S. 1941. "La Magie comme motif littéraire chez les Grecs et les Romains." *Symbolae Osloenses* 21:39–60.

Elliott, R. C. 1960. *The Power of Satire: Magic, Ritual, Art*. Princeton, N.J.: Princeton University Press.

Ferguson, John, ed. 1979. *Juvenal: The Satires*. New York: St. Martin's Press.

Fiske, George Converse. 1920. *Lucilius and Horace: A Study in the Classical Theory of Imitation*. Madison: University of Wisconsin Press.

Fraenkel, Eduard. 1957. *Horace.* Oxford: Oxford University Press.

Francis, Philip. 1746. *The Satires of Horace.* London.

Freudenburg, Kirk. 1993. *The Walking Muse: Horace on the Theory of Satire.* Princeton, N.J.: Princeton University Press.

——. 2001. *Satires of Rome.* Cambridge: Cambridge University Press.

Frischer, Bernard. 1982. *The Sculpted Word: Epicureanism and Philosophical Recruitment in Ancient Greece.* Berkeley: University of California Press.

Girard, Rene. 1979. *Violence and the Sacred.* Baltimore: Johns Hopkins University Press.

Goldberg, Christiane. 1992. *Carmina Priapea.* Heidelberg: Carl Winter.

Gow, James. 1901. *Q. Horati Flacci Saturarum: Liber I.* Cambridge: Cambridge University Press.

Gowers, Emily. 1993a. "Horace, *Satire* 1.5: An Inconsequential Journey." *PCPS* 39: 48–66.

——. 1993b. *The Loaded Table: Representations of Food in Roman Literature.* Oxford: Clarendon Press.

——. 2002. "Blind Eyes and Cut Throats: Amnesia and Silence in Horace *Satires* 1.7." *CP* 97:145–61.

Graf, Fritz, 1997. *Magic in the Ancient World.* Trans. Franklin Philip. Cambridge, Mass.: Harvard University Press. Originally published as *La magie dans l'antiquité gréco-romaine: idéologie et pratique* (Paris: Les Belles Lettres, 1994).

Gratwick, A. S. 1982. "The Satires of Ennius and Lucilius." In *Cambridge History of Classical Literature,* ed. E. J. Kenney, vol. 2, pt. 1, 156–71. Cambridge: Cambridge University Press.

Griffin, Jasper. 2003. "That Old Black Magic," review of *Greek and Roman Necromancy,* by Daniel Ogden, 2003. *New York Review of Books* 50 (7) (May 1): 3–45.

Habinek, Thomas. 1997. "The Invention of Sexuality in the World-City of Rome." In *The Roman Cultural Revolution,* ed. Thomas Habinek and Alessandro Schiesaro, 23–43. Cambridge: Cambridge University Press.

Hallett, Judy P. 1981. "Pepedi / diffissa nate ficus: Priapic Revenge in Horace, Satires I.8." *RhM* 124:341–47.

Hare, Thomas. 1737. *A translation of the Odes and Epodes {and Carmen seculare} of Horace into English verse.* London.

Henderson, Jeffrey. 1991. *The Maculate Muse: Obscene Language in Attic Comedy.* New York: Oxford University Press.

Henderson, John. 1989a. "Satire Writes 'Woman': Gendersong." *PCPS* 35:50–80.

——. 1989b. "Not 'Women in Roman Satire' but 'When Satire Writes "Woman.""" In *Satire and Society in Ancient Rome,* ed. Susan H. Braund, 89–125. Exeter: Exeter University Publications.

——. 1993. "Be Alert (Your Country Needs Lerts): Horace *Satires* 1.9." *PCPS* 39:67–93.

——. 1994. "On Getting Rid of Kings: Horace, *Satire* 1.7," *CQ* 44:146–70.

————. 1999. *Writing Down Rome*. Oxford: Oxford University Press.

Hendrickson, G. L. 1900. "Horace *Serm.* 1.4: A Protest and a Programme." *AJP* 21: 121–42.

————. 1911. "Satura—The Genesis of a Literary Form." *CP* 6:129–43.

————. 1927. "*Satura Tota Nostra Est.*" *CP* 22:46–60.

Hinds, Stephen. 1987. *The Metamorphosis of Persephone*. Cambridge: Cambridge University Press.

Hooper, Richard W. 1999. *The Priapus Poems: Erotic Epigrams from Ancient Rome*. Urbana and Chicago: University of Illinois Press.

Hopkinson, Neil. 1988. *A Hellenistic Anthology*. Cambridge: Cambridge University Press.

Ingallina, Salvatore Sergio. 1974. *Orazio e la magia (Sat. I 8; Epodi 5 e 17)*. Palermo: Palumbo.

Janowitz, Naomi. 2001. *Magic in the Roman World: Pagans, Jews, and Christians*. London: Routledge.

Johnson, W. R. 1993. *Horace and the Dialectic of Freedom: Readings in Epistles* I. Ithaca, N.Y.: Cornell University Press.

Keller, O. 1967, ed. *Pseudacronis Scholia in Horatium Vetustiora*. Vol. 2. Stuttgart: Teubner.

Kiessling, A., and R. Heinze. 1961. *Q. Horatius Flaccus: Satiren*. Berlin: Weidmannsche Verlagsbuchhandlung.

Knoche, Ulrich. 1975. *Roman Satire*. Trans. Edwin S. Ramage. Bloomington: Indiana University Press.

Konstan, David. 1983. *Roman Comedy*. Ithaca, N.Y.: Cornell University Press.

Kotansky, Roy. 1991. "Incantations and Prayers for Salvation on Inscribed Greek Amulets." In *Magika Hiera*, ed. Christopher A. Faraone and Dirk Obbink, 107–37. New York: Oxford University Press.

Krenkel, W. 1970. *Lucilius, Satiren*. Leiden: E. J. Brill.

Lacey, W. K. 1986. "Patria Potestas." In *The Family in Ancient Rome: New Perspectives*, ed. Beryl Rawson, 121–44. Ithaca, N.Y.: Cornell University Press.

LaFleur, Richard A. 1981. "Horace and *Onomasti Komodein*: The Law of Satire." *ANRW* 2.31.3:1790–826.

Laird, Andrew. 1999. *Powers of Expression, Expressions of Power*. Oxford: Oxford University Press.

Leach, E. W. 1971. "Horace's Pater Optimus and Terence's Demea: Autobiographical Fiction." *AJP* 92:616–32.

Lejay, Paul. 1911. *Oeuvres d'Horace: Satires*. Paris: Librairie Hachette.

Lesky, Albin. 1966. *A History of Greek Literature*. New York: Thomas Y. Crowell.

Lewis, Charlton T. and Charles Short. 1955. *A Latin Dictionary Founded on Andrews' Edition of Freund's Latin Dictionary*. Oxford: Clarendon Press.

Lodge, David. 1992. *The Art of Fiction*. London: Secker and Warburg.

Long, A. A., and D. Sedley. 1987. *The Hellenistic Philosophers*. 2 vols. Cambridge: Cambridge University Press.

Lowe, J. E. 1929. *Magic in Greek and Latin Literature*. Oxford: B. Blackwell.

Martindale, Charles. 1993. Introduction to *Horace Made New*, ed. David Hopkinson and Charles Martindale, 1–26. Cambridge: Cambridge University Press.

Marx, Frederick. 1904–5. *C. Lucilii Carminum reliquiae*. 2 vols. Leipzig: Teubner.

Mazurek, Tadeusz. 1997. "Self-Parody and the Law in Horace's Satires 1.9." *CJ* 93:1–17.

McNeill, Randall L. B. 2001. *Horace: Image, Identity, and Audience*. Baltimore: Johns Hopkins University Press.

Moles, John. 2002. "Poetry, Philosophy, Politics and Play: Epistles I." In *Traditions and Contexts in the Poetry of Horace*, ed. Tony Woodman and Denis Feeney, 141–57, 235–37. Cambridge: Cambridge University Press.

Morris, E. P. 1909. *Horace: Satires and Epistles*. New York: American Book Co.

Musurillo, H. A. 1955. "Horace's Journey to Brundisium—Fact or Fiction?" *CW* 48:159–62.

Nagy, Gregory. 1979. *The Best of the Achaeans*. Baltimore: Johns Hopkins University Press.

Nussbaum, Martha. 1994. *The Therapy of Desire*. Princeton, N.J.: Princeton University Press.

O'Connor, E. M. 1989. Symbolum Salacitatis: *A Study of the God Priapus as a Literary Character*. Frankfurt am Main: Peter Lang.

Ogden, Daniel. 2002. *Magic, Witchcraft, and Ghosts in the Greek and Roman Worlds: A Sourcebook*. Oxford: Oxford University Press.

Oliensis, Ellen. 1991. "Canidia, Canicula, and the Decorum of Horace's *Epodes*." *Arethusa* 24:107–38.

———. 1998. *Horace and the Rhetoric of Authority*. Cambridge: Cambridge University Press.

Palmer, Arthur. 1893. *The Satires of Horace*. 5th ed. London: Macmillan.

Parker, Alison. 1986. "Comic Theory in the Satires of Horace." Ph.D. diss., University of North Carolina at Chapel Hill.

Parker, W. H. 1988. *Priapea: Poems for a Phallic God*. London: Croom Helm.

Putnam, Michael C. J. 2000. *Horace's* Carmen Saeculare: *Ritual Magic and the Poet's Art*. New Haven, Conn.: Yale University Press.

Rawson, B., ed. 1991. *Marriage, Divorce, and Children in Ancient Rome*. Oxford: Oxford University Press.

Reckford, Kenneth J. 1969. *Horace*. New York: Twayne.

———. 1997. "Horatius: The Man and the Hour." *AJP* 118:583–612.

———. 1998. "Reading the Sick Body: Decomposition and Morality in Persius' Third Satire." *Arethusa* 31:337–54.

———. 1999. "Only a Wet Dream? Hope and Skepticism in Horace, Satire 1.5." *AJP* 120:527–54.

Richlin, Amy. 1992. *The Garden of Priapus*. Oxford: Oxford University Press.

Ricks, Christopher. 1976. "Allusion: The Poet as Heir." In *Studies in the Eighteenth Century*, ed. R. F. Brissenden and J. C. Eade, 209–40. Toronto: University of Toronto Press.

Rolfe, John Carew. 1935. *Horace: Satires and Epistles*. New York: Allyn and Bacon.

Romilly, Jacqueline de. 1975. *Magic and Rhetoric in Ancient Greece*. Cambridge, Mass.: Harvard University Press.

Rudd, Niall. 1955. "Had Horace Been Criticized? A Study of Serm., I,4." *AJP* 76: 165–75.

———. 1961. "Horace's Encounter with the Bore." *Phoenix* 15:79–96.

———. 1966. *The Satires of Horace*. Cambridge: Cambridge University Press.

Schröter, R. 1967. "Horazens Satire 1,7 und die antike Eposparodie." *Poetica* 1:8–23.

Scodel, Ruth. 1987. "Horace, Lucilius, and Callimachean Polemic." *HSCP* 9:199–215.

Seager, Robin. 1993. "Horace and Augustus: Poetry and Policy." In *Horace 2000: A Celebration, Essays for the Bimillennium*, ed. Niall Rudd, 23–40. Ann Arbor: University of Michigan Press.

Segal, Erich. 1968. *Roman Laughter: The Comedy of Plautus*. Cambridge, Mass.: Harvard University Press.

Shackleton-Bailey, D. R. 1982. *Profile of Horace*. London: Duckworth.

Steinby, Eva Margareta. 1996. *Lexicon topographicum urbis Romae*. Vol. 3. Rome: Quasar.

Stevenson, T. R. 1992. "The Ideal Benefactor and the Father Analogy in Greek and Roman Thought." *CQ*, n.s., 42:421–36.

Strubbe, J. H. M. 1991. "Cursed Be He Who Moves My Bones." In *Magika Hiera*, ed. Christopher A. Faraone and Dirk Obbink, 33–59. New York: Oxford University Press.

Sullivan, J. P. 1993. "Form Opposed: Elegy, Epigram, Satire." In *Roman Epic*, ed. A. J. Boyle, 143–61. London: Routledge.

Svenbro, Jesper. 1993. *Phrasikleia: An Anthropology of Reading in Ancient Greece*. Trans. Janet Lloyd. Ithaca, N.Y.: Cornell University Press.

Tambiah, S. J. 1968. "The Magical Power of Words." *Man* 3:175–208.

Tavenner, Eugene. 1916. *Studies in Magic from Latin Literature*. New York: Columbia University Press.

Ullman, B. L. 1913. "Satura and Satire." *CP* 8:172–94.

Van Rooy, C. A. 1965. *Studies in Classical Satire and Related Literary Theory*. Leiden: E. J. Brill.

———. 1971. "Arrangement and Structure of Satires in Horace *Sermones* Book I: Satire 7 as Related to Satires 8 and 10." *AClass* 15:67–90.

Warmington, E. H. 1938. *Remains of Old Latin*. Vol. 3. Cambridge, Mass.: Loeb Classical Library.

White, E. B. 1954. "Some Remarks on Humor." Reprinted in *The Norton Reader: An Anthology of Expository Prose*, ed. Arthur M. Eastman, 5th ed., 433–34. New York: W. W. Norton, 1980.

White, Peter. 1978. "Amicitia and the Profession of Poetry in Early Imperial Rome." *JRS* 68:74–92.

———. 1993. *Promised Verse: Poets in the Society of Augustan Rome*. Cambridge, Mass.: Harvard University Press.

Wickham, E. C. 1903. *Horace. The Satires, Epistles, and de Arte Poetica, with a Commentary.* Oxford: Clarendon Press.

Wickham, E. C., and H. W. Garrod. 1901. *Q. Horatii Flacci Opera.* Reprint, Oxford: Clarendon Press, 1955.

Williams, Gordon. 1995. "*Libertino Patre Natus:* True or False?" In *Homage to Horace: A Bimillenary Celebration,* ed. S. J. Harrison, 296–313. Oxford: Clarendon Press.

Witke, Charles. 1965. Review of *St. Jerome the Satirist: A Study in Christian Latin Thought and Letters,* by David S. Wiesen. *Satire News Letter* 2:135–37.

Woodman, Tony, and Denis Feeney, eds. 2002. *Traditions and Contexts in the Poetry of Horace.* Cambridge: Cambridge University Press.

Zetzel, J. E. G. 1980. "Horace's *Liber Sermonum:* The Structure of Ambiguity." *Arethusa* 13:59–78.

———. 2002. "Dreaming about Quirinus: Horace's *Satires* and the Development of Augustan Poetry." In *Traditions and Contexts in the Poetry of Horace,* ed. Tony Woodman and Denis Feeney, 38–52, 210–13. Cambridge: Cambridge University Press.

Index

Achilles, 82–83, 118
Adams, J. N., 160n8, 160n10, 162n17
alienation: of the audience, 6–7, 18; of the poet, 15
allusion: internal, 128; to Lucilius, 115, 118, 129–30; to Priapic poems, 92–93; to satire as genre, 24, 34
ambition, social, 56–57, 154n29
ambivalence, 77–78, 81–82, 99, 105–6
ancestry: authority as legacy of, 48–49; "Horace" as without ancestors, 68; literary, of Lucilius *vs.* Horace, 151–52n12, 152n14. *See also* status
Anderson, W. S., 11, 99–100, 102, 151n4, 151nn11–12, 160n2, 160n5, 162n19, 163n3, 163n8, 164n15, 165n21, 165n23
anger, 25, 35–36, 70, 138–39, 141, 142–43
Anthon, Charles, 159n14
Anthony, 64, 71–72, 73, 76
anus, 93, 98–99
Apollo, 18, 111, 118–20, 165n20
appetites, 4, 9, 23–25, 28, 30, 130, 166n3
Arbuscula, 140
Aristius Fuscus, 117–18, 119, 122, 125, 165n20
Aristophanes, 39
Armstrong, David, 156n15
audience: alienation of, 6–7, 18; bad poetry encouraged, 133–34, 140–41;

blame directed at, 5–6, 40–42; *Epistles* form and recognition of unavailability of interlocutor, 18; exchange and communication with, 17, 101, 142–43; expectations of, 7, 20, 41, 60, 70, 76; fear and hatred of poets by, 20, 40–42; flight of, 104; friends as, 43, 134, 139–41, 153n20; Horace as lacking an, 40, 42, 133–34; as insiders, 122, 123–24; instructed how to respond, 98, 106, 109–10, 141; invective or hostile speech practiced by, 107, 109–11, 121, 125–26, 141; limits to the speaking self established by, 80; Maecenas as, 139–41; menaced by satire, 5–6, 20, 90–91, 96, 122, 125; as other in poetic relationship, 36; persona as unthreatening to, 12–13, 15–16, 68; popularity of satire and Old Comedy, 41–42; as prize in poetic competition, 8, 42, 138–39; quality preferred to quantity, 139–41; relationship of speaker to, 10, 36, 122; satire as displeasing to, 40; shared power of satirist, 125–26; as silent interlocutor, 17; as spectators, 86–87, 96, 122; as sympathetic to or cooperative with Horace, 109–10,

other: audience as, 36; bad poets as, 11; blindness to faults in, 31–32, 136; desires of the, 20; desire to exploit failings of, 31; difference of, as evidence of selfhood, 33–34, 36; differentiation from, 80, 82–83; domination of, 35; happiness and, 136; as limit, 30–37; needs of, 36; right behavior in relation to, 32–34, 35; satire and requirement to recognize selfhood of other, 34; as a self, 30, 32–33, 83

Palmer, Arthur, 148n7, 155nn1–2, 157n16, 159n14
Parker, Alison, 148n8, 151nn4–5, 159n12
Parker, W. H., 160n4
parody, 39, 43, 59–60, 70, 72; Lucilius's use of, 137; mock-epic, 59–60, 63, 69, 70, 72, 82, 83, 157n18
patronage: father-son relationships compared with, 54–55; friendship as distinct from, 52; Maecenas as patron, 37, 38, 51–55, 73, 108; as political structure, 52, 54–55; power or domination, 54–55; in Roman society, 52, 54–55, 154n23
penis. See phallus or penis
Persius, 81, 85, 109, 115
personae: as absent in 1.7, 81–82; as artifice of poetry, 11–14; audience instructed by, 17; as balanced and respectful of limits, 8–9; as buffer for audience against dangers of satire, 6–7, 12–13, 36; Canidia as, 17, 160n2; character of "Horace" essential to satire, 56; comic elements of, 62, 66–68; crafted to fit requirements of genre, 9–10, 54, 56; critical distance dispelled by, 14; as distinct from the poet, 11–12; dual natures of "Horace," 74; envious detractors

as influence on, 54; as harmless or unthreatening, 12–13, 15–16, 61–62, 66–68; "Horace" as control structure for genre, 9–10; "Horace" as simultaneously insider and outsider, 15–16, 68, 81–82; "Horace" as worthy, 52–53, 119; humble status and limited social authority of, 15, 55, 68; identification of satire (genre) with, 13, 39, 56, 58; increasing development and expression of, 9–11; as model of Roman rectitude, 56; narrators used as substitute for "Horace," 90; poetic functions of, 11–14, 39; Priapus as, 160n2; as relatively powerless, 106; silence of, 121–22; sympathy of audience with "Horace," 121–22; as unthreatening, 61–62. See also narrators
"pest." See "interlocutor" in 1.9
phallus or penis: nickname applied to Horace, 107; phallic songs as magical speech, 102–3; Priapus as narrator in 1.8, 90–100; as voice of reason, 26–27, 90
Plotius, 62
poetics: limits as excessively restrictive, 132–33; meter, 48, 101, 134–35, 157n18, 162n21; poetry as fulfillment of poetic principals, 118; as reality based, 137. See also style
politics: commentary and criticism of, 73; as context for diplomatic mission, 64, 69, 75, 155nn1–2; friendship as political relationship, 72–73; omitted as poetic subject, 59–60; patronage as political structure, 52, 54–55; political violence in Rome, 3–4, 88
Pollio, 137, 138
Porphyrio (scholiast), 60, 111, 148n7, 166n10

WENDY J. RASCHKE, editor
*The Archaeology of the Olympics: The Olympics and
Other Festivals in Antiquity*

PAUL PLASS
*Wit and the Writing of History:
The Rhetoric of Historiography in Imperial Rome*

BARBARA HUGHES FOWLER
The Hellenistic Aesthetic

F. M. CLOVER and R. S. HUMPHREYS, editors
Tradition and Innovation in Late Antiquity

BRUNILDE SISMONDO RIDGWAY
Hellenistic Sculpture I: The Styles of ca. 331–200 B.C.

BARBARA HUGHES FOWLER, editor and translator
Hellenistic Poetry: An Anthology

KATHRYN J. GUTZWILLER
Theocritus' Pastoral Analogies: The Formation of a Genre

VIMALA BEGLEY and RICHARD DANIEL DE PUMA, editors
Rome and India: The Ancient Sea Trade

RUDOLF BLUM and HANS H. WELLISCH, translators
Kallimachos: The Alexandrian Library and the Origins of Bibliography

DAVID CASTRIOTA
Myth, Ethos, and Actuality: Official Art in Fifth Century B.C. Athens

BARBARA HUGHES FOWLER, editor and translator
Archaic Greek Poetry: An Anthology

JOHN H. OAKLEY and REBECCA H. SINOS
The Wedding in Ancient Athens

* 9 7 8 0 2 9 9 2 0 9 5 0 6 *